The Encyclopedia of Horror

The Encyclopedia of Horror

Edited by
RICHARD DAVIS

HAMLYN

First published in 1981 by
Octopus Books Limited

Published in paperback in 1987 by
Hamlyn Publishing
A division of the Hamlyn Publishing Group Limited
Bridge House
London Road
Twickenham
Middlesex
England

ISBN 0 600 553 590

Printed in Hong Kong

Contents

Foreword

According to a dictionary definition Horror is: ... a painful emotion compounded of loathing and fear; a shuddering with terror and repugnance; the feeling excited by something shocking or frightful ... not, I venture to suggest, descriptive of enjoyment in its true sense. But such is the fascination of the grotesque to a large section of humanity, that it has been the theme in every avenue of the Arts since time immemorial.

It is only the quality of writing that distinguishes the world's greatest authors from those of lesser degree, but some of the plots employed by Shakespeare to the comic-strip artists are fundamentally the same.

It seems an odd paradox that ghost and allied stories are firm favourites among the pleasures of Christmas-time. This may be due partly to the fact that such enjoyments are usually relished snug and safe before a comforting fire and within earshot of the family. But subconsciously there dwells the irrefutable knowledge that good always triumphs over evil in the long run. Subtract an 'o' from 'good' and add a 'd' to 'evil' and you have the two greatest protagonists the world has ever known. There lies, in essence, the attraction of the matter revealed in this Encyclopedia. Samuel Johnson wrote:

'Knowledge is of two kinds. We know a subject ourselves or we know where we can find information upon it'.

Here, then, in words and pictures, is a fascinating wealth of academic and general interest, which will delight and prove indispensable to novice and aficionado alike if they lean toward the macabre for their entertainment.

Peter Cushing

Introduction

Recently the Horror movie has developed a new and rather disquieting trend. We have been subjected to a spate of films in which the total plotline centres round the sadistic slaying of as many characters as can be managed in the film's running time. Coherent plots matter hardly at all: sexual titillation and violence, usually together, are the sole *raison d'être* for these works. These films have nothing to do with Horror as discussed in this book. Horror as we employ the term, pertains to the Realms of the Marvellous: extensions to the Known World whether in the genre of SF, the Supernatural, or Fantasy. Horror is a definition tinged for us with wonder. It has Poetry in it too, because at its best it heightens the reader's awareness. The movies in this sub-genre, suggested as many of them maintain by real-life crimes, are cynical attempts to cash in on Man's baser instincts of sadism and aggression. Most of them are poorly and cheaply made, their audiences voyeuristic accomplices. In contrast, the Horrors that we describe in this book try to extend, rather than narrow and blunt, Man's imaginative aspirations. Of course works of Horror must employ physical grue. But to appeal exclusively to your audience purely on the basis of physical sensationalism is to betray both him and yourself. It is ultimately in motivation that there lies the difference between art and pornography.

The Scream

Far right The supernatural atmosphere generated in this Goya masterpiece 'The Forcibly Bewitched', 1472, conveys the feeling of evil to the viewer with chilling clarity.

Below Matthias Grunewald (c. 1460–1528) created a nightmare scene of horror in 'The Temptations of St Anthony'. This altarpiece was obviously intended to impress the worshippers with its awesomeness and reflections of damnation.

No term emphasizes the divergence between fact and fiction as much as 'Horror' does. In no other genre are the attitudes of the general reader so firmly entrenched in opposition. The manifestation of factual horror arouses in us—invariably—revulsion so acute that we may only address it over a defensive barrier. Few of us can bring ourselves to follow the details of a factual murder, spread so gloatingly over the newspapers: we turn with relief to the latest book of spectral tales of ghosts and ghouls. How eagerly we escape into their fantasy world, how we relish the chills up and down our spine, the rise of the hairs on the backs of our respective necks. Hairs really do rise: this isn't merely a picturesque literary metaphor: there is a medical explanation for it.

And yet the horror for us, while we share it, may be, should be, just as real. Therein lies its effectiveness. So why do we love horror? What is it about fear that becomes so irresistibly attractive? Is it, as some maintain, a cathartic working-out of aggressive instincts? Do we savour it in a fictional context because by definition it is safely at one remove, tucked cosily between the pages of a book, or up on a cinema screen, and our enjoyment need not be tempered by feelings of voyeuristic guilt? The duration of our horrific experience is comfortingly ascribed within bounds so that when we close the book, leave the cinema or turn off the television set, we can return to our mundane world assured and protected in the knowledge that such things cannot be, the dead don't really walk. Dracula won't really visit us to suck our blood, or Frankenstein's Monster, if he exists at all—and who knows what results in the creation of life have really been achieved—is safely confined behind the locked doors of the Baron's laboratory. So here is our first paradox: horror works for us only if we are enabled to feel that it might be true, that the incidents described *might* conceivably happen, but if we know that they really do happen, that the 'horror' is true, then we rebel and protest. The rules of the game between author and reader are broken.

Perhaps our confusion arises from a misnomer. We've got so used to accepted literary definitions that we don't very often question them. But what really does our love of ghosts and the supernatural, of the piquant flavour of a spinechiller, have in common with the stupid, squalid murder stories that fill our newspapers? Why should they be bracketed together under the blanket term of horror? We use it—as we apply it to this book—for convenience's sake, because there is no other. We have been too lazy to invent one. People have compromised, but 'Tales of Terror' and 'Tales of Fear' are inadequate substitutes. The terms 'Fear' and 'Terror' are firmly anchored to the mere thriller: but all kinds of deeper connotations, explorations among the echoing vaults of the Unknown, worlds of the Weird, the Occult, the Macabre, are carried by the emotive term 'Horror', and shared with specious and ephemeral sensation because there is no other.

Fact and fiction confront each other over this issue: no compromise is possible. The horror fiction fan is concerned with realms of imagination; and for this he must approach the shelves of his local bookshop or library shamefacedly and apologetically. He must justify himself before his maiden aunt, or some other necessarily misinformed person, for the word 'horror' on his choice of reading material, and because of the lack of precision in definition his defence is nearly impossible to present coherently.

Of course physical horror has its place in the genre. There must be Darkness in order to

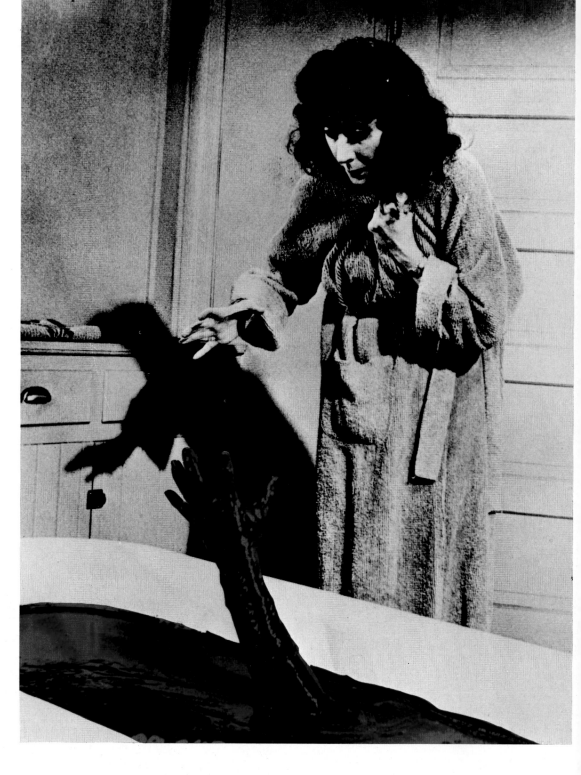

A victim of a monster crab extends his arm in a plea for help in The Tingler, *1959. Set in a cinema, Vincent Price warns the audience that the monster is loose. In the U.S.A. seats were wired so that selected viewers would 'tingle' through minor electric shocks!*

pinpoint Light. No-one would be foolish enough to deny any aspect of Total Experience. And there's no evidence that audiences at horror movies are any more violent or anti-social than those who go to see musicals. Self-appointed censors and guardians of our morals have always tolerated horror movies, albeit at times grudgingly. In reality there is very little violence, of the gratuitous variety. Human life is considered sacrosanct, and its deprivation is invariably given due and weighty emphasis. There is little casual shooting, as in for example Westerns, no balletic arrangement of falling bodies. The enormity of violent intrusion into a

non-violent situation is never discounted. The horror genre provides the last refuge of a Puritan morality in our tolerant society: Good and Evil are Absolutes, and there is little room for compromise. Hence there is little pornography in horror—if pornography is defined as a blurring of moral values.

But it is the type of horror in fiction which relies for its total effect on graphic depiction of physical gore: the type of story for which physical description is the sole raison d'être: this is the subversive subgenre which undermines and sabotages the whole category, and most nearly approximates to the factual counterpart of sensational journalism. Unfortunately this is the type of horror that sells the most. The notorious Pan collections are perennial best-sellers; more and more in recent years are the stories chosen seemingly for the amount of nauseous physical content they can cram into a limited space. They take less skill to write, and the fact that most horror fans wish to disown them is irrelevant. As long as people keep buying them—for the wrong reasons—they'll continue. Fact has corrupted fiction.

In this book we have explored horror in myth and legend as well as formalized fiction. In no way, of course, do myth and legend profess to be fact: though as allegory they point moral truths. Before we get involved in deep philosophical arguments as to what constitutes truth, let's just point out that allegory relates to the formation of religion, and that perhaps ultimate truth, if it could be apprehended, would extract ingredients from every known religion.

Allegory and fairy tale both explore regions of the Marvellous; they share with the more imaginative aspects of Horror a longing for a world unbounded by the limits of Reality as we perceive it. So does Poetry—or rather most aspects of it, in so far as it describes the Marvellous, and perhaps Horror is a mass substitute for Poetry.

In any event it is a vast subject: and there are many different ways of tackling it. Our contributors have not felt themselves bound to approach their own areas with any degree of artificially imposed uniformity. Sole considerations have been what was the most interesting, the most intriguing, the most important elements in the overall pattern. In this way we have hoped to build up as comprehensive a picture as we can in the allotted space.

Basil Copper in his piece on vampires and werewolves has explored both fact and fiction. Many readers, overfamiliarized with the respective myths through their treatment in the cinema, will be surprised to learn of the medical precedence of some of the symptoms. Richard Cavendish, one of the greatest authorities on satanism and the black arts, has approached his subject from the factual, traditional angle. With one or two rare exceptions, fiction has never managed to equal fact in interest value, and has for the most part resorted to formula cliché.

In the same way, the cinema has always been wary of treating the supernatural with much degree of depth. Film-makers have resorted to the more immediate, popular appeal of sensation and shock. Not so with the written word, of course, and Mike Ashley examines the rise of the ghost story—in many cases the epitome of the short story in its most perfect form. He concentrates almost entirely on fiction. The

Left The surrealist 'Ghost of a Flea' by William Blake. Blake's mystical drawings appeal more to the intellect than to the emotions but the eerie quality doubtless fascinated their 18th century audiences.

Below Salvador Dali's drawing of Lady Macbeth. Probably the best-known exponent of surrealism, Dali used symbols from dream life and hallucinations. This drawing seems to personify schizophrenia.

great body of ghostly literature holds incomparably greater fascination than the rather arid and bland accounts of so-called real-life hauntings. (I discount what appear to be cynically sensationalized accounts like *The Amityville Horror* which appear to me to be more of fiction than of fact, as has been subsequently proven). Factual ghosts always seem dull and predictable: even great men, original thinkers, when they remanifest themselves in the seance-room, can find nothing new to say, nothing of remotely comparable profundity to what they said when alive, and this after having passed through the greatest experience Man can know. I don't discount spiritualism. I merely wonder why spirits should bother to reappear.

Michel Parry, editor of the **Rivals of Frankenstein** short story collection, has chosen the same approach: though perhaps chosen is the wrong word to use. There are, as far as we know, no recorded instances of real-life Frankensteins creating real-life Monsters, though test-tube life, as we said above, might well be with us in the not too-distant future.

Frankenstein necessarily features in Douglas Hill's piece as well. He discusses how horror impinges on SF. The categories tend to be distinct in most readers' minds; though this I feel is, like so much else in the field, brought about by a basic confusion in terminology and definition. 'Horror' is a mood; SF is a category. Horror is more relevantly comparable to, say, comedy: SF to fantasy. In my own piece 'Zombies, Mummies and the Undead', while most readers know that mummies are incon-

testably real, they're not yet quite so certain about zombies. But many people claim to have seen them, particularly on the West Indian island of Haiti. I've cited examples of this, and tried to give a possible explanation as to what they really are. With mummies of course the approach is different. We all know what mummies are, but the process of mummification has some interesting features. With both categories of monster, I have also tried to present a general fictional survey, mainly though the cinema, because this is the only medium which has really done them justice.

Tom Hutchinson's 'Monster' piece is a general survey, discussing monsters and their significance in myth and fiction. He concludes that man makes his own monsters: that they are born out of a psychological need, not only to channel and confine his own aggressive instincts by externalizing them, but also to assign to the unknown, in the form of monsters and bogy-men, human qualities so that he can thus identify with, and tame them.

Horror remains on the whole untamed. The frisson of fear, the chasm of the Unknown, is man's constant companion. In our uncertain, precarious age, new cracks in the earth of knowledge open continually before him. The age-old paradox is never truer than today: the more he learns, the more there is to learn. Man walks on the edge of ever steeper precipices. He sees that the dark at the top of the stairs is evolving newer, ever more potent demons. It's almost with a sense of relief, that he turns back to the comfort of the older, traditional ones.

Above The classic artistic interpretation of death and damnation: 'The Garden of Earthly Delights' by Hieronymous Bosch.

Far left Aubrey Beardsley's 'Head of John the Baptist', an illustration for Oscar Wilde's Salome. *Influenced by stylized Japanese art, Beardsley manages to convey this macabre subject as a decorative design.*

Evil Monsters

In all of us there is the instinct to shun
that which is abnormal or strange in
others, and yet we are fascinated by it.
Given a fictitious monster to fear, we do
not, as often in real life, have to hide our
feelings of revulsion; we can allow ourselves
to enjoy being shocked and repelled. Tom
Hutchinson, film editor of *Now!* magazine and
SF reviewer for *The Times*, looks at the sublimi-
nal aspects of monsters and why they intrigue and
interest us so much. He examines the roots of the
monster myth in religious beliefs, mythology and
folklore, picking out such classic stories as Dr Jekyll
and Mr Hyde, the perennial monster theme made
more exciting by the frequent transformation of
human form into bestial shape. The demonic
Dr Moreau torturing human forms into nightmare beings never fails to bring a shudder
while Ray Bradbury, in **The Small Assassin**, conjures up an even more frightening
creature in the shape of a tiny baby who
kills its own parents. Modern cinema
gives a formidable dimension to the
credibility of monsters. Dinosaurs
spring to life in celluloid while
normally inoffensive invertebrates
such as ants, bees and spiders
take on aggressive roles and
threaten mankind. Finally one
cannot study monsters of
fiction without paying
homage to King Kong,
one of the most admired
monsters of them all.

Right A typical image created by an artist to convey the elements of evil and fear in horror.

Below Fascinated by the theme of the Devil and Hell, this time Goya shows Saturn devouring one of his children (detail).

Man Makes Monsters

The art of self-tormenting is an ancient one, with a long and honourable literary tradition. Man, not satisfied with the mental confusion and unhappiness to be derived from contemplating the cruelties of life and the riddle of the universe, delights to occupy his leisure moments with puzzles and bugaboos.

Thus Dorothy L. Sayers, no mean thriller writer herself, mused on humanity's irresistible urge to create monsters. As a race, we like nothing better than to huddle round the communal fire with our backs to the darkness and frighten the daylights out of ourselves with tales of the hideous. All that we perceive about us or within ourselves that is unnatural, incomprehensible, dangerous, frightening, evil or harmful we try to tame by giving it a name and weaving a tale about it. It has always been the same. Mead-soaked Anglo-Saxons thrilled to horrors conjured up by professional minstrels more than a thousand years ago. Today, millions willingly part with money to cringe before more palpable movie monsters.

Why do we do it? What is it that is so satisfying, so cathartic even, about creating something monstrous then allowing it to frighten us nearly witless? It is as though it is essential for us to summon up all our worst fears and externalize them, give them a local habitation and a name and at least some substance with which to embody our fears. As Ray Bradbury has pointed out, we fear that which has no name. If we can define the things that terrify us by giving them a name, then perhaps we can defeat them, contain them in the mind.

The need for monsters goes back so far that no-one would be foolish enough to expound authoritatively on its origin. But what are they? Are they folk-memories, distortions of beings that once walked the earth. Where did we get our pattern for monstrosity?

One of the *sine qua nons* of monstrosity is size. Monsters are always huge. This does not mean that everything huge is necessarily monstrous—in Wyndham Lewis's story 'The Human Age', the hero standing in a room sees 'the whole area of the window blotted from the outside, by something blue and green. It had curved lines all over it; it looked like glass . . . it appeared to be lighted from within. Then he saw that it was alive'. What he is looking at is a fraction of part of a vast eye—the eye of an angel. So monstrosity is popularly equated with size, as is physical deformity, to symbolize spiritual aberration: exemplified perfectly by Dorian Gray's portrait. But 'monster' derives from the Latin *monstrum*, a divine portent.

Divine Monsters

In western cultures it is the Greek creation myth that provides us with the template for monstrosity. The Titans were the precursors of the Olympic gods. They were the children of Uranus and Gaea, the heavens and the earth, were measureless to man and synonymous with enormity in all its senses. Led by Cronos, they turned on their father and tore him to pieces. Later, Cronos himself is warned that his own children—the product of an incestuous union with his sister Rhea—plan to usurp him in turn. So he eats them. Here we have parricide, incest, infanticide and cannibalism firmly linked to great physical size. Very early on in our folkmemory deformity of shape and deformity of spirit are united. Even centuries later, the myth has lost none of its power as can be seen in Goya's 'black painting' of Saturn (Cronos) greedily stuffing his children into his great maw.

Only one child escaped Cronos. That was Zeus. He set up his own team of immortals, the Olympian gods, to do battle with the Titans—Old versus New, Chaos versus Order, Death versus Immortality. The battle still rages.

Bestial Monsters

The Olympic gods were altogether more suited to human size and condition, but humanity's urge to make monsters remained undiminished. One of the most famous of these mythical monsters, one of the first man-made monsters was the Minotaur, at once frightening and pathetic.

The Minotaur was a man with a bull's head. He was born to Pasiphaë, the wife of King Minos of Crete, who fell in love with a great white bull that came out of the sea to her. The bull was possibly Poseidon but more likely Zeus, the world's most enthusiastic progenitor. Be that as it may, Pasiphaë had the craftsman Daedalus make her a model heifer in which she could hide to receive the attentions of the bull.

The resulting Minotaur was promptly walled up in a labyrinth (Daedalus again). The monster lived rather frugally on a diet of seven maidens and seven young men per year, provided by Athens as tribute to King Minos. He was finally overcome by Theseus who stood in for one of the intended victims and slew the monster with a magic sword. No hero, from Theseus to Luke

A baleful octopus with its buxom victim from Warlords of Atlantis, *1977, a monster-packed fantasy directed by Kevin Connor.*

Bruce, the giant shark surfaces in the poster for Jaws, *the most commercially successful monster movie produced to date.* Jaws *plays on basic human feelings of vulnerability in the water and fears about what might be lurking below.*

Skywalker, travels without his magic weapon.

In the case of the Minotaur it is easy to see how a monster may have been evolved from rather prosaic facts. Michael Ayrton, the writer-artist who had a great interest in all things Greek and Cretan, has defined myth as the 'gradual accretion of rituals and beliefs surrounding a core of remembered fact'. And it is a fact that Athens and Crete traded and warred together and that Athens sent a grain tribute to Knossos, Minos's Cretan palace. When this grain arrived, there were celebrations, significantly marked by a display of bull-dancing, a rather mind-boggling sport in which young men took the bull by

the horns, literally, and leapt over the animal's back. Thus the taurine connection was well established at Knossos and the myth grew up around it.

If it is easy to see how this myth evolved it is not so crystal clear why. One explanation may be the urge to make sense of the animal half of our nature. Man the poet and philosopher is much offended by man the belcher and fornicator. The bull is an undisputed symbol of potent virility. Perhaps the minotaur was created in an attempt to solve the perennial dilemma of the flesh versus the spirit, the ego versus the id.

Heroes and Monsters

If you create monsters out of all that is dark and dreadful, it is only logical to create heroes to fight them out of all that is light and noble. The prototype hero is, of course, Hercules, yet another son of Zeus—Hercules began in his cradle, strangling two snakes that his father, perhaps in a mistimed attempt at family planning had sent to crush him. He went on from strength to strength overcoming the Nemean Lion, the Stymphalian Birds and the Lernaen Hydra to name but a few. He had a grip of iron and the strength of ten.

Yet Hercules is hard for humans to identify with. He is brute strength personified. Human beings need rather more tangible heroes. After all it is easy—dull, even—to kill a monster if you are guaranteed invincible. A touch-and-go death struggle makes the hero more heroic and the monster more convincingly vanquished.

And so we come to the tale of Beowulf and the monster Grendel, one of the first hero and monster stories that we know of and a story that has set the pattern for the theme down the ages. It was written down in the 8th century, but is one of the major poems in the Anglo-Saxon oral tradition. Beowulf is a young Swedish prince who delivers the court of the Danish king, Hrothgar, from the menace of the monstrous Grendel.

Beowulf was one of the first heroes with human failings. He was not the son of a god; he was not immortal; he spent an inglorious youth not being particularly good at anything; and he was rather a show-off. Yet by the time he meets Grendel he has become very strong, with a grip that Hercules might envy. He is quite simply the best champion, warts and all, that humanity can put up against the forces of darkness.

The forces of darkness are incarnate in Grendel, the first modern monster. He is huge, he too has a grip like iron, a thick, spearproof hide, and he lives in a lake an outcast from the tightly-knit contemporary society represented by Heorot, the great hall of King Hrothgar. Apart from that he is deliciously spine chillingly nebulous. Despite his size he can slip in to invade the centre of that society, King Hrothgar's hall, and snatch men away to their doom. Grendel is all things monstrous to all men ... death, treachery or evil.

When Beowulf and Grendel meet it is with a clashing of symbols. They struggle to outgrip each other and Beowulf finally succeeds through superior strength and sheer tenacity. He tears off Grendel's arm and hangs it on the wall of Heorot for all to see. But this is 8th-century Europe, and people were a deal too sophisticated to expect one battle to win the war. There is no rest in the fight against evil.

Above The giant cephalopod attacks Captain Nemo's submarine Nautilus *in the Walt Disney production of Jules Verne's* 20,000 Leagues Under the Sea, 1954. *The film won an Oscar for its excellent special effects.*

Left A real-life monster from the deep? Photographs such as this have convinced many zoologists that there really is a monster of some kind living in the murky waters of Loch Ness.

Grendel's mother, if anything more fearful than her son, comes to avenge him. Beowulf has to fight her on her own ground—the bottom of a murky lake—and only succeeds in killing her with a magic sword suitably decorated with scenes depicting the destruction of the giants from Genesis.

The Anglo-Saxons were a realistic people with a strong grasp of despair. They knew that life was a very tenuous affair and to maximize their chances of survival they lived in small, tightly-knit and highly organized social groups centred on one lord or kinglet. These communities maintained a wary and precarious peace with each other by a complex system of marriages, diplomatic 'hostages' and treaties. Grendel represented all that they feared most: anarchy, unreason, the collapse of society in to its component parts of frightened and powerless individuals. Their insurance against such a horror was Beowulf, in many ways the prototype hard-drinking sheriff who talks with his fists who was later to become a folk hero in the capable persona of John Wayne.

Hic Draconis ...

At the end of his life, Beowulf perishes nobly, bisecting the dragon which has annexed the treasure hoard belonging to Beowulf's people. Dragons have a long and honourable tradition as monsters, the incarnation of effete power and sterile lust. Throughout folklore they are presented in a remarkably uniform way. They all fly, they all breathe fire, they all sit gloatingly on great hoards of treasure, they all live in stinking barrows and they all devour nubile maidens. J. R. R. Tolkein's Smaug from **The Hobbit** is the archetypal dragon.

In some parts of the world dragons became known as 'wyrms' or worms. And some will say that St George did not do battle with a fire-breathing dragon but with a monstrous worm. Perhaps the most famous of these is the Lambton Worm of Durham in the north of England, which coiled itself around a rock in the River Wear and by night 'twined round Worm Hill near Fatfield'. According to one folklorist he was thus two miles long—which is obviously a worm of some length and distinction. The more this worm devoured from the surrounding countryside, the more it demanded. Its appetite for human children grew from six a day

to at least a dozen, and it would milk up to a dozen cows or more as it fattened and bloated upon the misery of those around.

It is revealing how the reality of what happens to smaller worms is taken into account when we come to the defeat of the great worm. Sir John Lambton, returning to Lambton Castle from fighting overseas, determined to stop this monster's forays into his territory and, on the advice of those who were in the know, he decided to lure the creature into the River Wear and chop it up in the belief the onrushing current would then sweep away the lopped-off portions of worm before they had a chance to reform or become other worms. This was duly done amid a flurry and slither of battle. The Lambton Worm was thus destroyed, but a curse was supposed to have blighted the Lambton line thereafter.

One explanation for such beings could be that they did exist as some species of great saurian, the remnants of which still trailed behind in folk-memory to bewilder and frighten those who outlived them. Snakes they may have been; they became greater snakes in the telling and re-telling perhaps ultimately influenced by the primeval Serpent in the Garden of Eden.

Left The make up department at their very best produced this manifestation of evil.

Below More clever skills from the artists of the cinema screen.

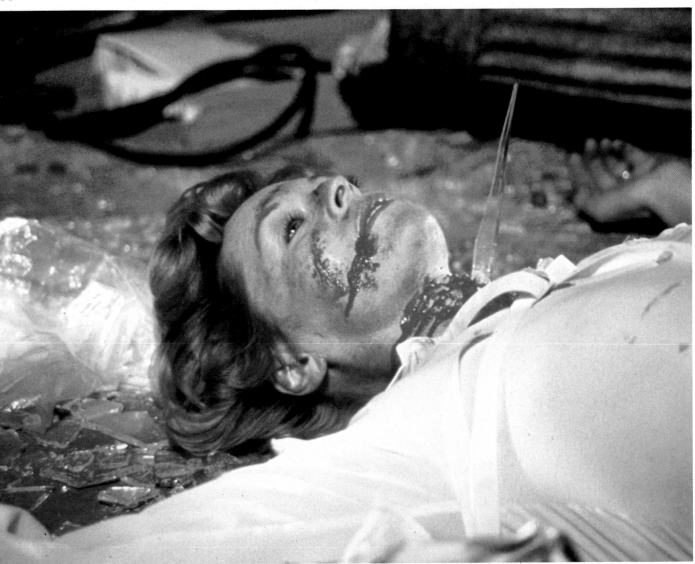

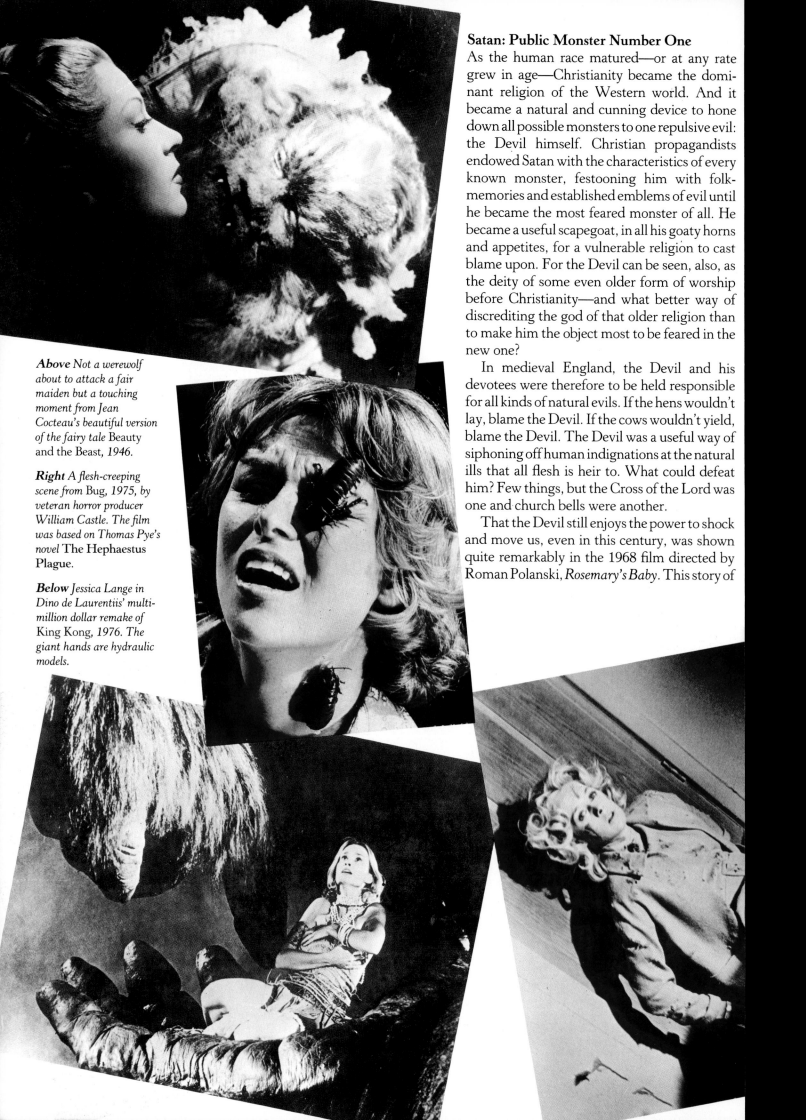

Above *Not a werewolf about to attack a fair maiden but a touching moment from Jean Cocteau's beautiful version of the fairy tale* Beauty and the Beast, *1946.*

Right *A flesh-creeping scene from* Bug, *1975, by veteran horror producer William Castle. The film was based on Thomas Pye's novel* The Hephaestus Plague.

Below *Jessica Lange in Dino de Laurentiis' multi-million dollar remake of* King Kong, *1976. The giant hands are hydraulic models.*

Satan: Public Monster Number One

As the human race matured—or at any rate grew in age—Christianity became the dominant religion of the Western world. And it became a natural and cunning device to hone down all possible monsters to one repulsive evil: the Devil himself. Christian propagandists endowed Satan with the characteristics of every known monster, festooning him with folk-memories and established emblems of evil until he became the most feared monster of all. He became a useful scapegoat, in all his goaty horns and appetites, for a vulnerable religion to cast blame upon. For the Devil can be seen, also, as the deity of some even older form of worship before Christianity—and what better way of discrediting the god of that older religion than to make him the object most to be feared in the new one?

In medieval England, the Devil and his devotees were therefore to be held responsible for all kinds of natural evils. If the hens wouldn't lay, blame the Devil. If the cows wouldn't yield, blame the Devil. The Devil was a useful way of siphoning off human indignations at the natural ills that all flesh is heir to. What could defeat him? Few things, but the Cross of the Lord was one and church bells were another.

That the Devil still enjoys the power to shock and move us, even in this century, was shown quite remarkably in the 1968 film directed by Roman Polanski, *Rosemary's Baby*. This story of foul fiendishness in modern New York should, by the rights of our so-called contemporary sophistication, have us slapping our thighs at its basic premise—namely, the impregnation of young newlywed Mia Farrow by the Devil temporarily incarnate in her husband, summoned by a coven of present-day witches. But people came to gawp as well as gasp; it was the biggest box-office attraction of its year.

Perhaps this was because of the way in which Polanski actually communicated his Devil to us: as something half-seen out of the corner of the eye. Its monstrousness was something to be guessed at, rather than viewed with full-frontal disgust, as those in medieval times might have depicted it. If anything, it was a creature more aligned to our own human shape and condition. In this adaptation of the Ira Levin novel the narrative is seen as the reverse and darkly bloody side of the Christian Nativity; the reverse side of the coin: from the spiritual to the obscene.

Even the Devil could not be blamed for the Industrial Revolution which smote 18th-century Europe, catapulting so many people from the grinding poverty of rural feudalism into the grinding poverty of the dark satanic mills. This was all man's own work. The repercussions have not been fully assimilated even today. Suddenly we needed new myths, new monsters, new heroes to explain ourselves to ourselves. The uneasy feeling that everything was running out of control frightened us then and frightens us now. Beowulf's simple, manly heroics were suddenly no match for the subtle monster we glimpsed, aghast, deep within ourselves. Man was creating his own literary monsters to symbolize these events with such inventions as Frankenstein's creature. And Man was moving even further into himself to gouge out the monstrous thing from the recesses of his mind.

Below centre The theme of the revolt of nature against mankind in The Birds. *Hitchcock based his film on a Daphne Du Maurier short story.*

Left The gill-man goes for Julie Adams in The Creature from the Black Lagoon, *1954, directed by Jack Arnold.*

Below Another version of the Missing Link turned up as a passenger on the Horror Express, *1972. Set entirely on a train crossing the Siberian wastes, this underrated horror movie was actually filmed in Spain.*

Right A talented artist produced this imposing illustration of horror. A face masked in evil.

Below In cinema life, the walking, talking portrait of a monster. Michael Brennan in the big screen version of Doomwatch.

The Monster Within

From the notion that man makes his monsters it has gradually come to be supposed that, if that is the case, then the monster must be within man. In the age of Buchenwald and Belsen, Hiroshima and Dresden, that is not so hard to imagine: but in the early 19th century, the personification of the evil within was not so easy to understand. It was a time, as novelist John Wain has written, that was:

> haunted by dreams and visions, when Western man felt himself to have passed through a cataclysm that had ended the old order and was not yet able to forsee the new, and when the tide of mytho-poetic imagination ran high.

Certain books carrried these ideas forward.

One such book was James Hogg's **Confessions Of A Justified Sinner**, a study of Scottish bigotry which was to have a profound effect on another writer who would produce one of the most famous books pronouncing on the monster within mankind.

Confessions begins on a low key, telling of a religious fanatic who gives birth to two sons—one of whom she believes to be profane and the other sacred. The sons grow up, one to believe that he has become possessed by the Evil One. It is a rigorous, highly individual idea, but one that was to be taken further by the psychiatrists: the concept of two personalities tied together as one; the physical yoking of good and evil in one body. Freudians defined it as schizophrenia and it formed the basis of many stories.

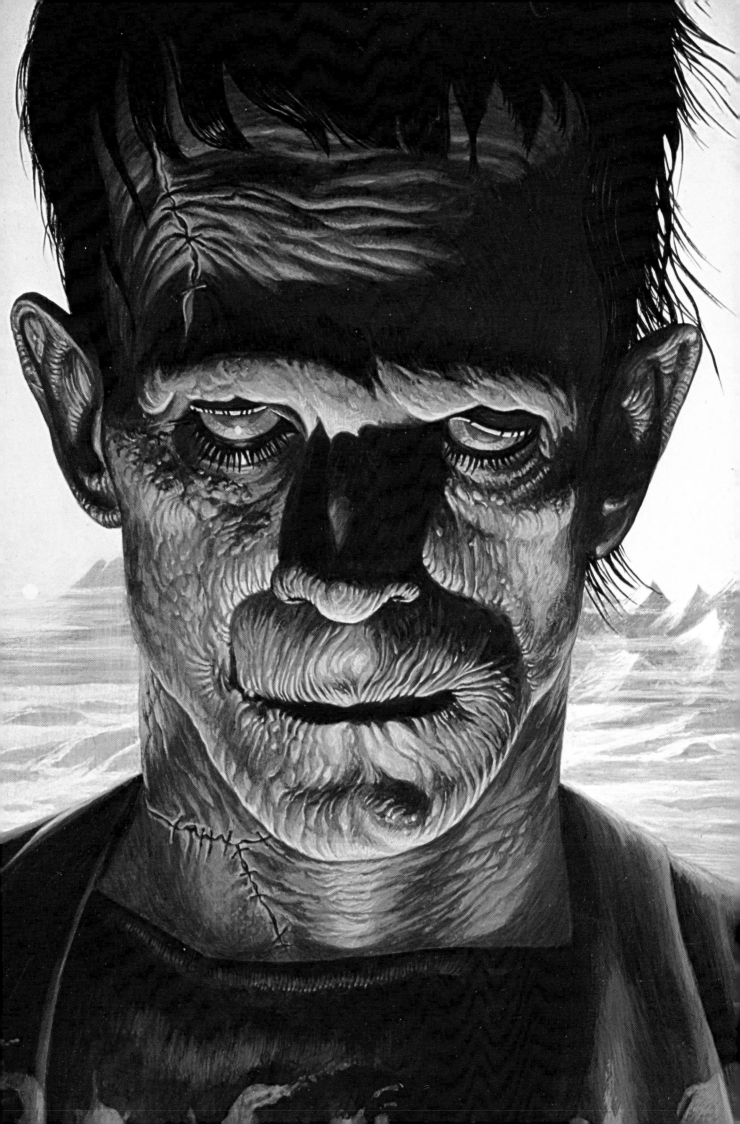

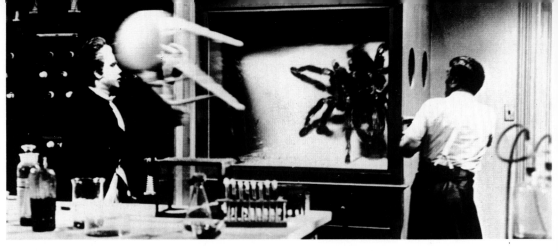

It was an idea which was most marvellously given literary shape in Robert Louis Stevenson's classic **The Strange Case of Dr Jekyll and Mr Hyde**. Movies were to take up the theme of dual personality made manifest and flesh with an avidity which proved that there was something stunningly saleable within its shocks, something that went straight to the heart. There was a version for John Barrymore in 1920; another for Frederic March in 1932; and yet another for Spencer Tracy in 1941. There were other later variations on the idea, some of which suggested that one side of the two personalities could be female.

Although the Jekyll and Hyde concept of personality is common enough these days, it is as well to remember that when Stevenson wrote it it was intended as a mystery; the revelation, in his own words at the end, by Dr Jekyll that he is also Edward Hyde who has killed so viciously, hunted as was any monster throughout the land—this revelation was to come as a horrific suprise. And Dr Jekyll had unleashed this monster with the best of all intentions, having become aware of 'the thorough and primitive duality of man ... It was the curse of mankind ... that in the agonised womb of consciousness those polar twins should be continuously struggling'. To separate these Siamese twins of the spirit was Jekyll's intention. Taking the draught of the drug that will promote the severance of the twain the result startles: 'My devil had been long caged, he came out roaring.' The rest is violence.

Man, His Own Monster

The notion of man becoming his own monster was contagious. Other writers cultivated the idea, tilling for images on the rich soil that later psycho analysts were to pick over. It reached one of its most fantastic and enjoyable definitions in the film *Forbidden Planet*, made in 1956.

This, ostensibly, is a science fiction reworking of Shakespeare's **The Tempest**. Dr Walter Pidgeon lives with his virginal daughter, Anne Francis, and robot-of-all-work, Robbie, on a planet which has enormous reserves of generated energy piped away in underground laboratories. Astronaut intruders camped nearby, are destroyed one by one by an invisible monster, a seemingly electrical presence. It is, in fact, the 'Monster from the Id'. A monster given shape and fearful violence by the stored energy which is conducted into the Doctor's subconscious. His jealousy and resentment at the intruders are thus given savage shape.

A more conventional but still untraditional version of **The Tempest** was that directed by Derek Jarman in 1979. Here the monster Caliban is a slavering, misshapen creature lusting after Miranda and yet never able to come to terms with its own animality. It, too, links with Jekyll and Hyde and so many other monsters in that there is, as Stevenson wrote, 'the haunting sense of unexpressed deformity with which the fugitive impressed his beholders'. Perhaps that stern impression was because the fugitive was the onlooker—but seen through a glass distortedly.

Perhaps mankind fears deformity because its monstrousness could easily take over his own body. Perhaps that is the reason why the great monster-maker H. G Wells—who started the **War of the Worlds**—also begat **The Island of Dr Moreau**, which was banned from cinemas in Britain when it was filmed as *The Island of Lost Souls* (1932). Here the monster is, in fact Dr Moreau (Charles Laughton) who is experimenting on animals to turn them into humans—and vice versa. The place of his experiments is called The House of Pain.

The paradox here is that it is the man who is the monster, because of what he does, and it is the seeming monsters who are sympathetic because of what has been done to them. The responsibility of man to the animals with whom he shares the planet and over whom he has the power of such ingenuity is here shown in a way that moves from the horrific to the poignant.

There is a horrendous corollary to the concept of man as monster, namely how can we know whether what we see is man or monster. If it looks human and normal how will we know if it is really monstrous? Gone are the days when monsters could be monsters, huge misshapen, appalling and very easily recognized. Now monsters can be disguised as our own children. What could be more horrific than John Wyndham's **Midwich Cuckoos**, a whole village of alien children the embodiment of every pregnant woman's most irrational, yet potent nightmare . . . that she is carrying a monster inside her.

Of course, the concept of the non-human masquerading as the human is not new, but in our world of test tube babies, genetic engineer-

ing, silent, unnoticed mutations—remember Harrisburg—it is a very potent image indeed. In the Ray Bradbury story, 'The Small Assassin', such a monstrous idea is given real power and horror because it is explained precisely why the four-month-old baby of the title kills first its mother and then its father:

What is more at peace, more dreamfully content, at ease, at rest, fed, comforted, unbothered, than an unborn child? Nothing. It floats in a sleepy timeless wonder of nourishment and silence. Then, suddenly, it is asked to give up its berth, is forced to vacate, rushed out into a noisy, uncaring, selfish world, where it is asked to shift for itself, to hunt, to feed from the hunting, to seek after a vanishing love that once was its unquestionable right, to meet confusion instead of inner silence and conservative slumber! And the child resents it!

Above The most frightening monsters are often those which retain some recognizable human characteristics. This 18th century illustration was claimed, by the artist, to be an accurate representation of a werewolf reputed to be at large in France.

Far left Up to his shoulders in worms in the Canadian horror movie Squirm, 1976, directed by Jeff Leiberman. He followed it up with the clever Blue Sunshine, 1977 in which former LSD users suddenly turn into bald homicidal maniacs.

Left A book jacket illustration enticing the reader to enter into the evil of the world.

Celluloid Monsters

Bradbury it was who was responsible for another famed cinematic monster, *The Beast From 20,000 Fathoms* (1953), one of those movies which declared that it was scientific man who made the monsters. In this case, an underwater nuclear explosion disturbed the prehistoric creature which then rampaged ashore to thresh around a New York that collapsed like the cardboard it was at its very presence.

In contrast, Bradbury's original story, upon which the film was based, was a quieter, more poetic idea—about a prehistoric monster which emerges from the depths because it is attracted,

in a way which approximates to love, by the lighthouse that gives the story its name. A delicate idea, not meant for the likes of the film that *The Beast From 20,000 Fathoms* aspired to be and very much out of place.

Within the Parthenon of monstrosity both Frankenstein and vampire-in-chief Count Dracula have chiselled out large niches for themselves. That they do not come within the scope of this chapter is because they are dealt with formidably elsewhere in the book. Besides they do seem to stand, entire within themselves, for certain aspects of the human condition and its relationship with supernormal forces. They are genres in their own rights.

Far left Poster for the Universal movie The Black Cat based on Edgar Allan Poe's classic spine chiller.

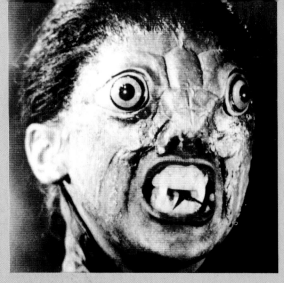

Right *The lovely Jacqueline Pearce incredibly concealed beneath the grotesque face of the Cobra Girl in Hammer's* The Reptile, *1966.*

Below *A Homunculus-style monster, with the face framed by the outsized hands.*

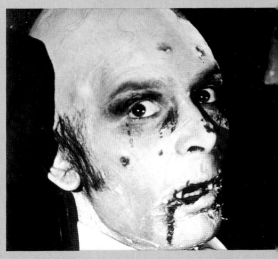

Four portraits of horror: *Peter Cushing (above) comes back from the grave for revenge in* Tales from the Crypt, *1971; while deformity repells with hunchbacked Carl (Victor Maddern) in* Blood of the Vampire, *1958. The troglodyte ape-man (Joe Cornelius) shows us (below) how we used to be in* Trog, *1970, while the evil vampire of* Twins of Evil, *1971 shows us just how unnattractive the Undead can be!*

After World War II there was an upsurge of interest not only in movies dealing with Frankenstein and Dracula, but also with films dealing with all manner of monsters. It was inevitable, because that war had seen exploded the most monstrous weapon ever devised by Man: the atomic bomb. In struggling to understand that awesome power, we had, as ever, to resort to fairy tale and films that could distance us from that fact and allow us to understand it.

There were euphemisms for the Bomb, of course—'radiation' or sometimes the effects of another star were blamed—to explain just how or why some organisms had been transmuted and mutated. What we were really talking about was 'The Bomb', putting it into syllables of understanding that could be best assimilated: the extraordinary, thus, to solve the monstrously ordinary. In so doing we were coming to our own terms with those viciously scarred survivors of Hiroshima and Nagasaki. And, as the relationships between East and West went into deeper cold storage and the possibility of yet another war did not seem *so* impossible, so we could align our fear at the prospect with the idea of invasion from outer space by monstrous entities.

Some were risible. *The Blob* (1958) was notable for being a very early film for Steve McQueen in which he was to be thanked by humanity for getting rid of a malignant fungus which had been dropped on to this planet from outer space. And that same year produced *I Married a Monster From Outer Space*—a title to sum up a fear, which was sometimes sexual, that the extraordinary could impose upon normality.

Despite its catchpenny title, this was a consistently and effectively eerie low-budget movie which had a bridegroom-to-be being taken-over by an alien who had landed in a flying saucer at a time when Unidentified Flying Objects were themselves becoming a further field of specialized hysteria. It was a film that had a power beyond its seeming means to achieve that power; it spoke directly to the human psyche threshing about in bewilderment wondering and worrying about the new technologies that turned men into monsters and drained them of whatever constituted their humanity.

Don Siegel's *Invasion Of The Body Snatchers* (1956) saw men as monsters by that simple fact of having lost their capacity to be human. From outer space came spores which, in one small American town to which Kevin McCarthy returns, assume human identity by duplicating the people who are already there. Vast 'pods' take on the likeness of the person to be assimilated; the result is one corporate creature functioning via many people, all thinking the one thought.

Below Claude Rains hides his acid-scared face behind an elegant mask as Erik becomes Erique in the second version of The Phantom of the Opera, *1943.*

Inset Herbert Lom as the third Phantom in Hammer's 1962 remake of The Phantom of the Opera *directed by Terence Fisher. Lom himself was sinister enough but his face, when revealed, was less scary than the mask!*

In a world becoming more and more uniform of thought, and conforming to so many different state or corporation dicta, this was a salutory warning. This brilliant film was seen as both an attack on the Right and the Left. Siegel claimed that it was merely a plea for individuality; an acquiescent monster seemed to him to be the most repulsive creature around.

It has always seemed, to those of us who cannot stand the sight or feel of a cockroach, that the most accessible monsters around are already with us—within the insect world. Post-war, there was a whole spate of movies that had to do with the tiny writ manifestly large. *Tarantula* (1955), for instance, directed by Jack Arnold, who specialized in this sort of thing: his view of a desert landscape dominated by a hill-high killer spider had the primal look of something taken from everyone's racial nightmares—from a time when most creatures seemed bigger than man himself, and all were malevolent.

This preoccupation with the insect world was notably impressive in the 1953 movie *Them!* where, again, the desert was the arena in which mankind would fight it out with a destiny that threatened to destroy him. A film with occasional passages of longeur, its most vital attribute was the raw energy of its idea . . . that tiny ants had been transformed by radiation from nuclear experiments into vast, violent creatures—once again working as a corporate organism to defend its territory.

The title comes from the only word that can be uttered by the small girl found wandering and in shock across the desert. From that first remarkable shot to the final journey into the tunnelled interior of the ant-world—where you can almost smell the formic acid—the film has a grip which is never less than compulsive. Its shocks linked only too easily with the unease felt by everyone about the way scientists were moving in their experiments with not only the atom—but our own futures. A film to symbolize our own age of anxiety.

The Creature From The Black Lagoon (1953), though, didn't bother with radiation or curses or any excuses for its monster, which was discovered as being a gillman in an inlet in the River Amazon. The film's only excuse was the simple one that it just wanted to put the frighteners on us, and it did just that, combining junk effects with competent direction.

Such monsters had as much to do with the skill of the make-up man as the scriptwriter's imagination. Indeed, the director Billy Wilder, in a sour comment on the sharp increase of films of horror combined with spills at speed, in the 1960s and 1970s said: 'Soon there'll be nobody left in the business but make-up departments and stunt-men'.

Centre Spanish inquisitor Vincent Price gloats over his next victim (John Kerr) in The Pit and the Pendulum, *1961, the second in Roger Corman's highly-successful series of movies based on short stories and poems by Edgar Allan Poe.*

Below Roy Stewart welcomes a visitor to his master's castle in the fast-paced Twins of Evil, *1971. This was the third in Hammer's 'Karnstein' series inspired by author J. Sheridan Le Fanu's vampire classic,* Carmilla.

King Kong: the Thinking Man's Monster

One of the most famous and effective of all monsters was not created out of make-up used on a human being, but owed his life mainly to special effects. He sprang fully grown from the minds of many people, including the British thriller-writer, Edgar Wallace. He has become one of the great folk-myths of the century; a folkloric creature about whom books have been written and other films made—though none as convincing as the first in 1933. His name: King Kong.

This is a quite splendid reworking of the Beauty and the Beast theme. Indeed that phrase is often encountered within the movie itself, a movie completely aware of what it is doing. Hence its monster gradually becomes one of the most likeable of all such creatures. Because it, too, conforms to something outrageous within us; something that is, at the same time, to be pitied.

Showman Robert Armstrong leads an expedition to an island inhabited by prehistoric beasts; with him are Bruce Cabot and the girl Fay Wray whose upward look of screaming anxiety was to become one of the most famous visual totems to the age. On the island, immense dark gates loom as though to emphasize the size of the monster that they keep out. He only appears to receive victims of sacrifice. One of those victims was to be provided by Fay Wray, when she is captured by the local natives and strung up to await the monster's bidding.

Here is the maiden of ancient legend staked out for destruction by the devouring dragon. But what happens now is that the monster falls in love with his prey, cradling her gently in his giant paw. Brought back to New York to

Left A monster of philosophy, Donatien Alphonse Françoise, Marquis de Sade, from whose name the word 'sadist' is derived. De Sade advocated the pursuit of pleasure through pain – other people's, of course. Fortunately, he mostly confined his ideas to his imagination and to such books as the much-filmed Justine, or the Misfortunes of Virtue and Philosophy in the Boudoir.

Below Sadism in the cinema: Charles Bronson (then called Buchinski) prepares to shorten Paul Picerni's life in House of Wax, 1953, a 3-D remake of the classic Mystery of the Wax Museum, 1932.

Monster with a heart of gold? The Incredible Hulk, the cartoon character come to life on the television screen, is a creature which can adopt both human and monster form; the monster element leaping into action to save innocents or right wrongs.

become a figure of exhibition and display it is for the girl's love that he escapes, and she for whom he climbs the Empire State Building—from which height he is eventually shot down and killed by fighter planes. There is never a dry eye in the house after *King Kong* has been showing and he must go down as the most heroic monster yet created.

Alien Monsters

The monster in *Alien* (1979), however inexplicable and terrifying in what it does, has no choice but to do what it must do; like the huge shark in *Jaws* (1975) it kills to eat to live. *Alien*, though, was more monstrously popular than most because of the credibility of the way it was constructed and realized as a box-office shocker.

Earlier, the writer Dan O'Bannion had col-

laborated with John Carpenter, of *Hallowe'en* fame, to create a science fiction movie called *Dark Star* (1974) which was about a group of clapped out, irresolute spacemen, tired of shuttling their spacecraft from planet to planet. It was this feeling of workaday, sweaty realism that seemed so genuine—as did the monster that was introduced.

This monster was almost laughable in its imbecility. It is nothing but a balloon with claws, a huge football-shaped creature from another world, whose very irrationality nearly brings about the deaths of those who are trying to look after it. But the humour of its sudden movements, the very illogic of whatever it does, eventually sours, in realization that it could be a killer—without realizing it. John Carpenter used his skill to cut one's laughter short.

The all-toothed horror of *Alien*, similarly, has no purpose other than to survive. The astronauts here encounter a vast spaceship and a dead creature. Scattered around are 'eggs', one of which attaches itself to a member of the party. In grisly fashion it devours him and then tackles the rest of the members of the crew.

The monster here is barely seen: all we know about it is that it is growing all the time, and that it needs flesh. But again, even here, in this alienated place, man makes monsters. For one of the crew members is revealed as a robot, an android whose loyalty is to the alien creature itself: it is the former's monstrosity that is seen as more evil, because it is he who has been given the element of human choice to combine with his own supernormal qualities of physique.

Thus our imaginings take root in our very ability to make them live. Like the alien we gorge upon monsters, like monsters ourselves, because they sustain the very lifeblood of our imagination. Perhaps it is part of some ancient folk memory, the drives of which have always to be nurtured and fuelled. For it is in their very strangeness and unknown danger that they are of use to us. Because we are still mentally poised between the cosy glow of Beowulf's fire-hearth and the alarm of the outside marshland, where nothing is warm and all is as chill as the universe we see about us. So we create monsters to give us that feeling that at once frightens us with its power and yet warms us.

There is another short story by Ray Bradbury in which a woman runs from something appalling along the highway. Frantic, she enters her house, slams shut the door and locks and bolts it. She hears from behind her the monster—which has been at home all the time and with whom she is now locked in!

It has always been so. Home is where the monster is. Because that is where *we* are.

Left Jerry Lewis jumps out of his seat in Scared Stiff, *1952, made when he was still partnered by Dean Martin. Directed by George Marshall, the film was an inferior remake of an earlier haunted house comedy directed by Marshall:* The Ghost Breakers, *1940.*

Below left Leatherface and company in Tobe Hooper's macabre and genuinely horrific The Texas Chainsaw Massacre, *1975. Like* Psycho, Chainsaw *was inspired by the bizarre crimes of necrophile-cannibal Ed Gein.*

Below The Addams family pose for a moment. Cousin It stands in the centre.

The Frankenstein Saga

To some, the ultimate horror must
always be a monster created by some
evil human genius. A bizarre parody of
Genesis, that instant of animation when
the creature's fingers tremble slightly, indicating to the audience that horror is about to
be unleashed, sending the nerves screaming
for cover. One of the most fascinating aspects
of Frankenstein's Monster, explored by script-
writer and novelist Michel Parry, is that the
original story was written by a teenaged girl. Mary
Shelley set out to capture in words the disturbed
images of her dreams, where she saw the 'hideous
phantasm of a man . . . show signs of life and stir'.
In doing so she unknowingly created a monster
of fiction which would fascinate and terrify
audiences for generations. Michel Parry looks
at the early stage productions of the story
and follows through to the unforgettable
portrayal of the monster by Boris Karloff.
The theme has had many interpretations, both as a monster movie and also
as a comedy and is still firmly established as a favourite horror classic.
Perhaps the continuing popularity
of the Frankenstein story in all its
varied forms is that it encapsu-
lates the perfect statement
about Man's pretensions. His
attempt to create artificial
life ends, reassuringly, in a
futile nightmarish failure.

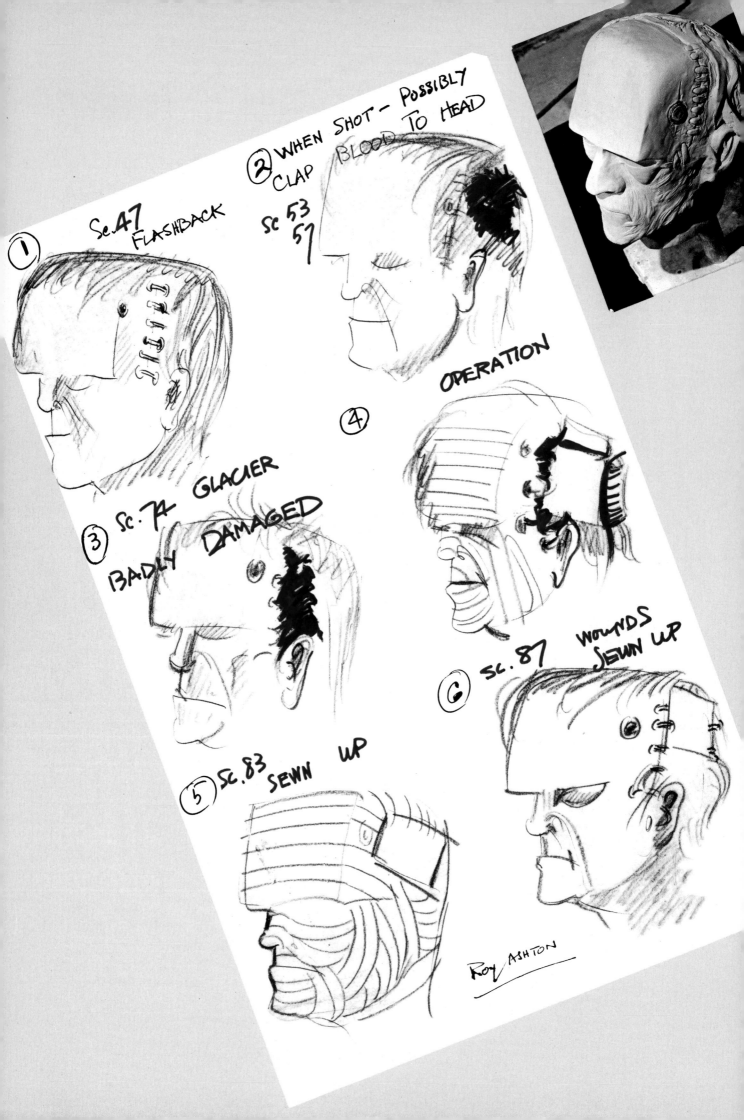

Frankenstein. Throughout the world the name is synonymous with horror, instantly conjuring up images of ugly, hulking monsters stomping murderously across our cinema and television screens. Most people, familiar only with the film Frankensteins, would perhaps be surprised to learn that the novel upon which these films are distantly based was written by a teenage girl. Mary Wollstonecraft Shelley was born in August 1797, the daughter of unconventional parents. Her father, William Godwin, was a political philosopher notorious in his day for his extreme revolutionary beliefs; he also wrote several outstanding gothic novels. His wife, Mary Wollstonecraft, was a campaigning feminist. Ten days after Mary's birth, her mother died. Godwin seems to have put the blame for his wife's death squarely on his daughter. His subsequent coldness toward her affected her deeply.

By most accounts, Mary was a sad child. Although she had stepsisters to play with, she preferred solitary pastimes—reading, 'scribbling' stories and, above all, daydreaming. No doubt she liked to imagine someone coming to take her away to a happier life. Eventually someone did. In 1814 she was introduced to her father's most idealistic disciple, Percy Bysshe Shelley; although only 20, Shelley was already gaining a reputation as one of England's finest poets. Two years later, Mary eloped with him to Switzerland.

The Nightmare

'We will each write a ghost story . . .'

With this impetuous suggestion, the eminent 19th-century poet Lord George Byron set into motion a train of events that would establish the two main traditions of horror literature and help shape the future of the yet unborn film industry. The setting was the Villa Diodati, an elegant mansion on the shore of Lake Geneva—Byron had fled there to escape a scandal back home in England—and the poet's guests that fateful July evening in 1816 were Percy Shelley and his 18-year-old mistress, Mary Godwin. (The couple were not to marry until after Shelley's first wife, Harriet, drowned herself the following December.) Also present that evening was Byron's young secretary-cum-physician, John Polidori. Confined to the house by bad weather, the four friends had been amusing themselves by reading aloud from **Phantasmagoriana** and other volumes of German ghost stories. One story, Mary later recalled, was about a gigantic, armour-clad ghost whose 'doom' it was to bestow the kiss of death upon each of his male descendants. It was the party's enjoyment of these stories which had prompted Byron's proposal.

The EDISON KINETOGRAM

VOL. 1   LONDON, APRIL 15, 1910   No. 1

SCENE FROM

FRANKENSTEIN

FILM No. 6604

EDISON FILMS TO BE RELEASED FROM MAY 11 TO 18 INCLUSIVE

The challenge was taken up with enthusiasm—which, unfortunately, proved short-lived. As Mary herself later put it: 'The illustrious poets . . . annoyed by the platitude of prose, speedily relinquished their uncongenial task.' Polidori attempted a tale about a 'skull-headed lady' fond of peeping through keyholes; he soon ran out of steam. However, inspired by Byron's abandoned vampire novel (a fragment of which appears at the end of his poem 'Mazeppa' (1819)), he persevered with another story, **The Vampire**, in which a young Englishman falls foul of a scandal-tainted nobleman, Lord Ruthven (a thinly-disguised Byron), who turns out to be a bloodsucking vampire. With this story Polidori introduced English readers to the now familiar convention of the suave, irresistible, aristocratic vampire, and so established the literary tradition that was to produce, among others, **Varney the Vampire** (1847) and **Dracula** (1897).

As for Mary, she busied herself to think of a story: 'One which would speak to the mysterious fears of our nature, and awake thrilling horror—one to make the reader dread to look around, to curdle the blood, and quicken the

Above A programme advertising, among others, the first screen Frankenstein *made by J. Searle Dawley for Thomas Edison Company in 1910. Charles Ogle plays the monster.*

Left Continuity sketches by Roy Ashton, Hammer's Head of Make-up, for The Evil of Frankenstein, 1964. These sketches help the film-makers to keep track of the various stages of the monster's appearance.

bed. Years later she described what resulted:

> When I placed my head on my pillow I did not sleep, nor could I be said to think. My imagination, unbidden, possessed and guided me, gifting the successive images that arose in my mind with a vividness far beyond the usual bounds of reverie. I saw—with shut eyes, but acute mental vision—I saw the pale student of unhallowed arts kneeling beside the thing he had put together. I saw the hideous phantasm of a man stretched out, and then, on the working of some powerful engine, show signs of life, and stir with an uneasy, half vital motion. Frightful must it be; for supremely frightful would be the effect of any human endeavour to mock the stupendous mechanism of the Creator of the world. His success would terrify the artist; he would rush away from his odious handiwork, horror-stricken.

Mary opened her eyes in terror, eager for the reassurance of familiar surroundings. With relief she realized she had her ghost story: 'What terrified me will terrify others, and I need only describe the spectre which has haunted my midnight pillow.' The following morning she set to work, beginning with the words, 'It was a dreary night of November...' (now the opening of chapter 5). Her first draft was little more than a summary of her nightmare. It was Shelley who found merit in the premise and encouraged her to expand what she had written into a full-length novel. Still only 18 years old, Mary sat down to write **Frankenstein or, The Modern Prometheus**.

Why did she choose the name Frankenstein? It has been suggested that Mary intended the name as an allusion to the American statesman Benjamin Franklin (1706–90), once considered something of a modern Prometheus for his invention of the lightning rod (he also made a study of electricity). Equally likely, she may have heard about—or even visited—an actual Castle Frankenstein in Germany. Buried in the grounds of the 13th-century castle, which was once the home of a notorious alchemist, is a certain Baron Georg. He was a brave knight said to have been killed saving a maiden from a ferocious monster. In some versions of the legend the monster resembles a giant boar, while in others it is manmade.

The Book

Frankenstein was first published in 1818 in a three-volume edition. Since no author's name was given, authorship was at first attributed to Shelley (in fact he wrote only the preface). Critical response was mixed. The popular novelist Walter Scott wrote:

Above The young lady Mary Wollstonecroft Shelley who wrote the monster classic, Frankenstein or the Modern Prometheus.

Far right Robot Frankenstein: The Colossus of New York, 1958, concerned a dying scientist whose brain was transplanted into a giant robot. In addition to super-strength, the robot was somewhat unwisely equipped with eyes that could shoot death rays.

beatings of the heart. If I did not accomplish these things, my ghost story would be unworthy of its name.' One evening, Mary listened, silent and somewhat in awe, as Shelley and Byron debated 'the secret of life', and whether that elusive secret would ever be discovered and applied by man. Much of their discussion centred around certain unorthodox experiments said to have been conducted by the influential physician-philosopher Erasmus Darwin (1731–1802). Darwin (grandfather of the more famous Charles) was even rumoured to have brought a piece of vermicelli to wriggling life! At this time electricity was still considered something of a mysterious novelty and experiments by Darwin and others, notably Luigi Galvani (1737–90), into the effects of electrical currents on organic matter (frogs' legs were a particular favourite) had led to speculation that living beings, humans included, were more or less 'natural machines' powered by electrical impulses. If this were so, it followed that electricity, correctly applied, could be used to reanimate a corpse—or even give life to an entirely new being composed of parts of different corpses...

It was with thoughts such as these running through her head that Mary finally retired to

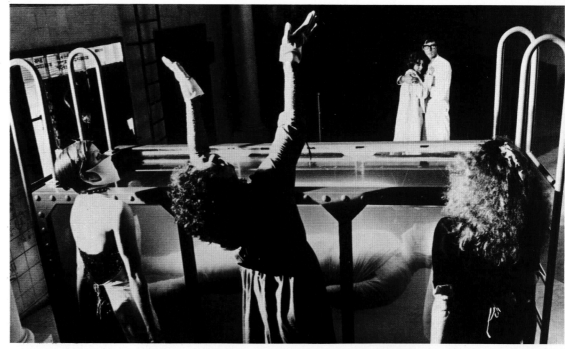

Top right *The diabolical Frank N. Furter (Tim Curry) prepares to give life to his latest creation, Rocky, in* The Rocky Horror Picture Show, *1975, by 20th Century-Fox. It was based on Richard O'Brien's hit musical. A sequel,* Shock Treatment, *followed in 1981.*

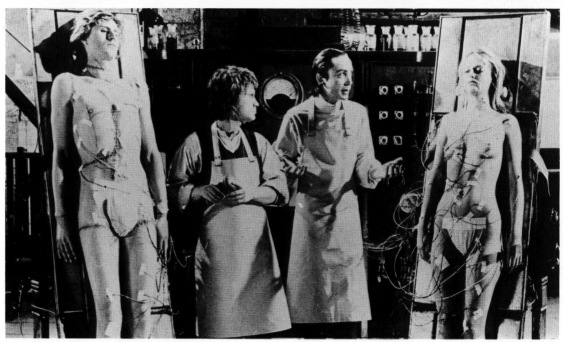

Centre right *Baron Frankenstein (Udo Kier) and assistant Otto (Arno Juerging) admire their handiwork in the gory, Italian-made* Flesh for Frankenstein, *1974. Crassly directed by Warhol associate Paul Morrissey, the film is best-known for its 3-D effects such as dangling various organs into the audience.*

Bottom right Coma, *1978 stared Genevieve Bujold as a concerned doctor uncovering a conspiracy to murder hospital patients and use their bodies in unorthodox experiments. The film was adapted from Robin Cook's novel and directed by doctor-turned-novelist Michael Crichton, who had previously ventured into Frankenstein territory with his story of androids on the rampage in* Westworld, *1973.*

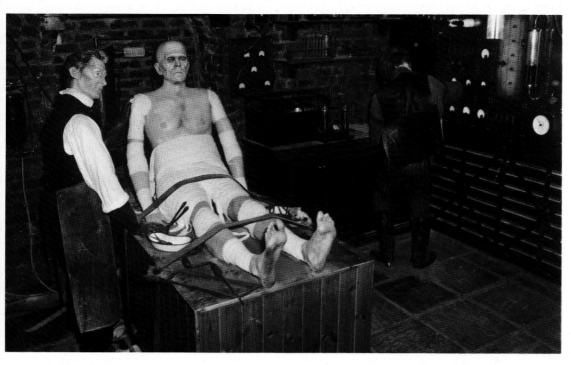

Left *The Frankenstein exhibit in London's Palladium Cellars, a waxworks museum devised by former head of Hammer, Michael Carreras. The Baron resembles Peter Cushing but his creation looks more like a bald Karloff than any of Hammer's monsters. Note the unmatching feet.*

'When we have admitted that **Frankenstein** has passages which appal the mind and make the flesh creep, we have given it all the praise (if praise it can be called) which we dare bestow. Our taste and judgement alike revolt at this kind of writing, and the greater the ability with which it may be executed, the worse it is.

Mary had undoubtedly achieved what she set out to write: a story that 'awoke thrilling horror'. Yet, in the writing, it had become much more than that. Where she showed genius was in the novel's challenging ambiguity. Frankenstein's creation is no mere bogy but a creature as tragic as he is ugly; so poignant a creature, in fact, that he has been seen as a symbol of the human condition. The reader feels torn between sympathy for Frankenstein and sympathy for his luckless, friendless monster. Paradoxically, the monster is made to seem more human than his maker: it is easier to relate to the monster's simple longing for acceptance than to Frankenstein's selfish, single-minded preoccupation with the 'secret of life'.

Frankenstein is really nothing less than a reworking of the biblical story of Adam with the monster taking the part of newly-created man and Frankenstein himself playing god. It's not coincidence that the book is dotted with references to John Milton's powerful account of the Adam and Eve story in **Paradise Lost**. In this case the monstrous Adam never even gets to set foot in the Garden of Eden (human society) and his vacillating god denies him even the companionship of an Eve. Small wonder that the monster comes to identify with Milton's rebellious Fallen Angel—as did Shelley and the other poets of the so-called 'satanic school'. The conflict between Frankenstein and the monster (God and man? God and Devil?) has all the disturbing resonance of a true archetype.

Like all great stories, **Frankenstein** is open to a wide variety of interpretations, including the notion that the monster is an embodiment of Frankenstein's own darker side—Mr Hyde to Frankenstein's Dr Jekyll, or Dorian Gray's portrait come to life. On a more personal level, it could even be said that the outcast monster represents Mary Shelley herself, with Frankenstein a projection of William Godwin, the obsessive idealist who denied her a father's love.

The popularly-accepted theme of **Frankenstein** is the age-old idea that man is unable to control what he has created: the Sorcerer's Apprentice syndrome. Yet it is not his playing at God that dooms Frankenstein but his failure to take responsibility for his creation when his experiment is successful. The moral of the story is (as Shelley succinctly put it): 'Treat a man ill, and he will become wicked.'

Frankenstein is now rightly regarded as a literary classic. Its influence has been detected in works as diverse as **The Hunchback of Notre Dame** (1831), **Wuthering Heights** (1847), **Moby Dick** (1851) and **Dr Jekyll and Mr Hyde** (1886) as well as innumerable tales of horror and science fiction. The book has been cited by Brian Aldiss, among others, as the very first science fiction novel (admittedly there is not much hard science in **Frankenstein**, but it is made clear that Victor is conducting a *scientific* experiment, not one of the occult rituals dear to the writers of gothic novels). It is also probably the only book of its period that has continued to sell in large numbers down to the present day. That fact alone speaks for its merit and lasting relevance.

In 1831, Mary Shelley revised **Frankenstein** to its present form and added an introduction revealing how the story came to her. By then she had written further books, the most interesting of which is **The Last Man** (1826). A science fiction story set in the year 2008, it describes the lonely existence of the last human on Earth after the rest of humanity has been killed off by a plague. His loneliness reflected Mary's: Shelley had drowned four years earlier, and most other members of her circle had also died prematurely. Mary herself died in 1851 aged 53. In her introduction to the revised edition of **Frankenstein**, Mary had bid her 'hideous progeny go forth and prosper'. Prosper it did, though not in a way she could possibly have imagined.

The Theatre of Frankenstein

Stage versions of **Frankenstein** were to become as popular with 19th-century theatregoers as with their cinema-going counterparts a century later. The first known dramatization was Richard Brinsley Peake's *Presumption; or, The Fate of Frankenstein*, which opened in London in July, 1823. Predictably, Peake took liberties with the original, notably having the monster die in an avalanche. The challenging role of monster was taken by Thomas Potter Cooke, an actor already popular for his villainous roles including Lord Ruthven in an adaptation of

Polidori's **The Vampyre**. As the monster, Cooke's face was painted yellow and green with black lips held unnaturally rigid; his black hair was long and unkempt, his exposed limbs a vivid blue. The play cannot have been too terrifying, however, as the action was interspersed with a selection of songs!

Mary Shelley herself attended a performance and passed judgement in a letter to the writer Leigh Hunt:

> But lo and behold! I found myself famous. *Frankenstein* had prodigious success as a drama, and was about to be repeated, for the twenty-third night, at the English Opera House. The playbill amused me extremely for, in the list of *dramatis personae*, came "——" by Mr T. Cooke: this nameless mode of naming the unnameable is rather good. . . . The story is not well managed, but Cooke played "——" extremely well; his seeking, as it were, for support; his trying to grasp at the sounds he heard; all, indeed, he does was well imagined and executed. I was much amused and it appeared to excite a breathless eagerness in the audience.

To help satisfy that eagerness, several rival productions were hastily mounted, including parodies with names such as *Frank-in-Steam* and *Frankenstitch*.

Above The monster (wrestler Kiwi Kingston) as he finally appeared in Freddie Francis' The Evil of Frankenstein, *1964, by Hammer.*

Left The first Hammer monster: Christopher Lee as the Creature in Terence Fisher's The Curse of Frankenstein, *1956. Lee had reservations about Phil Leakey's make-up, commenting that it made him look like a circus clown.*

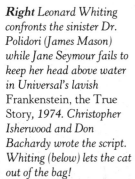

Right Leonard Whiting confronts the sinister Dr. Polidori (James Mason) while Jane Seymour fails to keep her head above water in Universal's lavish Frankenstein, the True Story, 1974. Christopher Isherwood and Don Bachardy wrote the script. Whiting (below) lets the cat out of the bag!

The next notable adaptation came in July, 1826, when *Frankenstein; or, The Man and the Monster*, opened at London's Royal Coburg Theatre. This version, by H. M. Milner, was 'founded principally on Mrs Shelley's singular work and partly on the French piece, '*Le Magicien et le Monstre*' (*The Magician and the Monster*) by Merle and Anthony, a French adaptation which substituted magic for the science of Mary Shelley's original. This time the monster was played by George 'O' Smith, another actor who seemed made for the part (*Punch* dubbed him 'Lord Frankenstein'). Milner relocated the story to Sicily, presumably to rationalize the play's spectacular climax: pursued to the summit of Mount Etna by Frankenstein and a troop of soldiers, the monster stabs Frankenstein, then leaps defiantly into the mouth of the simmering volcano! Perhaps the anonymous author of **Varney the Vampire** has this scene in mind, 20 years later, when he made Varney cast himself into the lava of Vesuvius (or perhaps the alliteration was irresistible). Other fates suffered by the monster in early dramatizations included freezing to death in an on-stage Arctic blizzard and, anticipating later film versions, expiring inside a burning church.

More light-hearted was *Frankenstein; or, The Vampire's Victim*, a comedy-musical of 1849. In a later parody, *The Model Man* by Richard Butler and H. Chane Newton, comedy star Fred Leslie played the monster as a bowler-hatted dandy with carnation and monocle! Probably the best-known adaptation is that by Peggy Webling, which premiered in London in 1927. Its sympathetic monster was played by Hamilton Deane, who had two years earlier played Dracula in his own dramatization of Stoker's novel. Deane later toured with both plays, playing Dracula and monster on alternate nights: perhaps the first close link between two characters who were to become increasingly interrelated. A timely lightning bolt put paid to this particular monster.

Perhaps the most bizarre stage Frankenstein was that performed by the Living Theatre commune in Europe and the USA in the 1960s. In this lengthy, rambling, largely improvised production devised by Julian Beck and Judith Malina, the monster (a symbol of oppressed humanity) was at times represented by a score of howling, near-naked exhibitionists clambering acrobatically over an enormous scaffold construction festooned with blinking lights.

A close contender for the title of most outrageous Frankenstein-inspired entertainment must be *The Rocky Horror Show*, a rock musical by actor Richard O'Brien in which nostalgia for old horror movies crashed head-on with the sexual revolution. The show's central character Frank-N-Furter, a lingerie-loving 'sweet transexual transvestite' from Planet Transylvania, sets out to create the perfect man (and bed-partner) in the shape of blond beach-boy-type Rocky. Disgusted by Frank-N-Furter's degenerate ways (picked up on Earth, naturally), his extraterrestrial butler, Riff Raff, finally zaps him and his creation with a ray gun. The show opened in London in 1973 and was still running seven years later. In 1975 the show's original director, Jim Sharman, made a film version, *The Rocky Horror Picture Show*, which, after a slow start, went on to make a fortune from midnight shows packed with vociferous enthusiasts dressed up as characters in the film.

In the late 1970s, following the successful Broadway revival of *Dracula*, several new Frankenstein plays opened in New York, *Love of Frankenstein* by Steven Otfinoski played briefly in 1978. As well as the usual characters, this comedy featured a werewolf and a strongly-accented vampire named Bela. More faithful to the original was *The Rage of Frankenstein* by Tim Kelly (who wrote the 1970 Vincent Price horror *Cry of the Banshee*), which opened the following year, as did Ken Eulo's *The Frankenstein Affair*. This last was set in the Shelley household in Switzerland at the time Mary was writing her book and drew a parallel between her creativity and the creation of Frankenstein's Monster (played by Alan Brunn).

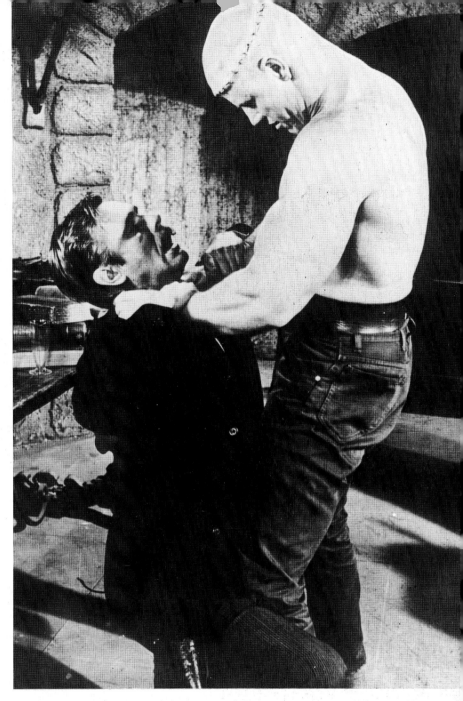

The Silent Monsters

Talking pictures were still almost 20 years away in 1910 when the first screen *Frankenstein* on record was made by J. Searle Dawley for America's Thomas Edison Company. Only one reel long, it packed the gist of the original into 25 brief scenes, some hand-tinted orange and yellow for extra dramatic impact. The aptly-named Charles Ogle portrayed an impressively grotesque hunchbacked monster with a lion's mane of frizzy hair (curiously, he wasn't made up of electrified leftovers as usual but was the product of a chemical reaction). The film sought to convey the notion that the creation of the monster was possible only because Frankenstein had allowed his 'normal' mind to be overcome by evil thoughts. When he married, his love for his bride overcame these negative impulses and the jealous monster simply faded away to nothing. A reviewer for *Motion Picture World* commented:

Above Rudolph Frankenstein (Steven Geray) meets his end in Jesse James Meets Frankenstein's Daughter, 1966. *Narda Onyx as Maria Frankenstein was the villainess of this curious companion-piece to* Billy the Kid Versus Dracula, 1966, *both directed by Hollywood veteran William Beaudine.*

Far right A moment of triumph for Frankenstein (Gene Wilder) in comedian Mel Brooks' affectionate spoof of the early Universal films, Young Frankenstein, 1974. Brooks even used some of the original sets and props from the 1931 Frankenstein, including the laboratory apparatus designed by Kenneth Strickfaden. The zipper-necked monster was amusingly played by Peter Boyle.

Below right Frankenstein (John Woodnutt) offers monster Frank (Bernard Taylor) a stein in this TV ad for lager. The monster has been used to sell everything from cars to breakfast cereal.

Below Comic horrors with Kenneth Williams and Fenella Fielding. Tom Clegg is the monstrous Oddbod in Gerald Thomas' Carry On Screaming, 1966

'The formation of the Monster in a cauldron of blazing chemicals is a piece of photographic work which will rank with the best of its kind. The entire film is one that will create an impression that the possibilities of the motion picture is reproducing these stories are scarcely realized.'

Prophetic words!

The next Frankenstein adaptation was *Life Without Soul*, a longer, more ambitious production made in the USA in 1915 by Joseph W. Smiley. Screenwriter Jesse Goldburg seems to have stuck fairly closely to the original except that Frankenstein shot his creation before himself expiring. The monster was somewhat disappointing: Percy Darrell Standing played him without make-up as a scowling, ugly man.

Next came *Il Mostro di Frakestein* (*The Monster of Frakestein* [sic]), made in Italy in 1920 by Eugenio Testa with Umberto Guarracino as the monster. Little is known of this film except that one scene depicted a confrontation between Frankenstein and his creation in a dark cave. Unfortunately, none of these early Frankenstein films have survived—we only know about them from reviews and a few rare photos.

The Golem: a Monster with Feet of Clay

Before moving on to later Frankenstein films, it is worth taking a look at the Golem, a rival monster appearing in a series of films that were to have some influence on Hollywood's approach to Frankenstein. There are many versions of the Golem legend in Jewish folklore, but the best-known concerns a Rabbi Loew who supposedly built a man out of clay and brought him to life to protect Prague's Jewish community in the 16th century. It has been suggested that Mary Shelley came across the story on her European travels and that it gave her the idea for **Frankenstein**.

The first film version of *The Golem* (also known as *The Monster of Fate*) was made in 1914 by the popular German actor Paul Wegener, who also took the title role. The lifeless Golem is discovered in an abandoned synagogue and reanimated by a scholar skilled in magic. The lumbering stone man makes a useful servant until it falls in love with the scholar's beautiful daughter. Rejected, it goes on a rampage, eventually plummeting to destruction from a high tower.

The Golem and the Dancer (Germany, 1917) was a comedy short in which Wegener disguised himself as the Golem to impress an attractive girl. Other Golem films were made in Denmark (1916) and Austria (1921) but best of all was *The Golem: How He Came Into the World* (Germany. 1920), Wegener's lavish full-length reconstructrion of the Golem's creation by

Rabbi Loew. Once again the artificial man falls in love with a beautiful girl (Loew's daughter) and goes on a jealous rampage—until a child innocently plucks the life-bestowing amulet from its chest, rendering it harmless. Outstanding sets, trick effect and photography as well as Wegener's performance make the film enthralling even today. A French version of the Golem story was made in 1936 and a Czech version, *The Emperor and the Golem*, appeared in 1951. The Golem turned up in London in *It* (GB, 1967) and promptly suffered a direct hit from an atomic bomb: its showed its disdain by walking off into the sea.

For all his endearing and enduring qualities, the Golem never came close to rivalling the popularity of the definitive Frankenstein Monster established by Universal's 1931 classic.

Karloff: the Thinking Man's Monster

In 1931 Universal Pictures announced that Bela Lugosi, star of the enormously successful *Dracula*, was to play the monster in a new version of *Frankenstein* based on the Peggy Webling stage adaptation. Director Robert Florey was assigned to shoot test footage of Lugosi in the part. Lugosi insisted on doing his own make-up. Accounts of his conception of the monster vary, some describing it as 'hairy', others as Golemesque, with smooth clay-like skin. In any event, the studio heads were not impressed—or frightened. Lugosi announced that he didn't want to play a non-speaking part anyway. Unlike Mary Shelley's talkative monster, the Universal monster was to be mute.

Robert Florey was replaced by James Whale, a 'hot' new director from England. He promptly cast another Englishman, Colin Clive, in the part of Henry Frankenstein (the name had been changed from Victor in the stage play, and it stuck.) For the part of the monster, Whale selected yet another Englishman, a gaunt, soulful bit-player he had noticed in the studio commissary one lunchtime. Early on in his career, this actor, born in 1887 as plain William Henry Pratt in the London suburb of Dulwich, had chosen for himself a much more distinctive name: Boris Karloff.

Universal's top make-up artist, Jack Pierce, began designing a suitably monstrous appearance for Karloff. It is largely to Pierce that we owe the popular image of the monster—square-headed, with bolts in the neck.

> I didn't depend on imagination, [Pearce was later to reveal]. Before I did any designing, I did some research in anatomy, surgery, criminology, ancient and modern burial customs, and electrodynamics. I discovered there are six ways a surgeon can cut the skull, and I figured Dr Frankenstein, who was not a practising surgeon, would take the easiest. That is, he would cut the top of the skull straight across like a pot lid, hinge it, pop the brain in, and clamp it tight. That's the reason I decided to make the monster's head square and flat like a box and dig that big scar across his forehead and have metal clamps hold it together. The two metal stands that stick out of his neck are inlets for electricity—plugs. Don't forget that the monster is an electrical gadget and the lightning is his life-force.

Frankenstein began shooting in August, 1931, and was premiered in December. In some areas it was released in green-tinted prints. The film opens with a joshing introduction by actor Edward Van Sloan (Professor Waldmann in the film), who warns the audience that they may be shocked and horrified by what they are about to see. Those who resisted his invitation to leave next saw Henry Frankenstein and his leering, hunchbacked assistant, Fritz (Dwight Frye), on a corpse-gathering expedition, robbing graves and gallows. Later, in his watchtower laboratory, Henry inserts a brain into the skull of his patchwork creation, little suspecting that the brain Fritz has procured for him is from an 'abnormal' criminal. Undaunted by the unexpected arrival of his fiancée, Elizabeth (Mae Clarke), and his old tutor, Professor Waldmann, Henry takes advantage of an electrical storm to complete his Promethean experiment. As lab equipment crackles and flashes spectacularly, the lifeless composite is raised up to an open skylight to receive the lightning's gift of life . . .

The first time we see the living monster is from the back. He turns. The camera cuts closer and closer until his dead-alive face—at once menacing and pathetic—fills the screen. These days the monster's features are perhaps too

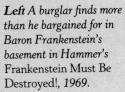

Left *A burglar finds more than he bargained for in Baron Frankenstein's basement in Hammer's Frankenstein Must Be Destroyed!, 1969.*

Below left *A family gathering in Munster Go Home, 1966, from Universal, a feature spin-off from the TV series in which Herman inherited an ancestral home in England. From left to right: Grandpa (Al Lewis), Herman (Fred Gwynne), his wife, Lily (Yvonne de Carlo), and their son, Eddie, the boy-werewolf (Butch Patrick).*

familiar to us to retain much of their original impact—but at the time of the film's first release, audiences had not seen anything so joltingly horrific since the unmasking of *The Phantom of the Opera* in 1925.

Despite his foreboding appearance (and criminal brain) the monster was basically a child-like innocent. Only when the sadistic hunchback baits him with whip and flaming torch does he reveal a more demonic side to his nature. He wraps a rope round Fritz's neck and

hangs him. While Henry prepares for his forthcoming marriage to Elizabeth, Waldmann prepares to dissect the monster. Not caring to be dissected, the monster strangles him, then wanders off into the forest where he meets a little girl, Maria, floating flowers on a lake. The monster attempts to do the same—with Maria. To his surprise, she drowns.

The wedding festivities are interrupted by the arrival of Maria's father with news of her murder. Search parties are immediately despatched to hunt the monster down. As luck would have it, Henry is the first to catch up with him. The monster knocks him unconscious and bears him off to the top of a nearby windmill. A crowd of torch-waving villagers converges on the building. When Henry tries to escape, the monster picks him up and hurls him down at the mob. Fortunately, one of the vanes of the windmill breaks his fall and the villagers help him down. With Frankenstein safely out of the way, they set fire to the mill. As flames engulf the building, a falling timber traps the now terrified monster. He screams his pain and fear, then, when the mill collapses, drops down into the inferno.

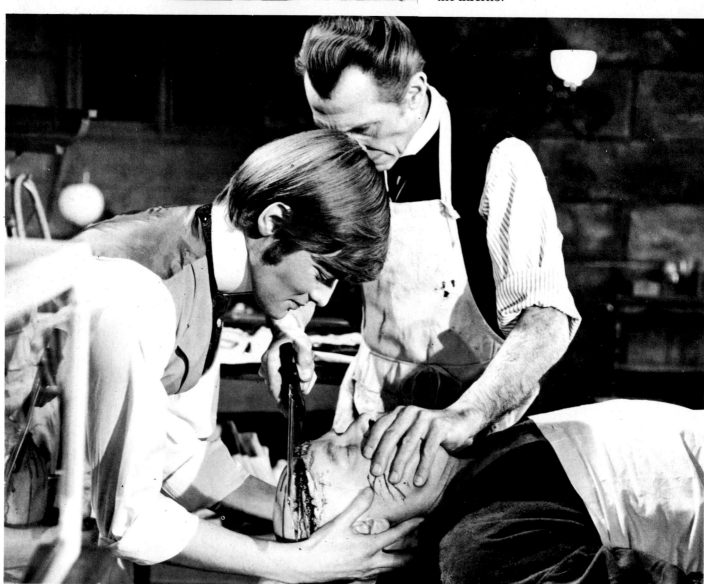

Holst, del   W. Chevalier, sculp

FRANKENSTEIN.

The Sons of Frankenstein

Frankenstein proved one of Universal's most successful films ever. Part of the credit must go to James Whale: his direction was (for the time) fluid and atmospheric, and set pieces such as the 'birth' scene remain impressive. But it was Karloff who stole the show. Despite being almost swamped by make-up, his sad, penetrating eyes conveyed a depth of pathos almost unique in the cinema. The film may be closer to the stage play than Mary Shelley's novel, yet, even mute, Karloff's performance somehow captured the spirit of the original. Karloff himself best summed up his approach:

> Whale and I both saw the character as an innocent one. Within the heavy restrictions of my make-up, I tried to play it that way. This was a pathetic creature, who, like us all, had neither wish nor say in his creation, and certainly did not wish itself the hideous image which automatically terrified humans whom it tried to befriend. The most heart-rending aspect of the creature's life, for us, was his ultimate desertion by his creator. It was as though man, in his blundering, searching attempts to improve himself, was to find himself deserted by his God.

Four years after *Frankenstein*, Karloff, now a star in his own right, returned to Universal to meet *The Bride of Frankenstein*. Like the earlier film, *Bride* also opens with an introduction—this time featuring Mary Shelley herself (Elsa Lanchester). In answer to their anxious entreaties, Mary assures Shelley and Byron that the monster did not die in the blazing mill after all. One of the villagers presently discovers this for himself when he enters the smouldering ruins to look for the monster's body. The monster had been saved when he fell into the water beneath the mill. He proves his continued good health by killing the villager, and the man's waiting wife, then stomping off into the woods to hide.

One of the most moving scenes in this or any other Frankenstein film comes when the Monster seeks refuge in a hermit's cottage. Unaware of the nature of his gruff visitor, the blind hermit (O. P. Heggie) welcomes him, plies him with food and drink and cigars, and even teaches him a few simple phrases. For the first time in his brief existence the monster has a friend. His contentment is rudely shattered by the sudden intrusion of two hunters (one of them future Dracula, John Carradine). In the ensuing battle the cottage is burnt to the ground. There's gratitude for you!

Meanwhile Henry Frankenstein teams up with the sinister Dr Pretorius (Ernest Thesiger), a splendidly eccentric power-seeking alchemist

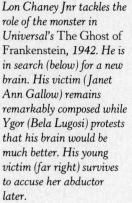

Lon Chaney Jnr tackles the role of the monster in Universal's The Ghost of Frankenstein, 1942. *He is in search (below) for a new brain. His victim (Janet Ann Gallow) remains remarkably composed while Ygor (Bela Lugosi) protests that his brain would be much better. His young victim (far right) survives to accuse her abductor later.*

who breeds tiny humans in glass jars the way other people breed goldfish. Pretorius proposes they use their combined skills to create a woman. 'That should be really interesting,' he gloats. The 'birth' of the female monster is the climax of the film: an even more impressive display of laboratory pyrotechnics than in *Frankenstein*. The male monster watches excitedly as the bandages are removed from his female counterpart (Elsa Lanchester). At last she stands revealed: seven feet tall with rigid limbs, vampire eyebrows and a backward-sloping beehive hair-do. The monster thinks she's beautiful. The reaction of the bride to the intended bridegroom, however, is one of horror—she recoils from his clumsy embrace. The monster has been rejected even by one of his own kind. 'We belong dead,' he sadly tells his 'bride', and pulls the switch that blows the laboratory sky-high.

In many ways *Bride* is an improvement on its predecessor. The characters are stronger and everything seems bigger, including the budget. Probably James Whale's best film, it is marred only by some ill-judged 'comedy relief' and the decision to have the monster speak (a decision heartily resisted by Karloff who felt it would make the character mundane and less sympathetic).

Karloff's objections evidently had some impact because the next in the series, *The Son of Frankenstein* (1939) directed by Rowland V. Lee, the monster has nothing to say (and, unfortunately, not much to do). Ygor (Bela Lugosi), a grotesque grave-robber with a broken neck (result of a botched hanging) discovers the unconscious body of the monster and persuades Henry's son, Wolf *von* Frankenstein (Basil Rathbone) to use his father's old equipment to revive him. Unfortunately, Ygor then uses the grateful monster to murder the jury responsible for his broken neck. In a climactic fight, Wolf atones for his bad judgement by toppling his father's creation into a pit of molten sulphur.

Despite a lavish budget and excellent cast (Lugosi giving his finest performance), *Son* is a disappointment, mostly because the weak script allows Karloff little opportunity to develop the human side of the monster. Sensing that his 'old friend' would soon be reduced to no more than a murderous 'prop', Karloff let it be known that he had played the part for the last time. The monster had made him a star—he owed him 'a little respect, a little rest.'

Universal had no intention of letting their top box-office monster rest for very long. *The Ghost of Frankenstein*, directed by Erle C. Kenton, followed in 1942 with Lugosi back as Ygor, Sir Cedric Hardwicke as another son of Frankenstein, Ludwig, and Universal's new horror star

Far right Elsa Lanchester
(in real-life Mrs Charles
Laughton) as The Bride of
Frankenstein, 1935, from
Universal. Her hair-style
was suggested by statues of
the Egyptian queen,
Nefertiti.

Below Not Dracula but
the manufactured man of
the title in the
Frankenstein-like
Homunculus, 1916, a six-
part serial made in
Germany by director Otto
Rippert from Robert
Reinert's novel. Intended as
a perfect man by his
scientist-creator, the
Homunculus (Olaf Fonss)
turned evil, using his
superior intellect to set
himself up as a dictator. It
took divine intervention in
the form of a well-aimed
bolt of lightning to remove
the tyrant.

Lon Chaney Jnr as the monster. Chaney had been sympathetic in *The Wolfman* (1941), but made a stolid monster. The following year, in *Frankenstein Meets the Wolfman* (directed by Roy W. Neill) Bela Lugosi finally took the part he had once derided. The script called for the monster to speak but also to be blind. When the film was released, however, all Lugosi's dialogue had been cut, along with any references to the monster's blindness—making complete nonsense of his groping portrayal.

Karloff returned in *The House of Frankenstein* (1944), directed by Erle C. Kenton, not as the monster, unfortunately, but as the mad scientist who thaws the monster out of a block of ice. The part that had made Karloff famous was played by Glenn Strange, a cowboy 'heavy' whose height and strong prominent features made him physically perfect for the role. Strange made a good-natured monster but somehow lacked impact. He was the monster again a year later in *House of Dracula* again directed by Erle C. Kenton.

The Universal monster had met Dracula and the Wolfman and the rest and survived. Finally, the monster (Strange again) met his nadir in *Frankenstein Meets Abbot and Costello* directed by Charles T. Baron in 1948. After that, he lay low for a very long time.

The Hammer of Frankenstein

The monster stayed dormant until 1956, and this time it wasn't Universal that resurrected him but a small, independent English company called Hammer Films. Hammer's success with an SF horror *The Quatermass Xperiment* (USA: *The Creeping Unknown*) had prompted the company to consider remaking the old horror classics. *The Curse of Frankenstein* directed by Terry Fisher, was its first essay into the gothic.

Like Universal's *Frankenstein*, *Curse* condensed the novel's sprawling action to one locale, Victorian Switzerland. In a prison death-cell Baron Victor Frankenstein (Peter Cushing) tells his story to a sceptical priest. In flashback we see how he attempted to create a perfect man and produced instead a hideous creature (Christopher Lee). The creature killed several people and finally abducted Frankenstein's fiancée, Elizabeth (Hazel Court). In trying to save Elizabeth, Frankenstein accidentally killed her. The creature, its clothes ablaze, fell into a vat of acid and was completely dissolved. Without its body, no one ever believes it existed and Frankenstein is condemned for its crimes. The film ends as he is led away to the guillotine.

A comparison between the Universal and Hammer versions is unavoidable. The difference in attitudes toward their respective mon-

sters is striking—the creature in *Curse* has far less importance. In both the novel and the 1931 film, the monster goes through a period of transition—the necessary brutalizing process—from neutral innocent to murdering fiend. In *Curse*, the creature's immediate impulse following its birth is to try to strangle its creator. It is a 'born', or rather constructed, killer. There is no possibility of it ever becoming anything other than what it is. This approach completely ignores Mary Shelley's idea that monsters are not born but made—by other people. Significantly, *Curse's* director, Terence Fisher, after directing a further four Frankenstein films for Hammer, would boast that he had never read the book and didn't intend to!

Hammer Films are not, of course, in the business of promoting philosophy but of provoking horror, specifically physical horror. The sort of surgical details that are only hinted at in the Universal films—incisions, severed heads, eyeballs, hacked-off hands—are lovingly dwelt upon in the Hammer films in garish colour. (*Curse* was the first Frankenstein film to be made in colour.) It was this aspect of the film that outraged British critics at the time of *Curse's* first release (one even suggested that it should be given a special 'SO' rating—for 'Sadists Only'). Seen today, the film seems tame beside the excesses of more recent films such as *Flesh for Frankenstein* (USA: *Andy Warhol's Frankenstein*). Despite (or because of) the critical outcry, *The Curse of Frankenstein* broke box-office records throughout the world.

There is also a fundamental difference in the look of the films. Universal's designers were

Below Roddy McDowall as museum curator Arthur Pimm, the man who brought the Golem back to life in It, 1966. Arthur obviously wishes he could do the same for his poor old mother.

fond of using weird architecture and symbolism to create a mood reflecting the strangeness of the drama that was unfolding. Even 'exteriors' were shot inside the studio to preserve the atmosphere that had been built up. Terence Fisher's Frankenstein films avoid this kind of artifice, placing emphasis instead on natural surroundings. If the settings are real, the horror will appear real too. Hammer's Frankenstein is *grand guignol* to Universal's passion play.

An even more important difference between the Universal and Hammer films is the approach to the character of Frankenstein. Mary Shelley's Victor was self-pitying, prone to frequent nervous breakdowns: not the stuff film heroes are made of. When not caught up in the excitement of his experiments, Colin Clive had a weak, neurotic side which permitted him to stand by and do nothing while Fritz tortured the Monster. Peter Cushing's Frankenstein, on the other hand, is strong, arrogant, ruthless: a man prepared to go to any lengths in the cause of his obsession. In *Curse*, he thinks nothing of murdering a scientist colleague to get a good brain for his creature. And when his mistress tries to blackmail him, he simply locks her in a room with the homicidal monster, then calmly sits down to breakfast. In the Universal films, only the *villains* did that sort of thing.

Cushing's Frankenstein is both a Byronic hero in the tradition of the gothic novels, and a modern antihero. Interestingly, Cushing has said that he models his interpretation on the 18th-century Scottish surgeon, Dr Robert Knox, the man who employed grave-robbers Burke and Hare to keep his dissecting room well-stocked; certainly a man who felt the end justified the means. Ruthless from the very beginning, Cushing's Frankenstein would grow steadily more so as the series continued.

The approach to the monster's appearance was different of necessity. Universal had taken the unusual step of copyrighting their famous monster make-up. Hammer's Phil Leakey came up with a messily gruesome face that was perhaps closer to Mary Shelley's description than was Jack Pierce's creation, but lacked impact except in close-up. As the creature, Christopher Lee—chosen for his imposing height—had his work cut out for him trying to bring a little humanity to such a determinedly homicidal being.

In the Universal films, it was the monster (always the *same* monster, even if played by different actors) which provided the link from film to film. Hammer's innovation was to make the baron the link-man. The monsters were to come in all shapes and sizes, often played by wrestlers or strongmen: strength before soul.

The first sequel, *The Revenge of Frankenstein*

(1958), opens with Frankenstein cheating the guillotine; the accompanying priest loses his head instead—a typical piece of understated Hammer humour. When next we see Frankenstein, he seems a reformed character. As 'Dr Stein' he devotes his time to treating the unfortunates in the workhouse hospital. Typically, it turns out that he is merely interested in them as an easy source of amputated limbs for the 'new' body he's building for his dwarfish accomplice. When his patients discover his real motive, they beat him to a pulp. Dying, he tells his assistant to transplant his brain into a spare body kept handy for just such an emergency. In the next scene, a sprightly 'Dr Frank' sets up practice in London, a fine example of a self-made man. Directed with great verve by Terence Fisher, and with an engaging perform-

Below A fine woodcut depicting Victor Frankenstein at work from a 1930 edition of the novel illustrated by the influential American artist Lynd Ward.

ance by Michael Gwynn as the monster, *Revenge* is the best of the Hammer Frankensteins.

Lacking the emotional charge of Fisher's films, *The Evil of Frankenstein* (1964), directed by Freddie Francis, is chiefly interesting because it was made for Universal and contains many references (monster in a block of ice, travelling showman, mobs of villagers) to the 1940s Frankensteins, even sharing their studio-bound look. For the first time, Hammer were also able to use a make-up based (vaguely) on the Jack Pierce concept.

Frankenstein Created Woman (1966), Ter-ence Fisher again, marked a return to the familiar Hammer look, but had the Baron showing an uncharacteristic mystical bent in his study of soul transference. The plot dwelt on the possibilities extended to a male soul 'transplanted' by Frankenstein into female body (Susan Denberg—easily the best-looking monster ever).

In the same year *Frankenstein Must Be Destroyed* begins with the Baron casually lopping off the head of a passerby for use in his latest brain transplant. Murdering and raping with abandon, Frankenstein now seemed more

Below It *again – this time it is Allen Sellers as the Golem with captive Jill Haworth in the 1966 movie by Goldstar.*

like a character from de Sade than Mary Shelley. An unusually sensitive scene had one of the Baron's transplant recipients (Freddie Jones) gazing longingly at the wife who no longer recognizes him.

Presumably there was some concern at Hammer that Cushing was getting too old to appeal to the youthful horror market any longer. *The Horror of Frankenstein* (1970) was a kind of 'I Was a Teenage Victorian Frankenstein' intended to introduce Ralph Bates as Cushing's young replacement. It was directed by Jimmy Sangster as a tongue-in-cheek remake of *The Curse of Frankenstein*, which Sangster had written 14 years previously.

Baron Frankenstein was his old self again in *Frankenstein and the Monster From Hell* (1973), directed by Terence Fisher, this time abusing his medical post in a lunatic asylum to procure parts for his latest creation. Inexplicably, the monster (Dave Prowse in his pre-Darth Vader incarnation) turned out furry. This film contained the most harrowing brain surgery scenes of any Frankenstein film. Perhaps too harrowing: after seven films in 15 years, *Monster* was the last in the Hammer Frankenstein series.

While hardly reflecting the spirit of Mary Shelley's novel, the Hammer Frankensteins did re-establish the monster's potency as a fright-image after he had been reduced to a coatstand for Abbott and Costello. It is interesting to note when *The Curse of Frankenstein* opened, 11 years had passed since the last real Frankenstein film. Within a year of the Hammer film's release, at least five new ones appeared—not *good* ones but Frankenstein films nevertheless. The history of the modern horror film industry begins with *The Curse of Frankenstein*.

For there's no doubt that despite the popularity of the Frankenstein story on the stage, it was with the motion picture that the legend found its ideal medium. We all respond more readily to the cinema's basic and immediate appeal: the theatre, with its artificial conventions, tends to confuse us, and the dramatic impact, however strong initially, is mitigated. In the cinema, the myth achieved universal relevance.

Below *A debonair Golem (André Reybaz) and admirer in a French TV version of the legend,* Le Golem, *1966.*

The Devil's Army

Fear of the Devil has gripped Mankind through countless ages. The Dark Power of Evil has apparently manifested itself to countless people in many guises although these days the visual interpretation of Satan tends to be a cross between Dennis Wheatley's horned horror in **The Devil Rides Out** and the towering menace of Milton's Beelzebub in **Paradise Lost**. Even though the idea of the Devil with horns seems faintly ludicrous in these enlightened times, it only takes a skilled contemporary author like Colin Wilson to bring the chill back into the tale. Richard Cavendish, author and leading authority on magic and witchcraft, describes the Devil, his hierarchy and the insidious ways in which his hold has, seemingly, been laid on our awareness. Black cats, goats and other horned beasts are all popular images associated with the Devil; these concepts are examined together with the traditional legends of the Dark Forces. The writer also looks at the origins of demons and their ability to possess human bodies. Finally we are introduced to the human element, Faustian black magicians and witches, drawn to serve the Devil for their own evil purposes; stories of these individuals shows exactly how strong popular belief in the Devil was at that time.

In 1976 in Lincolnshire, England, a man was tried for the murder of his eight-year-old daughter. Evidence was given that he was terrified of the Devil and believed he had been to hell and seen the Devil there. He became convinced that Satan had taken physical possession of the little girl, and in horror and revulsion he had cut her throat with a pair of scissors. In another case, at Zürich in Switzerland in 1969, five men and a woman were found guilty of beating a girl of 17 to death. They were members of a religious sect, to which the girl, Bernadette Hasler, also belonged. They suspected her of having dealings with the Devil. Under pressure from them, she wrote an account of how Satan came and made love to her—he was black and furry, she said—and promised that one day she would rule the world with him. In a desperate attempt to drive the Devil out of her, they beat her with walking sticks, a riding crop and a rubber truncheon, so savagely that she died.

Cases like this show that belief in the Devil is still far from dead. Official roman catholic doctrine, confirmed in statements issued from the Vatican, is that the Devil is real. Dennis Wheatley and Montague Summers, whose books have stirred an interest in the satanic in many thousands of readers, were both fully convinced of the existence of the Powers of Darkness. Writing in 1971, Wheatley said that their influence had 'formed a cancer in society'

The Powers of Evil

Though belief in the Devil is still alive today, it is much less common than it used to be, having declined in proportion to the decay of belief in God. However, Satan was for centuries a terrifying figure in the minds of millions in Europe and the Americas. He was a monstrous, ominous presence, malignantly hostile to God and to man, the fount and origin of all evil and wrong. Under his command an army of demons lurked everywhere, prowling and watchful, tempting and corrupting. They lured men and women into committing sins and crimes, to strengthen the power of evil against God and Christianity. They were always ready to seize on the slightest evil impulse in human minds and tend it as lovingly as a gardener his roses until it came to full bloom.

Demons crawled into people's minds and sent them mad. They encouraged black magic and witchcraft. They clustered in swarms round every deathbed, hoping to seize the soul and carry it off to endless agony in hell. They caused diseases and epidemics, failure of harvests, pestilence in cattle, plagues of insects, sterility, drought, famine, and misfortunes of every kind. Any harmful event whose cause was not immediately obvious was liable to be put down to their foul doing.

Until comparatively modern times, one of the principal reason for being a christian, in most people's minds, was to gain the protection of a powerful supernatural defence system against the machinations of evil. People crossed themselves against danger and bad luck. They made the sign of the cross over their children, cattle and crops to keep the forces of evil at bay. They used Christian spells and prayers to cure illness. Fields and crops, farm animals, ploughs and other implements, fishing boats and nets, were blessed by the local priest to give them the protection of the church. When storms raged, the church bells were rung to drive them away, or rather to drive away the evil spirits in the air which were believed to cause storms.

Although the powers of evil were horrifying and terrifying figures, they were psychologically and socially useful—as they still are for some people today. They provided an explanation of undeserved suffering and misfortune. If

Below Four witches, *by Albrecht Dürer, 1497. A witch is usually thought of as an evil old hag, hideously ugly and malevolent. Alternatively, however, she may be young and comely for the witch represents all the evil attributed to woman in a society dominated by men.*

Left A satirical treatment of the witches' sabbath, the orgiastic gathering at which male and female witches were believed to worship the Devil. Satan is shown here as a grotesque figure playing the bagpipes.

Below Sketch by the Spanish painter Goya, showing an old and a young witch rising into the air on a broomstick. With them is an owl, a bird of darkness and ill omen. Witches were believed to smear themselves with a special ointment which enabled them to fly.

something harmful or tragic happened to you which you had not brought on yourself, instead of questioning the justice of God or society, you could blame it on the Devil and his minions. Evil spirits also supplied an explanation of mental illness in an age which had no concept of the unconscious mind. And because they could be blamed for leading people astray, they were often made scapegoats for crimes. This tradition is not yet exhausted. In 1974, in a trial at the Old Bailey in London, a man who had raped a girl argued that he was not responsible for his actions at the time, because the Devil had seized control of him and driven him to assault her. The judge did not take kindly to this plea and it was eventually withdrawn.

Enemy in Sight

Over the centuries, a vast mass of tradition and popular belief grew up about the forces of evil, as fears and fantasies were projected onto them. Satan, or Lucifer as he was called before his fall, was the Prince of Darkness, the supreme Enemy, hurled headlong from his high seat in heaven long ago when he led a rebellion against God. According to medieval writers, he was infinitely cunning, maliciously intelligent, patient and subtle, a master of lies and deceit, cold hearted, ruthless and appallingly powerful. He was not as powerful as God, but God for His own inscrutable purposes allowed Satan to tempt and corrupt and destroy. Under him stood rank upon rank of evil spirits, from the great satraps and viceroys of the night down to minor imps and hobgoblins.

Much of the time, Satan and his subordinates

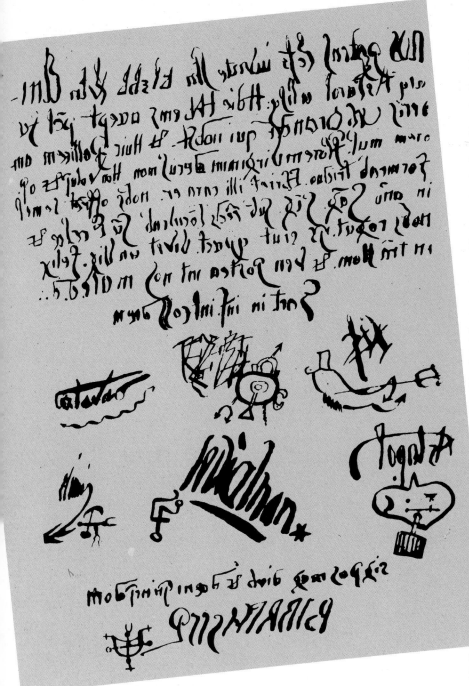

remained invisible, their presence sensed perhaps in a sudden, inexplicable atmosphere of terror, in the creaking and rustling of trees in a dark wood, in night fears and frightening dreams, in an icy tingle down the spine. Often, however, they would appear in visible form. Medieval writers said that it would have been counterproductive for them to show themselves as they really were, for they were unimaginably revolting and loathsome, but as they were skilled in disguise they could appear in any shape they liked, making themselves counterfeit bodies out of smoke or noxious fumes.

Satan himself, it was believed, frequently appeared to human beings as a man, often a 'black' man, meaning darkhaired and swarthy, and wearing black or dark clothes, as a hint of his connection with night and the dark. He might be tall and handsome, and by long tradition he was a gentleman. He spoke all languages fluently and he particularly enjoyed discussing knotty points of theology. He had a sardonic sense of humour and he loved cruelty for its own sake. In 1578, near Soissons in France, a woman named Catherine Darea cut off the heads of two little girls, one of them her own daughter, with a sickle. Before she was executed, she explained that the Devil had come to her in the form of a dark man, ordered her to do the grisly deed and handed her the sickle.

The symbolic connection between good and light—and conversely between evil and darkness—is old and deeply rooted, and survives in modern fiction. In John Dickson Carr's thriller **The Devil in Velvet** (1951), where Satan appears early in the story, there is something dark, smoky and impalpable about him. He sits in a chair in a shadowy corner of the room, his outline seems unstable, and when he speaks his words are not audible in the normal way but

sound in the hero's mind. In J. R. R. Tolkien's **The Lord of the Rings** (1954–55) the great evil power is Sauron, the Dark Lord, ruler of the black and barren land of Mordor, 'where the shadows lie'. His chief lieutenants, the grim Ringwraiths, are invisible but clothed in black, like darkness itself:

> The Black Rider flung back his hood, and behold! he had a kingly crown; and yet upon no head visible was it set. The red fires shone between it and the mantled shoulders vast and dark. From a mouth unseen there came a deadly laughter.

Such was the Devil's subtlety and skill that he could disguise himself convincingly as a friend, a neighbour or a relative. The idea that someone close to you might be the Enemy in ambush is one of the most frightening ever conceived about the Devil, and there are still cases of people who see the eyes of Satan looking at them from a familiar face. For all his skill in disguise, however, the Devil might be betrayed by the fact that he limped, or by some other deformity, especially of the foot, such as a tell-tale cloven hoof. The limp was the consequence of the injury he suffered when he was hurled down from heaven. Deformity is a sign of Satan's warped nature, and a deformity of the foot symbolically means that the foundation on which a creature stands is twisted and defective. It is apparently a legacy of this tradition that in modern adventure stories and films a limp or a club foot is sometimes the mark of a peculiarly sinister villain.

The Black Goat

Besides appearing in human form, the Devil could disguise himself as any animal he chose,

Above right *A Walpurgis Night procession. This satirical picture is based on the old belief that huge numbers of witches and demons used to meet to hold high Satanic revel on St Walpurga's night, the night of the first of May.*

Centre right *Another satire on traditional beliefs. Three witches, like those in* Macbeth, *are cooking a noxious brew in a cauldron held by the Devil, while a black cat sits jauntily by.*

Below right *The* Nightmare, *from Collin de Plancy's* Dictionnaire Infernale. *In the past anything mysterious and frightening tended to be put down to evil spirits. The 'mare' in nightmare is the Old English word for the evil spirit which attacks people in their sleep and causes bad dreams.*

Far right *'An Incantation Scene' by Frans Fracken Junior, 1606, a typical version of a seventeenth-century theme – witches and demons at their evil ceremonies. Above the fireplace, top right, is the name of the famous semi-legendary sorcerer, Doctor Faustus.*

for he was master of the animal, brutish impulses in nature and the human soul. Witches, who were believed to worship Satan, were reported to have seen him as a black goat, a black cat or a black dog, and in many other animal shapes. Some of the descriptions suggest that when the Devil appeared at the sabbaths, or gatherings of witches, he was a man dressed up in an animal costume and mask. At Poitiers in France in 1574 the Devil was a goat who talked like a man. At Brecy in 1616 he was a black dog who stood on his hind legs and talked. In Guernsey a year later, a woman who went to the witches' sabbath saw the Devil as a dog with horns. It spoke to her, bidding her welcome, and took her by the hand with one of its paws, which she said looked like hands.

Satan is also traditionally linked with the bat, with its love of the dark and its grotesquely ugly face. He is sometimes portrayed with the wings of a bat, as in Gustave Doré's 19th-century illustrations to Milton's **Paradise Lost**. It was once widely believed among blacks in the American South that the Devil had the form of a bat, and in Sicily bats used to be burned to death or hung as incarnations of Satan.

In popular tradition, however, the Devil's best-known animal form is that of a huge black goat, or often as a creature half-man and half-goat, with the torso of a man but with a goat's head and horns, shaggy loins and legs, and cloven hooves. This is the form in which he appeared in the film version of Dennis Wheat-

ley's occult thriller **The Devil Rides Out**. Why there is such a close link between Satan and the goat is not entirely clear, but the animal shares with the Prince of Darkness a reputation for unbridled lust, an ungovernable temper, anarchic destructiveness and a foul smell. The goat is also the possessor of a sinister and disquieting slanted eye, and the New Testament established a firm connection between the goat and evil in the scene of the Last Judgement, when the righteous are likened to sheep and the wicked to goats.

The idea of a creature part-human and part-goat seems to have been influenced by the Greek god Pan and the spirits called satyrs, which were symbols of wild nature and the animal in man, of intelligence blended with a darker power. It was when he appeared in this caprine form that witches were believed to adore and copulate with their Master in orgiastic revelry at their gatherings. Whether as a goat or in some other shape, Satan was also commonly believed to have horns, which are symbols of animal vigour, brute force and the rampant sexuality of male horned beasts—bull, goat, ram and stag.

Like the Devil himself, the subordinate demons, the officers and other ranks of the army of evil, could make themselves visible in a huge variety of forms and shapes. They could manifest themselves as men, as beautiful lascivious women, as animals, birds or insects, or in mixed forms combining human and animal elements. Christian artists have given their imaginations free rein in depicting demons as fantastic and nightmarish beings, covered with fur or scales, with bulging eyes and gaping mouths, with fangs and tusks, with heads too heavy for spindly bodies, with horns, tails, feathers, wings, claws and talons, with the heads or beaks of birds, with too many faces, eyes, arms or legs, or too few. These creatures are monsters, frightening supernatural beings portrayed in a literally super-natural way by joining bits of different animals together and combining human and animal forms. They are images of chaos, anarchy and the demonic mutiny against the order of nature and society, the order established by God.

The Fall of Lucifer

Christians believed that God was stainlessly good, with no particle of evil in His nature. They also believed that God had created the world and the first human beings as perfect as Himself, as described in the book of Genesis, which says that God looked upon His creations and saw that they were good. Unfortunately, common human experience showed that there was evil in the world and in human nature in full measure—death, disease, pain, starvation, sinfulness, cruelty, undeserved suffering and tragic

Far right *Satan, with the wings of a bat, in an illustration by Gustave Doré to Milton's* **Paradise Lost**. *In Christian tradition the Devil was once a great archangel called Lucifer, 'light-bearer', but he was expelled from heaven for rebelling against God and his name became Satan, 'adversary'.*

Below *According to Julius Caesar, in the first century BC some of the Celtic tribes used to build colossal images of wickerwork which they filled with criminals and set on fire as a sacrifice to the gods. Scene from* The Wicker Man.

Towards the coast of Earth beneath,
Down from the ecliptic, sped with hoped success,
Throws his steep flight in many an aëry wheel.

Book III., lines 739—741.

misfortune. But how could evil have crept into a world made and ruled by a good God, and into humans who were made in God's image?

An answer was provided in two myths, the story of the fall of Lucifer and the story of Adam and Eve, both of them based on passages in the Old Testament. Long ago before the beginning of time, God ruled on high surrounded by his court of angels. The highest of them was the archangel Lucifer, 'light-bearer', the name which the Romans gave to the morning star. According to some writers, he was the chief of the angelic order of Seraphim. So high and mighty was he that in his insane pride he thought himself the equal of God and rebelled against him. He was followed by many of the other angels, whom he had corrupted. There was war in heaven, Lucifer and his cohorts fighting against the angels who remained faithful to God, who were led by the archangel Michael. Lucifer was defeated and thrown down from heaven to Earth, and his angels were cast down with him, to become his subordinate demons on Earth and in hell. On Earth Lucifer's name became Satan, 'adversary' or 'enemy'. (The Hebrew word *satan* was also translated into Greek as *diabolos*, 'slanderer', from which our word Devil comes.)

The scriptural authority for the Devil's downfall was the famous passage in Isaiah (14:12): 'How art thou fallen from heaven, O Lucifer, son of the morning!' Christians connected this with the words of Jesus: 'I saw Satan as lightning fall from heaven' (Luke, 10:18). The story of the war in heaven is told in the book of Revelation (12). This myth gave the Prince of Darkness his character as the arch-rebel and traitor, bent on overturning the whole established order of nature and society. He was driven to rebel by pride, the first and deadliest of the seven deadly sins, a towering egotism which made him unwilling to accept second place, even to God. The name Lucifer suggests that the story may have stemmed from the observation that the morning star is the last proud star to defy the sunrise, but as the sun's rays gain in strength, the light of the morning star fades.

To explain how evil had infected the goodness and beauty of God's world, the story of Lucifer's fall was combined with the much older tale of Adam and Eve, in Genesis. According to the christian myth, when God created the first human beings and gave them the beautiful Garden of Eden to live in and dominion over all the animals, the Devil was passionately jealous. He feared that these creatures made of mud might succeed to his own lost state, or in some versions, having no woman himself, he envied Adam the possession of Eve. He decided to

engineer their downfall by inspiring in them the same arrogance which had caused his own fall. He took the form of the serpent, the wiliest of animals, or else he used the serpent as his agent (there is no suggestion of this in the original story in Genesis). The serpent at that time had four legs and could talk. It told Eve that if she and Adam ate the forbidden fruit, the apple from the tree of knowledge of good and evil, they would become as powerful as God. The poison of ambition entered Eve and she ate the fatal apple and persuaded Adam to eat some too. As a result the evils of death, pain, hard work, guilt and shame were brought into the world. Adam and Eve were expelled from the beautiful garden, as the Devil himself had been expelled from heaven. The serpent was condemned to slither on its belly all its days. All mankind, descended from Adam and Eve, inherited what Christian theologians called 'original sin', a slimy taint of wickedness endemic in human nature.

It was to rescue mankind from death, the grip of sin and the power of the Devil that God sent His Son into the world as Jesus Christ. Satan tried to corrupt Jesus, as he had corrupted Adam and Eve, tempting him with the promise of earthly power, glory and riches. But Jesus was proof against temptation, and the Devil's grasp on human beings was broken by the triumph of Christ on the cross. Since then, Satan has never

Above Ernest Borgnine is the evil horned figure, from The Devil's Rain. *Horns are a traditional mark of Satan and suggest the Devil's lordship of the animal world and the animal impulses of human beings.*

Above left *Still from* Jaws of Evil. *A sorcerer conducts a black mass, the Christian ceremony perverted to the worship of the Devil.*

Left *The heroes of* The Devil Rides Out, *made from Dennis Wheatley's well-known thriller, get some rest inside a magic circle which protects them from attack by evil supernatural forces. In the rim of the circle are various traditional names of God.*

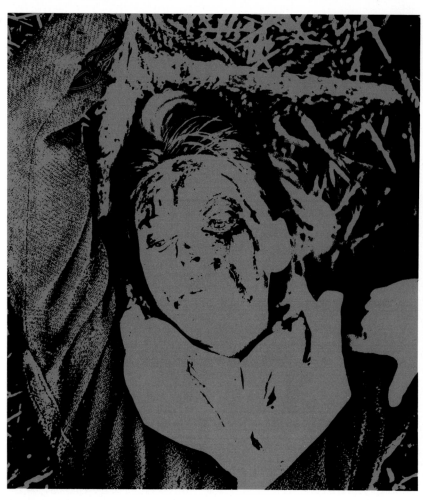

Above left Still from the film Witch-finder General, *showing one of Matthew Hopkins's victims, a suspected witch who has been beaten up to make her confess. Hopkins's career as a witch-finder lasted only a few months until public opinion turned against him.*

Above right Sissy Spacek in Carrie. *Symptoms which used to be attributed to possession by evil spirits are nowadays explained in terms of hysteria, mental illness and split personality.*

rested in his efforts to get human souls into his clutches again, to rebuild his lost empire and deny them to his enemy, God. For many centuries Christians expected the Devil to send a son of his own into the world as the Antichrist, a messiah of evil who would seek to enslave mankind. The idea has been used in modern novels and films. In Polanski's *Rosemary's Baby*, (1967) for instance, the birth of a son to Satan by a human woman is a diabolical imitation and parody of the birth of Jesus to the Virgin Mary. A sign of the demonic nature of the coming child is that his pregnant mother has a desperate compulsion to devour raw meat, and when he is born, he has horns, traditionally a mark of both the Devil and the Antichrist.

The Demon Hierarchy

Medieval writers believed that enormous numbers of demons were at large in the world. It was deduced from Revelation that a third of the angels had fought on Lucifer's side in the war in heaven. Estimates varied, but some writers calculated that there were originally 399,920,004 angels in heaven, so that the number of fallen angels was 133,306,668.

It was recognized that some of these fallen beings ranked higher than others. The names of most of the Devil's chief lieutenants came from the Old Testament, where they were gods worshipped by the neighbours and enemies of

the Israelites, or other formidable supernatural beings opposed to the true God. The most important deity to be transformed into a demon was Baal, the principal god of the native fertility cult in Palestine when the Israelites settled there. His consort, the fertility goddess Asherah, turned into a male demon named Astaroth, who was alleged to have bad breath.

Beelzebub was originally Baal-Zebul, a god of the Philistines. The name means 'lord of flies' and divination by the flight of flies may have been practised by the god's priests. Beelzebub was the chief of evil spirits in Jewish popular belief at the time of Jesus, and subsequently the lord of the flies became a well-known henchman of the Devil. The title was sometimes used as an alias of Satan himself. In 1582, at Avignon in France, a group of witches was condemned to death for worshipping 'Beelzebub the Prince of Devils in the shape and appearance of a deformed and hideous black goat'. Some writers thought there was a supreme trinity of evil, rivalling and parodying the Christian trinity, and consisting of Satan, Beelzebub and Leviathan. They are the first three fallen angels in **Paradise Lost**. Leviathan was originally a huge sea-monster, said in the Old Testament to have done battle against God. Two other fallen angels who were drawn from Jewish folklore were Asmodeus, the demon of lust, and Belial or Beliar, the demon of lies.

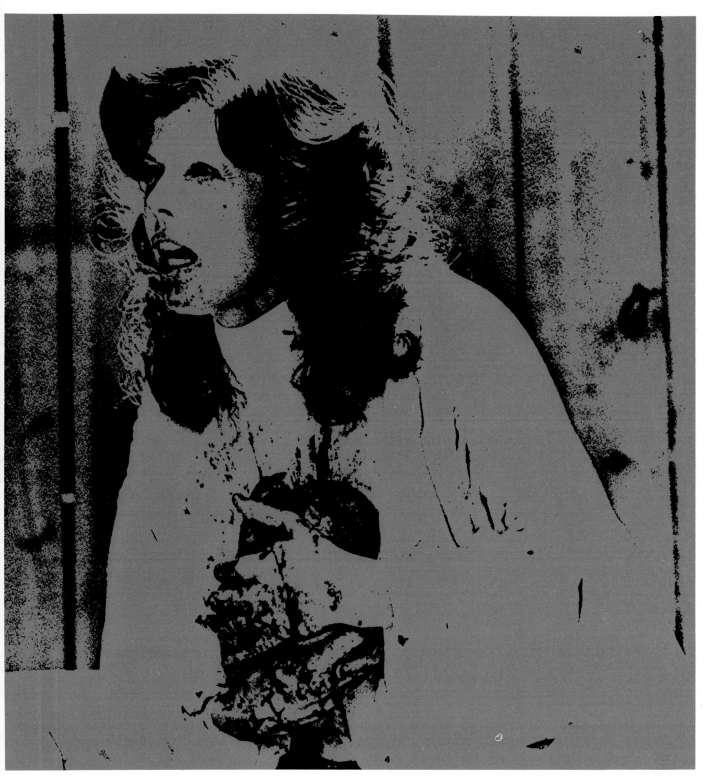

Possession

The most convincing and dramatic evidence of the existence of these evil intelligences came from cases of so-called demonic possession. In the 1630s, for example, some of the nuns at a convent in the French town of Loudun began to behave in an extraordinary and hysterical way. They went into convulsions, arching and heaving, screaming and raving, making lewd gestures and pouring out floods of foul language. At times their heads hung limp as if their necks were broken and their tongues lolled out of their mouths. Rolling and writhing on the floor, they would shriek abuse at God, Christ and the Virgin Mary. It seemed clear that they were in the grip of evil spirits, and determined and eventually successful efforts were made to cast the demons out of them by exorcism. People came from considerable distances to watch their startling performances, which have also attracted modern film producers in search of audiences. A film called *Mother Joan of the Angels* was made about the Loudon case, as was Ken Russell's *The Devils*, and a French film, *La Religieuse*, was about a young girl in a convent who became the prey of demonic powers.

The outbreak at Loudun was only one of many cases of the same kind. At a time when there was no concept of the unconscious mind, it is not surprising that the forces of evil were

Above A moment of pure terror in another possession type movie The Brood *with Samantha Eggar.*

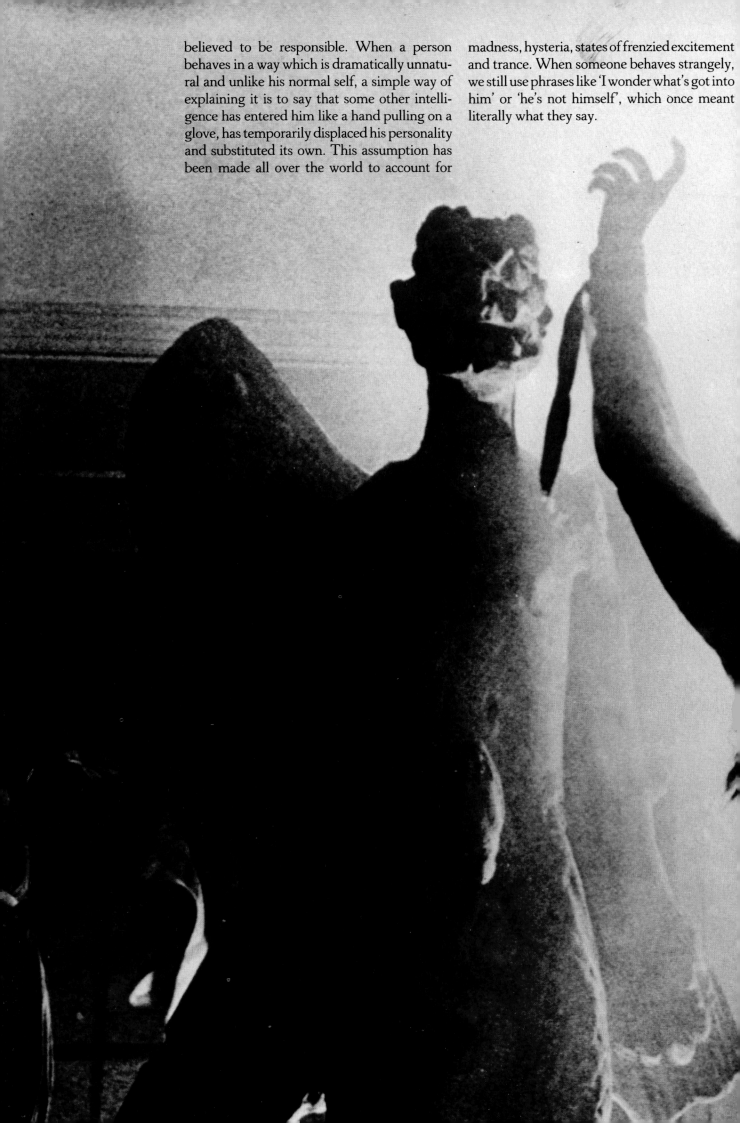

believed to be responsible. When a person behaves in a way which is dramatically unnatural and unlike his normal self, a simple way of explaining it is to say that some other intelligence has entered him like a hand pulling on a glove, has temporarily displaced his personality and substituted its own. This assumption has been made all over the world to account for madness, hysteria, states of frenzied excitement and trance. When someone behaves strangely, we still use phrases like 'I wonder what's got into him' or 'he's not himself', which once meant literally what they say.

Astonishing numbers of demons were sometimes believed to have entered possessed patients. At Vienna in 1583 no less than 12,652 evil spirits were said to have infested a girl of 16. In 1610, it was discovered that a nun in a small convent in Aix-en-Provence was possessed by 6,666 demons (a very significant number), headed by Beelzebub, Leviathan, Baalberith, Asmodeus and Astaroth.

The cases which must have been the most convincing and frightening of all were those in which the possessed person spoke in a different voice, or sometimes several different voices, which appeared to be those of the possessing spirits. In Germany in 1830 a peasant woman suddenly began to suffer from convulsive fits, during which she spoke in a voice entirely unlike her own. Her normal personality vanished and was replaced by a different one, which shouted, raged, swore and cursed at God and everything sacred. After five months a second 'demon' joined the first inside her and in her fits they swore, laughed, barked like dogs, mewed like cats and made a horrible din. She grew painfully thin because if she tried to eat anything except a mush of black bread and water, a demon would cry out through her mouth, 'carrion should eat nothing good', and make her thrust the plate away, the food untasted.

'Possession' cases are now explained in terms of mental illness, hysteria and split personality. Part of the patient's personality has somehow become separated off from the rest. It speaks in a different voice and has its own distinct character. It gives the impression of being, and genuinely regards itself, as a different person altogether. It often makes disparaging and contemptuous remarks about its 'host'. The older explanation has been a long time dying, however. There was a horrible case in County Tipperary in Ireland in 1894. A man named Michael Cleary came to suspect that his young wife, Bridget, had been spirited away by the fairies and that the thing pretending to be his wife was an evil spirit. He and some of the neighbours, including Bridget's father, tortured her to force the evil intelligence to admit what it was. They finally held her over the kitchen fire and burned her so badly that she died. More recently, in 1975 at Leeds in England, 31-year-old Michael Taylor was found guilty of murder, but insane. He had killed his wife, the mother of their five children, after becoming convinced that she was possessed by a demon. At the trial a local clergyman gave evidence that Michael Taylor himself was possessed by numerous evil spirits and that attempts to exorcise him had been unsuccessful.

So many cases of alleged demonic possession have occurred in recent years that the old ecclesiastical rites of exorcism, which had almost fallen out of use, have had to be revived. Scene from The Exorcist.

The Kingdom of Hell

When Lucifer and his angels were cast out of heaven, they created a kingdom for themselves in hell, deep down in the bowels of the earth, where they torture human souls wicked enough to fall into their clutches. Hell in the traditional christian picture is a gruesome counterpart and parody of heaven: it is the ultimate abyss, where heaven is the ultimate height; dark and shot through with fire and smoke where heaven is radiant with pure light; filled with hatred, brutality and agony where heaven is filled with peace and joy. The landscape of hell is black, barren, jagged and murky. Often it is entered through a gigantic mouth, the gaping maw of the Leviathan. Just as heaven means living for ever in the sublime presence of God, so the essence of hell is living eternally in the hideous presence of the Devil.

James Joyce wrote a terrifyingly powerful sermon on hell in **A Portrait of the Artist as a Young Man** (1916), based on what he had been taught at school in Ireland. The longest and fullest desctiption of hell is Dante's **Inferno**, written in the 14th-century and so vivid and detailed that some people at the time believed that the author must actually have been there. Dante's hell is an inverted cone, reaching down to the centre of the earth and divided into nine circles or layers. The greater a sinner's wickedness in life, the deeper in the pit he or she is consigned and the more terrible is the punishment. The souls of gluttons are clawed and flayed by a three-headed monster. The wrathful are trapped in festering ooze, naked and smeared with slime, tearing each other with their hands and teeth. Heretics are roasted in fire, murderers are submerged in boiling blood, pimps are flogged by horned demons, swindlers are sunk in boiling pitch and jabbed by demons with pitchforks, thieves are confined in a snake-pit, liars are stricken with leprosy and covered with sores and itching scabs.

Many of the punishments, as was traditional, are tortures of fire and heat, but the ninth and lowest circle of all, furthest from the light and warmth of the sun, is the hell of ice reserved for those guilty of the foulest of all crimes, treachery. Here in the utmost depth is the colossal figure of Lucifer himself, the arch-traitor, the rebel against God. Covered with matted hair, he is encased in ice up to his chest, his huge bat's wings soaring up towards the roof of the cavern. As the infernal parody of the trinity, he has three heads, and in one of his mouths he mangles the body of Judas Iscariot, who betrayed Christ.

In the Middle Ages, pictures of hell were painted and carved in churches as grim warnings of the horrors that awaited sinners if they did not mend their ways. Preachers, writers and artists let their sado-masochistic impulses run wild in picturing the torments of hell—burnings, flayings, impalings, throttlings, floggings, multilations and agonies of every conceivable kind. A peculiarly unpleasant legacy of the tradition occurs in some 19th-century children's books, where hell is used as a deterrent to misbehaviour. In one of them, a roman catholic priest named Furniss describes the pains of hell for his youthful readers. A girl who preferred going to the park on Sunday to going to church is condemned to stand for eternity on a red-hot floor in her bare feet. A boy who drank and kept bad company is immersed in a perpetually boiling kettle. The blood of a girl who made the mistake of going to the theatre seethes in her veins and her brain is audibly boiling and bubbling in her head.

Preposterous and repulsive cruelty of this kind brought its own reaction. Nowadays, many christians no longer believe in the traditional hell of physical torture. They regard hell as a psychological condition, the hopeless misery and despair of being cut off for ever and through one's own choice from God.

The Black Magician

In popular belief, besides his storm troops, the Devil maintained a fifth column of agents and allies among human beings. These were sorcerers and witches, drawn to Satan's service by their own evil natures and their hunger for power. In the European tradition, the master magician is not a servant of the Devil. He wields power of his own and if he conjures up evil spirits, it is as their superior, not as their slave. To the Christian church, however, evil magic depended for its success on demons, not on any human power, and a sorcerer was one who had surrendered himself to the forces of darkness and sworn allegiance to their leader.

The black magician in league with the powers of evil survives as a horrifying figure in modern fiction. One of the classic examples is Canon Docre, the sorcerer and Satanist in **La Bas** (1891), by the French novelist Joris-Karl Huysmans. Docre is an ageing and villainous priest, who is described celebrating a Black Mass—the mass perverted to the worship of Satan—in a chapel in a private house. There are black candles on the altar, above which is a picture of a derisive Christ, whose bestial face is twisted into a mean laugh. Docre himself wears a dark red robe beneath which he is naked, and a scarlet cap with two horns of red cloth. He says the mass in honour of the Devil, reviling Jesus and subjecting the consecrated host to disgusting indignities. The congregation scream and writhe in hysteria and the ceremony culminates in an indiscriminate orgy.

Right 'St Wolfgang with the Devil' by Michael Pacher, 1483. In art the Devil is often portrayed in a literally 'super-natural' way by combining together bits and pieces of different creatures. Here he has the horns and hooves of a stag, and a second face on the buttocks.

Above *A witch is burned at the stake, in* Jaws of Evil. *In real life it was unusual for condemned witches to be burned alive. They were normally strangled before the pyre was lighted.*

Right *The unfortunate Urbain Grandier (Oliver Reed) was hideously tortured to make him confess. He did so, but later withdrew his confession despite being ruthlessly tortured again. He was finally burned alive in the presence of a large crowd which scrabbled and fought for his ashes and cinders, believed to have magical power. Scene from* The Devils of Loudun.

The original of Canon Docre was Father Louis Van Haacke, a roman catholic priest of the chapel of the Holy Blood at Bruges in Belgium. Huysmans believed him to be a satanist who enticed young people into his clutches, corrupted them and initiated them into black magic. He was said to have crosses tattooed on the soles of his feet, so that he continually trod on the symbol of Christ.

In one of the best of the James Bond thrillers, Ian Fleming's **Live and Let Die** (1954), the villain is Mr Big, a massive and awe-inspiring black master criminal, who uses the terror and sorcery of voodoo to keep his followers in fear of him. In his library, where the hero meets him, stands a white wooden cross, nearly as tall as a man. The arms of the cross are thrust into the sleeves of a dusty black frock coat. Above this is a battered bowler hat, pierced by the vertical bar of the cross, and around the cross's neck is a starched white clerical collar. An elegant cane leans against the cross and at the base are a pair of lemon yellow gloves and an old black top hat. This evil scarecrow is the symbol and effigy of the dreaded Baron Samedi (Baron Saturday), the voodoo god of death, master of cemeteries and lord of the zombies, the walking dead.

The black magician of fiction and folk belief is a frightening figure because he is a kind of monster, joining together things which ought not to be united. Though human, he has linked himself with alien, unhuman, hostile beings. Through them, he has abnormal gifts—he can cause injury and harm by willing it, he can know what is happening far away, he can read minds, he can dominate, hypnotize and destroy. He also reflects fear and resentment of unauthorized and unnatural power. Influence in human society is normally gained through recognized channels—it is inherited or worked for—but the power of the sorcerer is acquired by routes which are secret, devious, unlawful and unholy.

In H. P. Lovecraft's novel **The Case of Charles Dexter Ward** (1927), sinister influences from the past reach eerily into the present as the hero comes more and more to resemble his dead ancestor, a black magician. Dennis Wheatley wrote a thriller called **They Used Dark Forces** (1964), in which 'they' are Hitler and the Nazis, represented as Satanists using, and used by, the powers of evil in pursuit of their evil ends. (In reality, Hitler had little time for magic of any kind, though his SS chief, Heinrich Himmler, was deeply interested in the occult.) The sorcerer in the story is a Jew named Dr Malacou, whose lair is an old ruined castle in Germany. Malacou is in his fifties, tall, gaunt and slightly stooped. As befits a disciple of Satan, he is dark in colouring. He has black and hooded eyes, a swarthy complexion and black hair flecked with grey. He also has a deceptively pleasant smile and a hypnotic stare which subdues the strongest will. Profoundly versed in astrology, the lore of numbers and the magical system known as the cabala, he performs perverted rites in honour of the Devil. The theme of the monster in human flesh is underlined when his rituals culminate in an act of ceremonial incest with his own daughter.

Faust and Frankenstein

Wheatley's Dr Malacou has made a pact with Satan, and this is an example of a theme which crops up frequently in both fiction and popular belief, the story of the man who signs himself over to the Evil One. In return for worldly power and advancement, wealth, pleasure and the love of women, he formally pledges his body and soul to the Devil either at death or after a stated number of years. The agreement is recorded in a document written in the signer's blood, which is more than just a gruesome touch, for his blood symbolically conveys his life into Satan's hands. On the Devil's side, the Prince of Darkness is driven by his hunger for human souls to make a bargain in which, according to the stories, he is often cheated.

Roger Bacon, the 13th-century scientist and experimenter, reputed inventor of gunpowder and spectacles, was believed to have signed a pact with the Devil, promising Satan his soul if he died neither in the church nor out of it. The agreement seemed watertight, but the crafty Bacon constructed a cell in the wall of a church, neither inside nor outside it, and took care to die there, thus escaping the Devil's claws.

Less happy was the experience of a priest named Urbain Grandier, who in 1643 was accused of bewitching the possessed nuns of Loudun and enslaving them to Satan. Produced in evidence at his trial was the pact which he had allegedly made with the Devil, written in his own blood. Also produced was a formal acknowledgement, with all the words spelled backwards, signed by Satan, Beelzebub, Leviathan, Astaroth and other demons. The unfortunate priest was found guilty and condemned to burn alive.

In Germany in 1677 a painter named Christoph Haizmann fell into convulsions and pleaded to be taken to a nearby shrine of the Virgin Mary. He said that nine years before he had made a pact with the Devil, who had appeared to him as a man with a black dog. Written in blood from the palm of his right hand, the agreement read: 'I sell myself to this Satan, to be his own bodily son, and belong to him body and soul in the ninth year.' Haizmann was in terror because the term of the pact was

about to run out. He was taken to the shrine and there, after three days and nights of exorcism, he saw the Virgin forcing Satan to surrender the pact. The repentant Haizmann spent the rest of his life in a monastery.

The semi-legendary sorcerer Faust was also reputed to have sold his soul to Satan. Faust was a charlatan who travelled about Germany claiming to be a great magician and astrologer. Stories began to spread about him and after his death, in about 1540, various protestant clergymen announced their belief that he had made a pact with the Evil One in return for magical power. This swelled the charlatan's reputation into something far more sinister and impressive. Lurid tales circulated about his death, when the Prince of Darkness claimed his bargain. According to one story, the Devil came for Faust one night at midnight. The whole house shook, and in the morning the sorcerer was found strangled, with his face twisted round to the back. In another version, a fearsome wind shrieked round the house and Faust was heard screaming, 'Help! Murder!', but no one dared to go to him. When dawn came, the magician's mangled body was found in the yard near the dung heap. His room was swimming in blood, brains and teeth, and his eyeballs were stuck to one wall.

The legend of Faust has inspired plays by Marlowe and Goethe, music by Gounod, Ber-

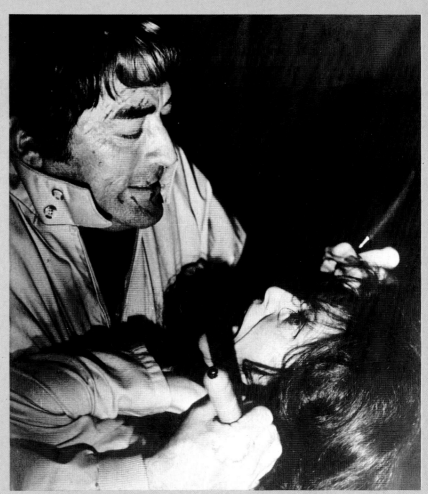

Above Film producers have frequently exploited the theme of 'possession', in which a person is apparently taken over by an evil supernatural being or force. In the old days cases of supposed demonic possession were important in stimulating belief in the Devil and his army. Still from The Omen.

modern fiction principally as a frightening bogy
in stories for children. The wicked witch in Walt
Disney's film of *Snow White* has sent chills
down the spines of several generations of
audiences. There is another in *The Wizard of
Oz*, and even in this supposedly materialist and
rationalist age few children are altogether
immune from the fear of the witch.

What gives the witch her special terror for
children, perhaps, is that she is an evil caricature
of the mother figure. The belief that witches eat
children's flesh is centuries old, and where the
loving mother nourishes and comforts children,
the witch has a more sinister appetite for them.
Often in stories the witch displays a spurious
tenderness and affection for her prospective
victims, a fawning parody of mother love
intended to lure them into her clutches.

The witch in the well-known German folk-
tale 'Hansel and Gretel' catches her prey in a
kind of stickily alluring fly-trap. The two
children, whose own mother has died, are
abandoned in the forest. They come to a dear
little house made of gingerbread and sugar, and
break off bits of it to eat. But the house belongs
to an evil old witch, who locks Hansel in a cage
and fattens him up to cook him and eat him. She
is outwitted by Gretel and in the end the
children shut the witch in her own oven and
escape, but the moral of the story is that evil may
lurk behind the most innocent and pleasant-
seeming of appearances. Despite the happy
ending, what sticks in the mind is that the
cannibal witch and the loving mother are two
sides of one coin.

There are several different types of witch in
traditional popular belief. One is the local white
witch or 'wise woman', who uses herbal rem-
edies and spells to cure ailments, banish warts
and heal diseases of cattle. She also provides
love charms, identifies thieves and locates
stolen property. Much of what she does is
beneficial, but she can work destructive magic as
well and she is a frightening figure, approached
with respectful caution, because she has uncanny powers. It is often believed that she
comes from a long line of witches and has
inherited her magic from her mother or grand-
mother. She has an accepted place in the
community and has survived, here and there,
down into the present century.

The second type is the black witch, who is
totally evil and a social outcast. She is filled with
inward spite and malevolence, which she projects at anyone who offends her by ill-wishing
them, and she also uses poisons, spells and
repulsive concoctions. The stereotype is the
hideous crone—bent, wrinkled, scraggy, dis-
figured with hairy warts and chin, often lame or
otherwise crippled—muttering curses as she

lioz and Liszt, and a novel by Thomas Mann,
among many other works. It is the tale of the
man who swears allegiance to the Devil because
he hopes to gain supreme intellectual mastery.
Faust signs the pact because he wants to know
everything there is to be known. Like Lucifer
before him, he tries to rise too high and he
challenges the prerogatives of God, who alone is
master of all knowledge.

Faust represents the dangerous determi-
nation of man to understand and control
everything around him, with catastrophic
consequences. The same concept appears in
modern thrillers in the character of the mad
scientist, whose brilliance and passion for
knowledge drive him into megalomania. It is
the central theme of the Frankenstein story first
told in Mary Shelley's novel **Frankenstein**,
which came out in 1818. The central character is
deeply versed in the occult sciences. Setting out
to rival God's creation of Adam and Eve, he
fashions and brings to life a monster, a hideous
caricature of a human being, made of bits of
dismembered corpses. He cannot control his
own creation and the monster eventually murders him. The scientist here replaces the black
magician and the Devil in typifying the perils of
overweening pride and ambition.

The Evil Witch

Another horrifying figure of traditional belief is
the witch. The hideous crone with her hooked
nose almost meeting her chin, her skinny
fingers, beady eyes and malevolent cackle, her
broomstick and her black cat, survives in

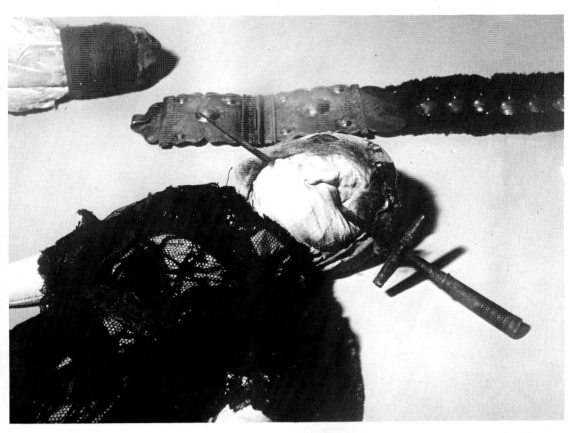

Above left There is an old and widespread belief that witches can harm people by making a doll to represent a victim and then maliciously torturing it, piercing it with nails or, as here, driving a dagger through it. The victim is supposed to suffer the same pain in reality.

stirs a noxious brew in a cauldron, like the witches in **Macbeth**. However, a witch of this type is not always old and ugly. She may be young and beautiful, or she may seem so, for it is not entirely clear whether she is human or whether her human appearance is a disguise worn by an alien being. She can readily change shape, especially at night, when she turns into a carnivorous creature—a bird of prey or a cat or a wolf—and sallies out with others of her kind to stifle babies in their cots, attack adults, cause nightmares, damage crops and harm farm animals. Tales of someone wounding a cat or a wolf and the next day finding that a woman of the neighbourhood has the same injury are found all over the world.

These beliefs helped to create a third type of witch figure, the satanist witch. During the Middle Ages the church became convinced that witches were human but were in league with the Devil and his demons. They worshipped Satan at the witches' sabbath, to which they flew by night on broomsticks or demonic animals, and it was through their monstrous alliance with evil powers that witches were able to work harmful magic. Just as demons could be blamed for accidents and disasters, so could witches. They were believed to cause storms, floods, destructive fires, drought, poor harvests, disease, madness, unexplained deaths and misfortunes of every kind.

In a climate of this kind, it was easy to suspect any old woman who was solitary, ugly, quarrelsome and perhaps not quite in her right mind of being an evil witch. In many cases, people began

to believe they had been bewitched after a falling out with a neighbour. But suspects were not confined to the old, to social rejects, or even to women. In the 16th and 17th centuries large areas of Europe were swept by a panic fear of witchcraft that sent thousands of innocent suspects, men and women, old and young, rich and poor, to torture and death. Anything from a quarter of a million to a million people are believed to have fallen victim to the witch panic. It was a savage demonstration of the grip which the Devil's army once held on human minds. Modern fiction and films, as well as occasional court cases, show that the hold has not yet been fully broken.

Above Many popular beliefs about magicians and witches in Europe may go back ultimately to a very early period of history when shamans, or professional magicians and healers, had a recognized role in society. Shamanism survives to this day in Siberia and this picture shows a Siberian shaman in his hut.

Vampires & Werewolves

The legend of Bram Stoker's **Count Dracula** must rank as one of the foremost horror stories of all time. Undoubtedly, much of the appeal comes from the overt sexuality of the theme of a male vampire sucking the blood of a nubile maiden. The basic theme has many adaptable elements: the return of the vampire to his crypt at sunrise; the transformation of innocent victims into other evil vampires, sometimes without our realising it; the ritual death of the central vampire figure. All of this provides endless scope for suspense and terror. The werewolf legend is, itself, also fascinating because of its shadowy basis in fact. Lycanthropy has long been recognised as a medical condition suffered by the demented who believe that they are wolves. People living in earlier, God-fearing times would have taken very little convincing of the existence of werewolves when confronted by a ravening human whose face was contorted into the likeness of a snarling wolf. Basil Copper, former journalist and newspaper editor, has made a special study of both vampires and werewolves and has written nearly 60 books in the macabre, fantasy and horror genres. In this chapter he studies the origins of the legends and disquietingly leaves us to wonder whether legends are facts or facts are legends.

The Myth of the Blooddrinker

'Villagers near the West Pakistan town of Okara are reported to be sleeping indoors, in spite of fierce heat, because they believe vampires are about. They attribute recent deaths among sheep to the vampires'.

An extract from a modern film script? Or a notation for a piece of fiction? Nothing of the sort. Sober facts extracted from *The Times* newspaper as recently as 1969. Proving once again that the vampire, together with the werewolf and the zombie, is one of the most potent and enduring of western myths. Just why this should be so is not clear. Certainly the vampire as a piece of mythic horror is an apparition to conjure with. Although wreathed in the mists of time, it has become a powerful sexual symbol in fiction and particularly in the modern cinema where the virile and masterful image projected by such artistes as Christopher Lee sets the fans queuing and the producers beaming all the way to the bank.

But how many people have given any thought to its origins or its exact definition in supernatural terms? Most people have, it is true, heard of Bram Stoker and his famous **Dracula** but it is fairly safe to say that few of the thousands who so glibly evoke its name have actually read it. Which makes it even more curious why such a badly written and clumsily constructed Victorian novel should have such irresistible appeal today.

Rarer still are those who know much about the actual medical condition of vampirism, or the horrific deeds of those suffering from haematomania. This is literally a blood-lust which impels them to monstrous crimes beyond their control and which leads them to

Right One of the origins of the vampire legend must undoubtedly be the story of Countess Elizabeth Bathory of Hungary (1560–1614). She was reputed to have had such a lust for blood that, at her trial, the prosecution alleged that she had murdered and drunk the blood of several hundred young girls.

Below Another source of the legend, the vampire bat, Desmodus rotundus which ranges from Mexico to Paraguay. It attacks sleeping mammals, even humans, biting with its razor-sharp incisors and sucking the blood.

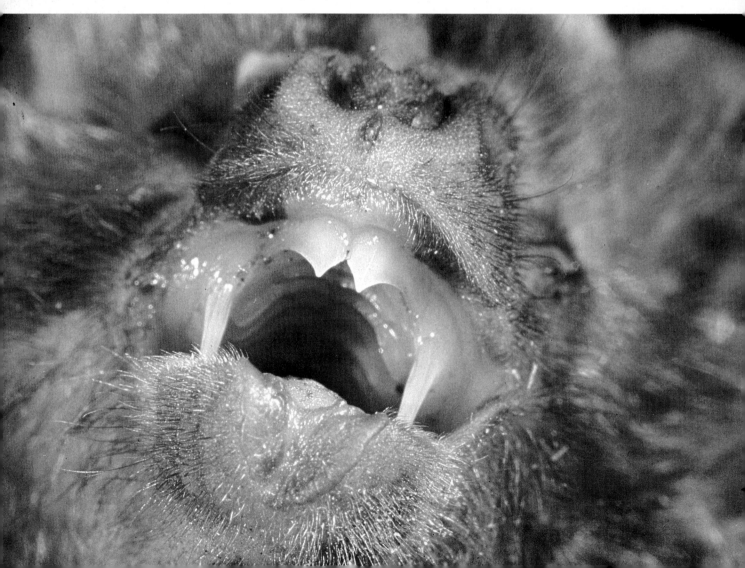

Above An evocative image from Universal's Dracula's Daughter, *1936, as Countess Marya Zaleska (Gloria Holden) stands beside the funeral pyre of her father. Edward Van Sloan as Van Helsing brings about her downfall.*

Left The horror of youth and beauty instantly being corrupted by the ageing process is part of the main theme of Captain Kronos: Vampire Hunter, *1972. This interesting variation stars Horst Janson as the hunter complete with vampire-slaying kit and dwarf assistant.*

Following pages Over the centuries many artists have been inspired by the subject of vampirism. Celebrated painter Edvard Munch captures the sensual element in his study 'The Vampire'.

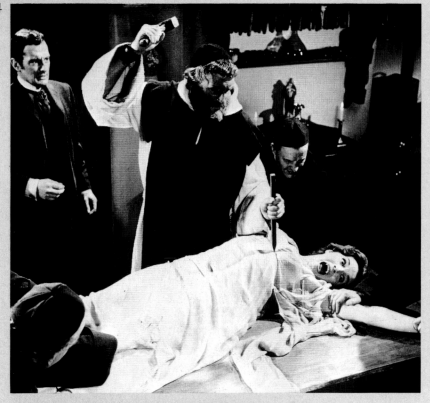

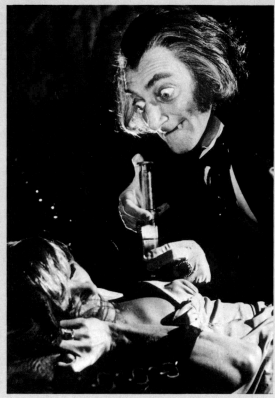

slake their unnatural thirst with the blood of the living or—worse still—with that of the newly dead. Of such a terrible company were the historical figures of Countess Elizabeth Bathory of Hungary and Gilles de Rais in France. Those suffering from a medical condition which made them behave in the classical tradition of the vampire are just as mercifully rare as the vampire itself, and there are only a handful of authenticated cases this century.

What is a Vampire?

The vampire of myth and legend is a person whose life was wicked and who, after 'death' lives on to prey on others by sucking their blood, so sustaining his or her unnatural existence. The source of the legend is lost in time. No-one can say how or where it began though it is common to most countries and races which have written languages and known histories. In Eastern Europe the term 'nosferatu' was used to denote the vampire and in other countries and at other times it had a wide variety of names; but whatever the terms used, it meant only one thing to people of an earlier, simpler age; the Undead-dead.

The vampire was impotent and lifeless between the hours of sunrise and sunset, but after dark would be free to rise from its coffin or burial place and seek out its prey. Together with its supernatural powers went other attributes; the ability to change itself into a wolf or bat— the latter being a particularly useful form in which to gain entrance to bedrooms at night; the power to mesmerize its victim until its sharp incisors had done their work; and its impervi-

ousness to the ills that beset mankind.

Providing it could satisfy its unnatural thirst, the vampire had the power to prolong its life for centuries, remaining eternally young. It could only be destroyed by a silver bullet or by a stake, traditionally of aspen or hawthorn, driven through the heart, after which it would dissolve into unspeakable corruption and finally dust within a short space of time. Those of its victims who were not delivered by the crucifix and holy water were doomed themselves to become vampires in turn, and so the plague spread.

The vampire had some limitations, it is true. Apart from vulnerability to silver bullet or stake, beheading or fire, it could not cross water, and if wolfs' bane or garlic were placed outside the potential victim's window or round the bed, it would not be able to pass.

Vampires boast particular physical features. Their ears might be pointed; they might be unnaturally lean, white-faced and have piercing eyes; their finger-nails are long and sharp; their breath stinking; and, of course, their long, sharp, pointed teeth are difficult to hide. The crucifix would burn their skin if placed upon it; and they return no reflection in the mirror, an aspect that film and stage have made great play with over the past 40 years.

The legends were embellished further by facts of natural history; notably by the nasty habits of the vampire bat of South America and other tropical countries. This is the only known creature which carries rabies without itself falling victim to it. A more recently discovered horror is the vampire moth, the *Calyptra eustrigata* of Malaya, which behaves in a similar

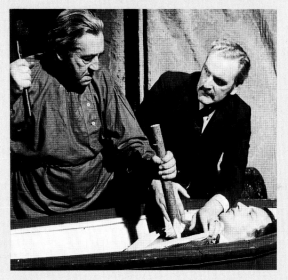

manner to the bats, but instead of teeth uses its proboscis like two tiny saws to penetrate the victim's skin. There is even a vampire cat, a potent symbol in Japanese legend, which was often evoked in medieval folktales, and is still a portent of evil.

The mystic vampire was to come to terrifying life in the persons of a number of mercifully rare individuals who, in an age not noted for its gentleness performed deeds which sent a shock of horror round the civilized world.

Vampires in History

The first of these monsters was Gilles de Rais, a 15th-century French baron whose name became a byword for sadism and perverted cruelty. He suffered from an irresistible urge for blood which compelled him to commit the most atrocious crimes. He drank human blood when seized with his murderous impulses, which

Opposite page: ***Top left*** *Justice is meted out to one of the brides of Dracula in Hammer's* Dracula, Prince of Darkness, *1965.*

Top right *Comic version of the theme with Marty Feldman seen on television using a hypodermic to extract his ration of blood.*

Centre *The vampire-slayer's inept assistant (Roman Polanski) misses the stake as he practises the final stroke. Polanski's hilarious* Dance of the Vampires, *1967 is a splendid parody of the whole vampire genre.*

Below *Werner Herzog's 1979 remake of Murnau's silent film* Nosferatu, *1922, was an almost exact copy of the original.*

This page: ***Top*** *David Niven in the unusual role of a vampire, menacing his victim in the comedy* Vampira, *1974.*

Centre *The classical method, again, of dispatching a vampire in BBC Television's adaptation of Richard Matheson's* No Such Thing as a Vampire, *1968.*

Far left A nightmarish artistic interpretation of a werewolf with vestiges of human form apparent under the lupine mask.

Left A page from a 15th century German pamphlet depicting Vlad Tepes, notorious sadistic military governor, dining among his impaled enemies.

Below Stylized television drama interpretation of Bram Stoker's Dracula in a 1979 series Tales of Mystery and Imagination produced by Thames Television.

were quite beyond control. His orgies of sadism, in which women and boys were used by the Black Baron and his friends turn about, were combined with sacrificial torture. Some of de Rais' crimes were too horrific to detail and included disembowelling living children and simultaneously drinking their blood.

The Baron was a weird blend of decadence and courage, as famous for the latter trait—he fought alongside Joan of Arc in her victorious campaigns against the English—as he was notorious for his pederasty and sadism. The world was well rid of Gilles de Rais, who included human sacrifices to the Devil among his revolting activities, when the aptly named Black Baron was executed in 1440.

His female counterpart emerged in the 16th century in the person of the Countess Elizabeth Bathory, a Hungarian noblewoman who became a sort of vampire queen. She was alleged to have murdered and drunk the blood of several hundred young girls, her activities having inevitable lesbian overtones.

The Countess, born in 1560, was brought to

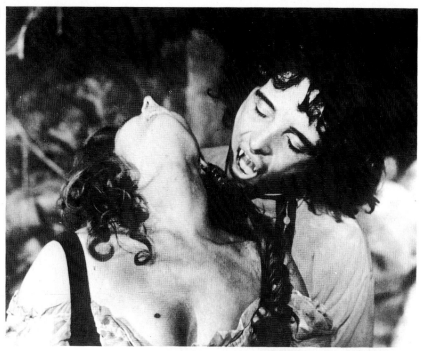

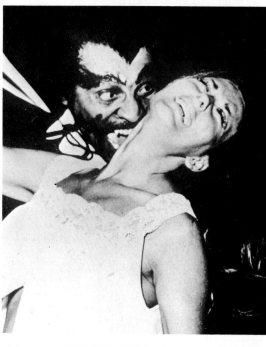

Above *A vampire strikes in a scene from Hammer's* Vampire Circus, 1972. *Adrienne Corri is the vampiress poised to bite the lovely neck of Elizabeth Seal.*

Centre *The screen's first black Dracula, William Marshall, manifests himself in William Crain's film* Blackula, 1972. *A bite from Dracula transforms an African prince who then goes to America and causes havoc in Los Angeles.*

Right *The maestro at work, Christopher Lee the most famous vampire of them all stalking yet another victim, this time in a modern setting* Dracula A.D. 1972.

Far right *The tragic disease lycanthropy inspired novelist Guy Endore's* The Werewolf of Paris, *filmed by Hammer as* The Curse of the Werewolf, 1961. *Here young Leon is locked up by his guardian to prevent him from roaming in the night. The grown Leon was impressively played by Oliver Reed.*

trial in 1611, after the countryside round her castle had been aroused by her excesses. The authorities raided the building during an orgy and found, to their horror, girls chained in the dungeons and apparently used as human cows, being 'milked' of their blood as needed. It was said at her trial that the Countess' blood-lust was first aroused when she scratched her maid with a comb in a fit of temper and was tempted to drink the blood she found on her hands. She had the impression that blood did her skin good and actually bathed in it.

Although her accomplices were beheaded, Elizabeth Bathory's own fate befitted her horrific crimes: the judiciary formally condemned her to life imprisonment and she was walled up in her own bedroom, dying four years later, on 25 August, 1614.

Of more interest to followers of the modern vampire cult was Vlad Drakula although ironically he had even less to do with true vampirism than Bathory and de Rais. Vlad Drakula, known as Vlad Tepes—Vlad the Impaler (1431–76)—was a Wallachian monarch and supersadist, who impaled his enemies on spears and ruled as king for three periods, notably from 1456 to 1462, when he became a national hero in his wars against the Ottomans. A despot and master of torture Drakula was the cruel model on which Stoker based his fictitional Count Dracula, the vampire hero of the perennial bestseller which first appeared in 1897.

Modern Vampires

Even more germane to the true theme and to the fictional and cinematic evocations of vampiric monsters are three horrifying *causes célèbres* from more recent times.

The first began in Paris in 1849 when graves in the Père Lachaise Cemetery, where some of the greatest artists and composers are buried, were found opened and corpses violated. The atrocities continued for some while and public alarm grew when it was alleged that vampirism was involved. Guard was mounted on the cemetery and the depredations ceased, but later suburban cemeteries were entered, the coffins of the newly-dead being broken open and the bodies mutilated. Amid a mounting wave of horror the necrophilist moved the scene of his operations to Montparnasse Cemetery.

In a *grand guignol* finale, the French Army kept watch at Montparnasse in July that year and a soldier fired at a dark figure which glided away among the tombstones. In scenes reminiscent of a gothic novel, the soldiers followed a blood-trail which led over the cemetery wall and down the boulevard outside. Their search ended at the Val de Grace Military Hospital where Sergeant Victor Bertrand of the 74th Regiment, badly wounded, admitted that he was the phantom of Montparnasse.

Bertrand, who became known throughout Europe as 'Le Vampyr' was a necrophiliac and addicted to vampiric practices which made him a real-life forerunner of Stoker's supermonster. At his subsequent courtmartial he was sentenced to a year's imprisonment and, after emerging from the darkness into the limelight of international publicity, returned to the darkness again.

Clinical vampirism was not to evoke horror on such a scale until 1924 when Fritz Haarman of Hanover, a sexual pervert, mass murderer and self-confessed cannibal stood trial. Haarman was in the habit of picking up destitute refugee boys at Hanover railway station, taking them back to his squalid quarters over a cook shop in the old section of the city and then murdering them after gratifying his desires.

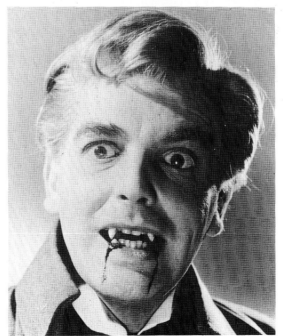

Above *Christopher Lee again portraying the immortal Count, this time looking balefully from his coffin in a scene from Hammer's* Dracula, 1958. *Peter Cushing plays Van Helsing.*

Two faces of vampirism *A very convincing set of teeth (centre), created for Thames Televisions' interpretation of Dracula, based on the incisors of the vampire bat. David Peel (below) has rather more conventional vampire teeth but manages to convey an expression of horrific blood-lust in his Dracula role in* Brides of Dracula, 1959.

Far left *This wolf-man, Oliver Reed, has a somewhat neanderthal look about him which greatly enhances his credibility as a werewolf.*

Above *Hours of painstaking work in the make-up chair resulted in this amazing transformation of Lon Chaney Jr. for Universal's* Frankenstein meets the Wolfman, *1943.*

Right *The impressive make-up of Michael Landon was one of the best aspects of Universal's* I was a Teen-age Werewolf, *1957.*

Far right *The incredible visage of Lon Chaney Jr. again, this time starring in* The Wolfman, *1941. Make-up artist Jack P. Pierce spent several hours each day working on Chaney's features to achieve this extraordinary effect.*

He was encouraged and abetted by a youth called Hans Grans, who was even more decadent than Haarman himself. Haarman murdered his victims by holding them down by hand and then killing them with one bite on the throat: this led him to be dubbed by the popular press of the day as the 'Hanover Vampire' when his atrocious crimes were discovered. It was believed that as many as 50 murders—all the victims being young men between the ages of 12 and 18—could be laid at his door in five years of criminal activity. Haarman added cannibalism

to his crimes as he sometimes cooked human meat in his kitchen and ate it, while human flesh was also sold as ordinary meat to unsuspecting hausfraus in the shop below.

The remains of the victims were thrown into the river which flowed close by the fiendish pair's quarters. Once the body of a victim was hidden in a newspaper behind an oven, but was not discovered when the police made a perfunctory search of the premises. Haarman, who was also a police informer, was charged with 27 murders when brought to trial after a quarrel with a potential victim at Hanover Station.

Grans, his equally infamous companion, escaped with life imprisonment, later commuted to 12 years' penal servitude, but Haarman, the Hanover Vampire, was, appropriately, decapitated by sword in April 1925.

In the true vampiric mould was the atrocious John George Haigh, executed in 1949, after confessing to eight murders, though he was charged with one only, that of Mrs Olive Durand-Deacon, whom he dissolved in a drum of sulphuric acid in a storeroom at Crawley, Sussex. A feature of his crimes, which were labelled 'the Vampire Killings' by the world press, was his repeated statement that after death he took a wine-glassful of blood from the neck of each of his victims and drank it.

Though monetary gain was the motive behind all of the 40-year-old company director's crimes, he undoubtedly had a strange, distorted nature in which obsession with blood was dominant: in his confessions he spoke of weird dreams in which a man cut the trunks of trees to draw off blood in a cup. He told the police, 'once more I saw the forest of crucifixes which changes to trees dripping with blood'. In an odd parallel with Elizabeth Bathory, his own blood-lust began, he said, when his mother spanked him with a hair-brush which drew blood; he sucked this and acquired a taste for it. As a choirboy at Wakefield Cathedral he used to sit in the twilight for hours and gaze at the figure of Christ bleeding on the cross, and during the war, in a road-accident, he sustained a head-wound, causing blood to pour down into his mouth. Though many of his strange dreams and the other stories he put forward in court were discounted by the prosecution, there is no doubt in my mind that Haigh's vampiric traits had a factual basis.

Lord Dunboyne said in his well-argued study of Haigh, 'No other reported case seems traceable to suggest that a murderer drank, or claimed to have drunk, the blood of the murdered, as an end in itself, unassociated with any sexual perversion.' It is this trait alone which makes Haigh, who was hanged at Wandsworth Prison on 6 August 1949, mercifully unique.

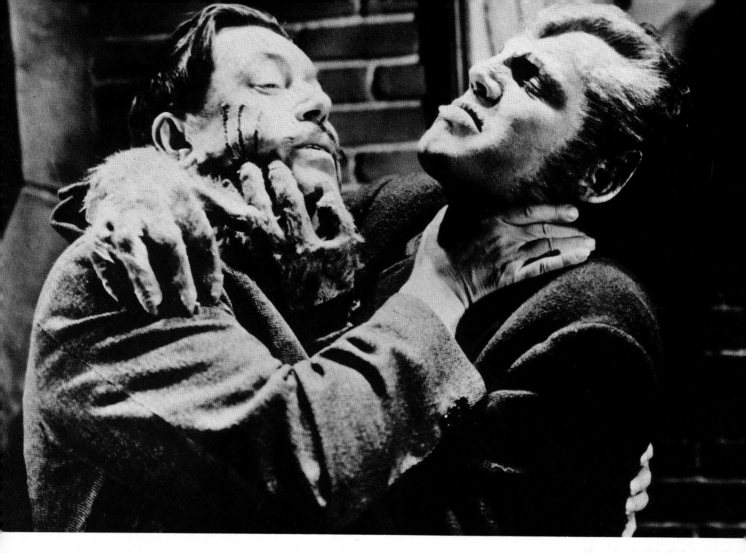

Above Werewolf meets werewolf in Werewolf of London, *1935. Werewolf Dr Glendon (Henry Hull, right) grapples with Dr Yogami (Warner Oland) another victim, after finding the latter in his laboratory snipping off blooms of the antidote plant.*

Vampires in Fiction

The vampire first entered seriously into literature in the early 19th-century, when John Polidori, a young physician and friend of Byron was involved in a discussion with the poet and his two friends, fellow-poet Percy Bysshe Shelley and his mistress, (later wife) the novelist Mary Wollstonecraft. The occasion gave birth to an undoubted masterpiece, Mary Shelley's novel **Frankenstein** and, a little later, Polidori's horrific pot-boiler **The Vampyre**. At first, this was thought to be the work of Byron and it swept Europe, going into edition after edition.

The enormously long tale, featuring a demoniac villain in the vampiric Lord Ruthven, first appeared in a monthly magazine in 1819 and started a trend which shows no sign of slackening, more than a 150 years later.

As in the case of the screen versions of Dracula long afterward, women felt a strong sexual attraction to the vampiric central character, and the tradition was carried on by the prolific Thomas Preskett Prest, whose **Varney the Vampire** came almost 30 years later, providing a link between the Polidori piece and Bram Stoker. **Varney** ran to no less than 868 pages, although it was a modest work by Prest's scale. One of the most fertile authors and pamphleteers of the 19th century, he thought nothing of turning out novels of more than a thousand pages. **Varney**, subtitled **The Feast of Blood**, appeared in penny parts, broken down into 220 chapters and was an enormous and popular success.

If this book launched the vampire novel, the seal was set on its popularity by Bram Stoker, born in County Dublin in 1847, and for many years business manager to the great Victorian actor, Sir Henry Irving.

Yet to my mind Stoker's genius resides in his handful of short stories, among which 'The Burial of the Rats', 'Dracula's Guest', 'The Squaw' and 'The Judge's House' are masterpieces of horrific literature.

Enter Count Dracula

Much of **Dracula** was dull and rambling, even for the period in which it appeared. Nevertheless its peaks of horror are very fine indeed and Stoker's vivid prose style rises to respectable heights in the first third, and best portion of the book, which sets the scene and introduces the Count in his wild, Transylvanian castle. The early chapters have the faded charm of a pre-package tour travelogue and increase the feeling of claustrophobic horror as the commonplace details of the journey gradually give way to the hinted terrors of the wild country. At Bistritz, the post-town at which the nominal 'hero', Jonathan Harker changes coaches for the sinister Borgo Pass, the young estate agent finds a letter from his client, Count Dracula—My Friend—Welcome to the Carpathians—which sets the tone and the scene that has served filmmakers and writers so well over the years.

The first five chapters of the book are brilliant in their mounting horror, particularly in sequences depicting Harker's coach journey to the Count's castle: the long-delayed entrance of the Count himself—'His face was strong ... the mouth, so far as I could see it under the heavy moustache, was fixed and rather cruel-looking, with peculiarly sharp white teeth'; and in a fine moment of terror when Harker sees the Count emerge from a window below him and crawl down the castle wall over a tremendous abyss with his cloak spread out like wings.

Unfortunately, Stoker is unable to maintain this standard in a very long and uneven book which is given over to interminable diary entries concerning the two somewhat pallid heroines; although even here there is ingenuity with some of the narrative being carried by Dr Seward's Phonograph Diary. But the Count's arrival at Whitby on the death ship is finely done and the book gains ground in the last third with the grim duel between the unholy powers of the Count and the materialism of Dr Van Helsing.

Stoker's methods, with climax after climax, would pall on stage or in the cinema, but they seem perfectly appropriate in their period and context. One must take the dross with the gold in order to appreciate the full flavour of this unique novel. Stoker's value is that his achievement is unrivalled in his own field and it seems fairly safe to say that another century might still roll away before the Count's image grows dim in contemporary folklore.

Dracula in the Theatre

It fell to Bram Stoker's friend, Hamilton Deane, the son of the author's childhood companion, to be the first to bring the evil Count to life on the stage. His dramatization was not given to the world until after Stoker's death at the age of 65 in 1914. For various reasons it was not until 1925 that Dracula began its stage career in Wimbledon, of all places.

A little later, Dracula went to New York the title role being played by Bela Lugosi, the man who *is* Dracula for millions. John Balderston adapted the novel for the American stage and it was on this version that the famous Lugosi film was based.

Dracula in the Cinema

The first cinema version of the piece came from Germany in 1922 when the great director F. W.

Left A portrait of the sinister Vlad the Impaler who was said to be the model for Bram Stoker's Dracula. Vlad Tepes was ruler of Wallachia in the 15th century and had a reputation for cruelty and sadism.

Above F.W. Murnau's silent masterpiece Nosferatu, 1922, had superb camerawork by Fritz Arno Wagner and Gunther Krampf as this still shows. Count Orlok (Max Schreck) makes his way to the heroine's room. Schreck's frightening make-up was closely copied by Herzog for Klaus Kinski in the 1979 remake of Nosferatu.

Above right The terrifying demise of the one-legged soldier in Carl Dreyer's early sound classic Vampyr, 1932. The celebrated cameraman Rudolf Maté filmed through gauze throughout to give the effect of a white mist. This low-budget production, made in France, has become a cult film. The soldier, one of the helpers of the vampiric old woman and sinister village doctor is destroyed with them in the finale of the film.

Far right An illustration of bats taken from a Victorian natural history book, including an interpretation of the vampire which was known to exist in parts of South America.

Murnau pirated Stoker's story for his film *Nosferatu*, in which Dracula was thinly disguised as Count Orlok. Though the film has some deficiencies of style and technical blemishes it is still very impressive today, mainly due to the performance of the German actor Max Schreck who, in horrific make-up, dominates the film and is responsible for its greatest moments. Fellow German Werner Herzog paid tribute to Murnau's achievement in his 1979 remake of the film. Many of the scenes were shot exactly as the original and Klaus Kinski as Orlok based his horrific make-up and characterization on Schreck's pioneering performance.

But it was Lugosi, who was to go on playing Dracula in one form or another for something like 30 years. He made the biggest impression in Tod Browning's 1931 film, which is still an immensely satisfying achievement, even if it does seem a little slow and stagey to modern, more thrill-bent audiences.

The best film on a vampiric theme is undoubtedly Carl Dreyer's magnificent *Vampyr*, a strange, haunted nightmare, shot through gauze by one of the world's great cameramen Rudolf Maté, and based on Sheridan Le Fanu's *Carmilla*, though it uses none of the Irish master's material except for the fact that the vampiric presence is a woman.

Though nothing remained of *Carmilla* in Dreyer's early (1932) sound film, shot in France and with only two or three professional players in the cast, it is still the vampire film par excellence and its major moments, notably the coffin-dream of its hero, David Gray (played by the film's backer, the young Baron Nicholas de Gunzburg), remain pre-eminent.

It was down to the British company, Hammer Films to start the modern vogue for the ignoble Count, a lead which the producers of cheap Spanish and Italian films were not slow to follow. They began with *Dracula* (1958).

The Hammer of Dracula

Hammer at their best can be very good indeed and the stock companies, led by Christopher Lee and Peter Cushing in the Dracula and Van Helsing roles, have the advantage of opulent decor, distinguished casts of supporting players and a zest in the hands of directors like Terence Fisher which make their audiences thrill to these ancient, primeval themes of vampire and victim, blood and death.

Some of the best of the Hammers include the originating production of 1958, *Brides of Dracula*, particularly recommended, notably for distinguished performances by Cushing and the late Martita Hunt; and one of the most original, *Kiss of Evil*.

The enthusiasm for vampire films, novels, plays and even LP records shows no signs of abating. There are even Dracula Societies and only a few years ago there were seriously-intentioned vampire hunts in Highgate Cemetery. Some of these manifestations are definitely unhealthy but it is a tribute to a myth that, like Dracula himself, refuses to die.

The Curse of the Werewolf

Like that of the terrifying vampire, the curse of the werewolf is an equally ancient myth. It has existed as a potent legend in almost all countries and all ages. Indeed, in most cultures where there was a written language, the werewolf will be found.

Unlike the vampire, which rose from the dead to prey upon the living, the werewolf/victim was not necessarily a person of evil life. Neither did he have to be bitten, like the prey of the vampire, in order to succumb. The curse of the werewolf, a sort of mania or disease, could descend without warning and turn men into ravening beasts. And unlike almost every evil spirit of folklore, from the vampire, demon and witch, to the sorcerer and goul, the werewolf alone had an element that was unique in his

The Bat

The Vampire

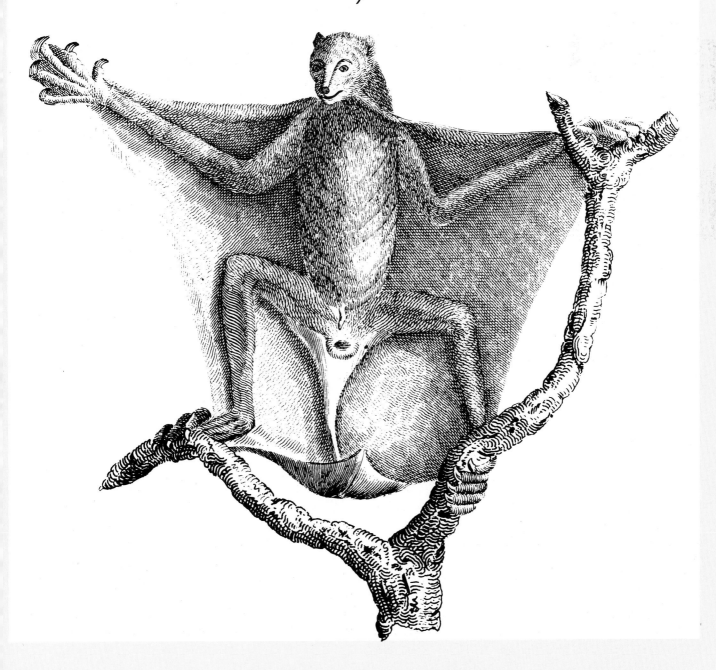

makeup; he was as much victim as villain and he aroused compassion and pity even amongst his potential victims. Why was this so? What was it about the werewolf that made him unique? And just what is a werewolf, not only in legendary but in clinical terms?

What is a Werewolf?

Lycanthropy, to give the condition its proper term, means literally the power to change from man into wolf. Although learned men through the ages have argued as to whether it was actually possible for a human being to change

Below An illustration from Varney the Vampire, *a serialised novel by Thomas Preskett Prest. This massive 868 page work thrilled Victorian readers when published in 1847.*

his shape into that of a beast, there is no doubt that in the minds of primitive, medieval populations this was an established fact.

More plausible was an actual medical condition which 'made men melancholy' and turned them into ravening beasts. Ancient records speak of men who were changed at the turn of the moon and gathered in graveyards, baying at the moon and causing havoc among the interred corpses. In modern times, a distinguished doctor has put forward an ingenious theory which might well account for many examples of the 'werewolf disease' which caused holocausts of judicial revenge in the Middle Ages. We shall be examining this later.

The legend of the werewolf lies somewhere between these various extremes and there is no doubt that in medieval times, when veritable plagues of werewolves were reported, the judiciary reacted in a fashion typical of the time: the result was a welter of denunciations, with trials, hangings, mass-burnings and decapitations. In dark age Europe, when neighbour denounced neighbour, mass hysteria often took over, something like the Salem witch-hunts.

But what were the symptoms of the werewolf? And how could the victim be infected? The latter question is somewhat difficult to answer; by the bite of another werewolf, certainly, but there is evidence from old records,

Right Bela Lugosi, perhaps the best-known Dracula in film history. Tod Browning's 1931 version of Bram Stoker's novel was notable for its fine camerawork by Karl Freund. Browning created a superb atmosphere for the film, enhanced by the restrained performances of Lugosi and other principals.

Abb. 403. Ein Währwolf, der angeblich 1685 in Neuses im Markgrafentum Onolzbach aufgetreten ist. Kpfr. München, Kupferstichkabinet.

that men metamorphosed their shapes for no discernible reason at all. Hence its treatment as a disease in some more enlightened countries.

The victim would first feel ill: he would have a dryness of the chest and an unnatural thirst; a burning desire to divest himself of his clothing; his features would physically change; his complexion turn yellow; his eyes become bloodshot and inflamed; the hands and nails would become gnarled and claw-like; hair would grow on his hands, body and face, and sometimes the sign of the pentagram, the dark, blurred, five-pointed star that was the mark of the beast, would appear on his chest.

Then the werewolf victim would be powerless to act of his own volition until after the fit had left him. Unless he were locked in, secure behind bolts and bars, he would roam the night, killing and savaging anyone he came across. If unable to gain the open air he would roll on the floor like a wild beast, biting and tearing in an agony of mind and body until dawn released him from the frenzy.

The full moon was the worst time, so the tales ran, and that was a period particularly feared. Close relatives of a suspected lycanthrope would make sure their loved one was well secured at these periods and unable to run free in the night.

Like the vampire, the werewolf had many names in different parts of the world: wehr-wolf in England and Scotland, loup-garou in France, werwolf in Germany, and volkodlak in Eastern Europe. But the term meant only one thing, a beast/victim whom death alone could stop. Many were the safeguards devised against the werewolf. Like the wolf himself he was said to have superhuman cunning. Often he would live unsuspected in the community, killing by night and returning to his house before dawn.

People with slanting eyes or long, claw-like hands were particularly at risk when the finger of suspicion pointed. One horrible manifestation of the werewolf hunts was the cutting into a suspect's skin which the inquisitors attempted to turn inside out, on the theory that the werewolf turned his skin, wearing it with the fur inside during the day. Thousands of innocents must have perished over the centuries in this barbarous fashion. Once the wolf/man had shifted his shape he roamed the night, terrorizing and killing. He could only be destroyed by a silver bullet but once he had resumed his human form he became mortal.

A holy crucifix would burn the werewolf's skin like the vampire's, if placed upon it. Many alleged werewolves were condemned on circumstantial evidence, such as when a wolf was

Above A curious and interesting old print of 1685 which was published in Munich. It shows a werewolf first being driven into a well in the town of Eschenback and then being hanged for its crimes.

*Der in seiner Menschlichen Wohnung noch
stets rasende des Verbannt, und gefangenen,
so genanten Menschen Wolffs; und
Geist.*

Neufer

Left *Another engraving of
the alleged werewolf of
Eschenback, Germany in
1685 about to claim a
victim. It is interesting to
note that a similar study to
the previous engraving is
shown in miniature on the
wall.*

shot at by a member of a hunting party and a neighbour was later found to bear a bullet wound in a corresponding place. In these cases coincidence was often ruled out and the party, guilty or otherwise, was summarily tried and condemned to the flames.

Unlike the vampire the werewolf could not return to haunt the earth again after death. Almost alone among the dark creatures of myth and legend he was as much victim as slayer and remorse played a big part in his makeup. He really had only one thing to look forward to: merciful death. For there was no known cure for his condition; that was the most horrifying thing about it.

From such haunted regions have come the folklore and fairy tales of such seemingly-innocent narratives as 'Puss in Boots' and 'Beauty and the Beast' and 'Little Red Riding Hood'. But the werewolf was a very real phenomenon to medieval man, and the 16th-century author of the famous **De la Demon-omanie des Sorciers**, Jean Bodin, who published his work in Paris in 1580, gave his opinion of lycanthropy unequivocally. He maintained that the Devil could change the shape of a man into a beast, but that he could not alter his essential human nature. Many painters, such as Goya, depicted scenes in which such monsters as werewolves were assuming their beast-shapes, and revolting concoctions were evolved by evil-minded people who really wished to change themselves into wolves.

Werewolves in History

Let us now turn to some examples of the depredations of werewolves from ancient re-cords. One of the most horrifying concerned a man called Gilles Garnier who was brought to trial in France in the 16th century for lycan-thropic practices. He admitted attacking and devouring young children, using his teeth and his claw-like hands as a ravening beast. Dozens of people gave witness at his trial in 1573 when it was stated that he had eaten part of his victims. Garnier would appear to have been a medical case; a victim of lycorexia, which turned him into a brute beast, and he confessed to attacking and murdering over a dozen children. He was condemned by his judges to be bound to the stake and burned alive; later, his ashes were scattered to the winds and the district was troubled by werewolves no more.

In 1598, in the Conde district of France, local people were terrified at the activities of a wolf-man; villagers saw wolves feeding from the body of a small girl. With considerable courage a party went out to drive the animals off; later, a ragged-looking man with long hair and staring eyes was discovered behind a bush and taken before the local magistrate.

The man's name was Jacques Rollet and at his trial he claimed to be able to change his shape into that of a wolf by means of an ointment. He stated that the other two wolves at the scene were his brother and sister. In a remarkably humane decision for the times the judges commuted Rollet's death sentence.

In one of the most famous werewolf trials, that of Michel Verdun and Pierre Bourgot at Poligny, France, in 1521, the accused confessed that they had changed into wolves' forms by shedding all their clothes and anointing their bodies with a special salve. Common ingre-dients included soot, bat's blood, deadly night-shade and various types of oil, though modern

Far left *Artist Simon
Vedder's impression of a
werewolf which was
published in Pall Mall,
London in 1901. The
werewolf is prowling on a
winter's night outside a
lonely homestead, possibly
in an Eastern European
setting.*

scientific opinion, of course, states that none of the elaborate concoctions would have the slightest effect in changing shape when applied to the skin. Verdun, Bourgot and another confederate were executed after confessing to hideous crimes including cannibalism.

Only three years earlier, Jean Peyral, who was executed for his crimes, confessed that he had murdered a number of people while bodily transformed into a wolf. He admitted having intercourse with wolves and of having assumed the shape of the beast through a pact he had made with the Devil.

Another case, which appears in several versions concerns a landowner in France whose friend called upon him and asked him to come hunting. He was unable to go because he was expecting his lawyer, but later in the day he decided to seek out his friend.

He saw him coming down the hillside, agitated and covered in blood; he told the landowner he had encountered a gigantic wolf, had fired at it and missed. The beast sprang on him and in the life-and-death struggle which followed he had managed to hack off the brute's right forepaw. He had brought it back with him in a sack. He shook it out on the grass of the garden to show his friend. The landowner was consumed with horror when not a wolf paw but a human hand tumbled from the sack. He recognized it, from the ring with a peculiar stone on its finger, as being that of his wife!

The landowner returned to his house but was told by his steward that his wife was resting and could not be disturbed. He had the door of her chamber broken down and found her in bed, white, ill and covered with blood. He summoned a doctor when it was found that her right hand was hacked from the wrist. Somewhat unkindly, it may be felt, he denounced her to the authorities and she was publicly burned as a werewolf. The story is one of the best of its kind and may serve to stand for a host of others in ancient records.

Such cases were common throughout Europe and Russia in earlier times and the waves of trials and public executions went on for several hundred years until the ages of reason and science put an end to them. Certainly, there was something behind the legend of the werewolf and a sort of mass-hysteria impelled people to confess. There is no doubt also that a number of the accused had an affinity with wolves of the forest and an actual frenzy, recognized by medicine, seized them. Of course, many of the wilder stories and confessions were no doubt due to torture and may be safely discounted in the light of modern knowledge.

A Medical Explanation

An English doctor has recently put forward a remarkably convincing explanation for the 'werewolf disease' which afflicted Europe in the Middle Ages and in other periods. Dr Lee Illis of Hampshire presented a paper on the subject to the Royal Society of Medicine in October, 1963, and I am indebted to him for his generosity in putting his findings at my disposal and to the Royal Society itself for their permission to make use of their Proceedings.

Dr Illis' paper, 'On Porphyria and the Aetiology of Werewolves' is a well-documented and, to my mind, unassailable argument to the effect that the outbreaks of lycanthropy which afflicted Europe and other parts of the world at various times had a solid medical basis. Dr Illis maintains that the majority of so-called werewolves of the past may have been suffering from congenital porphyria. This extremely rare

Below The cover of the first issue of **Varney the Vampire** *serialised from Thomas Preskett Prest's novel. This book, first published in 1847 containing nearly 900 pages, was one of the first literary works to portray the subject of Vampirism.*

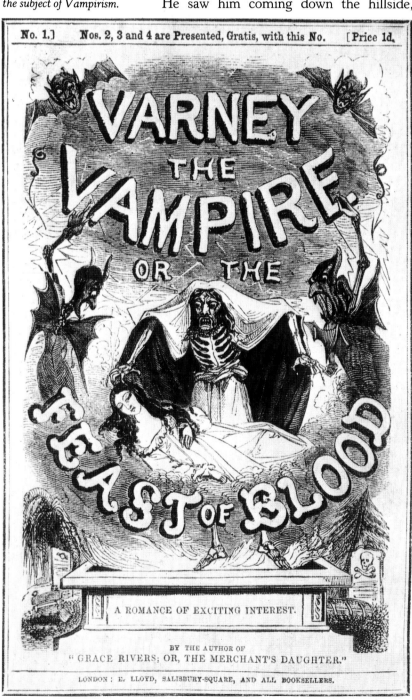

No. 1.]   Nos. 2, 3 and 4 are Presented, Gratis, with this No.   [Price 1d.

VARNEY THE VAMPIRE. OR THE FEAST OF BLOOD

A ROMANCE OF EXCITING INTEREST.

BY THE AUTHOR OF
" GRACE RIVERS; OR, THE MERCHANT'S DAUGHTER."

LONDON : E. LLOYD, SALISBURY-SQUARE, AND ALL BOOKSELLERS.

disease afflicts the patient with all the outward signs and symptoms which passed for lycanthropy in those far-off times. The type of porphyria with which Dr Illis is dealing is caused by a recessive gene which leads to sensitivity of the skin so acute that the patient breaks out in a superficial patchy inflammation when subjected to strong light, particularly sunlight. Ulcers form, there are mutilations to the nose, ears, eyelids and fingers abnormal pigmentation of the skin occurs, and the teeth may become red or reddish-brown. Many of these medical symptoms are classic signs through which the werewolf was identified by the superstitious in ancient times.

The patient would wander about at night, which the victim of porphyria would find more bearable than exposure to daylight; the lesions to the skin of the face and hands were typical of the werewolf who had been bitten by wild animals; and the derangement of the nervous system by the disease, leading to mental disorders and epilepsy, fitted closely all the manifestations believed to be typical of the werewolf; all would have been enough, in mediaeval times, to condemn such a poor wretch to the execution block as a proven werewolf.

This rare type of congenital porphyria occurs in modern times in certain places and districts in countries like Sweden and Switzerland, but Dr Illis emphasises that only about 80 such cases have been reported in recent times in world medical literature. He adds '[they] should not be confused with a common and widespread type which has nothing whatever to do with the subject of lycanthropy. One type of porphyria is relatively common and occurs in all countries.

Werewolves in Fiction

The werewolf entered into literature in the early 19th century through the medium of the penny dreadfuls of the day. One of the most prolific authors in the genre, George William Reynolds, though predated by others, put the werewolf on the map in fictional form with **Wagner the Wehr-Wolf**, 77 chapters of blood-curdling excitement. The vivid and racy story, typical of the gothic thrillers of the period, enthralled its readers and was the first really sustained effort in the genre. It originally appeared in penny parts in 1857, being published by Edward Lloyd of Salisbury Square, Fleet Street, one of the early partwork kings.

As so often happens, Reynolds was not a pioneer. He had merely taken themes already used by other hands, and in so doing made a great popular success. For earlier writers had not seen the possibilities in the werewolf.

They had included the clergyman, Charles Maturin, whose **Melmoth the Wanderer**, an

almost indigestible gothic masterpiece, had enormous success in 1820. Maturin had used a werewolf episode in his **The Albigenses**, though it seemed only dragged in to be in the fashion of the time.

Other 19th-century writers who used the theme but without realizing its true potential were N. Weber in his **The Tribunal of Blood** (1806), and Alexandre Dumas in **The Wolf Leader** (1857). Perhaps the most successful writer in the genre, before Reynolds, was Sutherland Menzies whose exciting and well-written **Hugues, the Wer-Wolf** appeared in 1838. This was another partwork and, unusually for the period, was set in Kent, then a remote rustic waste. As the years passed other, more literate pens took up the theme, particularly in the short story field, among them such masters as Ambrose Bierce ('The Eyes of the Panther'), Robert Louis Stevenson ('Olalla') and Rudyard Kipling ('The Mark of the Beast').

The finest novel on the theme—and there are many—is Guy Endore's fascinating **The Werewolf of Paris**, published in the early 1930s and the nearest thing to a classic in the genre. It stands austere and solitary. It is an extremely well-written work of literature, as well as an exciting and carefully observed clinical study of a young man called Bertrand, whose lycanthropic history rises to a grim climax against the background of the Franco-Prussian War and the Siege of Paris.

Above Not a set created by Hammer Films but a view of London's Highgate cemetery which has been the scene of desecration, vampire hunts and even devil worship. This famous Victorian cemetery, where Karl Marx is buried, has an extraordinary atmosphere, attracting attention from sensation seekers who have smashed tombs, violated graves and even disinterred corpses.

Above Some vampires, it seems, prefer their blood on draught. Actor Daniel Massey becomes blood on tap in Vault of Horror, *1973 produced by Milton Subotsky.*

Yet it has been unjustly neglected since its first appearance in England in book form in 1934 and it is only comparatively recently, with its reappearance in paperback, that Guy Endore's gripping tale is beginning to take its rightful place in the literature of the genre.

Guy Endore was born in New York in 1900 and was the author of many successful books on classical subjects, as well as being an extremely successful Hollywood scriptwriter who worked on major films in the 1930s. He died in America in February, 1970, and his passing evoked little comment, which was a pity as he had created many distinguished books in a long and hardworking literary life. A writer of fastidious imagination he achieved his effects on a delicate scale without any of the coarseness which marred the work of lesser writers. Endore also created many fine stories on macabre themes and the passage of nearly 50 years has done little to dim the effect of his masterpiece.

The cinema was not to discover the theme until fairly late and though there is nothing comparable to *Vampyr* and the original *Dracula*, those classics of vampirism, lycanthropy has actors as diverse as Lon Chaney Jr, Henry Hull, Bela Lugosi and Oliver Reed recreating the curse of the werewolf for the screen for our entertainment.

Werewolves on Screen

The mist stirs sluggishly; gaunt tree branches shiver in the rising wind. From the edge of the swamp, birds scutter and then burst upward in alarm as a figure bounds from the fog. He glances round desperately, his fangs glinting in the dim light, his covering of rough fur silvery, as the sound of hounds baying is brought to the pointed ears.

The music rises on the sound-track; the treeboles of Universal Studios have never looked gaunter or the mist more menacing. Once again Lon Chaney Jr is walking the night, fangs ready to rend and tear as the unfortunate Lawrence Talbot runs amok.

Creighton Chaney, son of a famous father, Lon Chaney Sr, donned the makeup reluctantly, not wanting to cash in on his father's name. He played the Wolfman more times than any other actor, and finally came to love it. Certainly audiences took to it and Chaney's creation was the best of its day, though it was predated by Universal's own *Werewolf of London* in 1935.

Pedestrian direction by Stuart Walker and an unconvincing performance by Henry Hull in the title role—reputedly he had no patience for the makeup sessions at the hands of Universal's special effects man Jack Pierce—combined to make this a limp and unconvincing exercise in the genre. But there are striking sequences, though they have little to do with Hull. One is the performance of Warner Oland as Dr Yogami of 'the University of Carpathia'. This Swedish actor has seldom been better than in his appearance as the half-sinister, half-pathetic lycanthrope. Valerie Hobson heads a better than average supporting cast but almost the best things in the film come from an imaginative episode concerning the restlessness of wolves at the London Zoo; and the extraordinary performance of a cat who becomes aware of Hull's lycanthropic tendencies and reacts in spitting, snarling close-ups.

Lon Chaney Jr had better luck in *The Wolfman* (1941) and his name had considerable lustre following his triumphs both on stage and in the cinema as the pathetic Lennie in Steinbeck's *Of Mice and Men*. Though *The Wolfman* nowhere rises to great heights of terror, and is again vitiated by Universal's curious notions of British police procedures, it has perhaps the most distinguished cast for a film of this kind.

Chaney did well as the doomed Talbot and went on playing the part for Universal in less and less impressive productions, beginning with *Frankenstein meets the Wolfman* and *House of Frankenstein* (1944), ending up with *House of Dracula* in 1945. Though the casts were stuffed with first-rate artistes, the material given Chaney became increasingly shoddy, though he still managed to make his Talbot a pitiable figure.

Nina Foch appeared as possibly the screen's first female lycanthrope in Columbia's *Cry of the Werewolf* in 1944. This one had some entertaining moments, Miss Foch very sensibly metamorphosing into a she-wolf offscreen.

The theme petered out in B-features in the 1950s and 1960s, although a London-based American producer, Milton Subotsky, made an interesting werewolf film, *The Beast Must Die*, in 1974, based on a story by the SF writer James Blish.

Perhaps the nearest thing to a classic in the genre and one in the traditional mould was Hammer's *The Curse of the Werewolf* (1961), in which Oliver Reed gave an anguished performance in the impressive central role. The screenplay utilized parts of Guy Endore's novel **The Werewolf of Paris**, but transferred the entire locale to Spain. Handsomely mounted in colour and with outstanding artwork, the production also had first-rate supporting actors, of which Anthony Dawson and Richard Wordsworth were particularly effective. Later to be TV's Alf Garnett, Warren Mitchell had a cameo part as a frontier guard and other notables in the cast include Clifford Evans and the former Lucas of

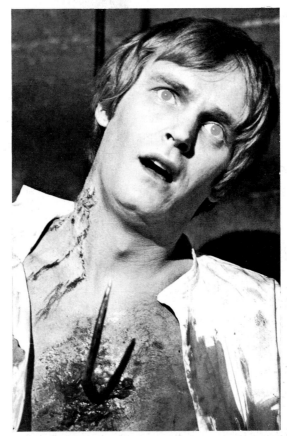

Christopher Matthews falls victim to Christopher Lee as, Dracula in Hammer's Scars of Dracula, *1970*

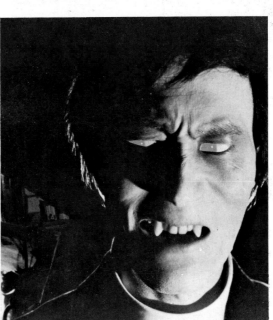

Japanese Dracula looking very authentic in Lake of Dracula *produced by Tohofilms in 1971.*

TV's Maigret series, Ewen Solon. The film, which is occasionally revived on television, is the closest the cinema has yet come to truly evoking the shadowy figure of the pathetic man-beast.

Together with the symbols of the vampire, the sorcerer, the zombie and the manmade monster, the werewolf continues as one of the most powerful mythical figures of our time. Long may their shadows linger and their literary and cinematic evocations continue to thrill, the vast audiences that this genre invariably attracts. The excitement will always keep the fans entertained—the unexpected and unexplained.

The Supernatural

It is probably Man's ego which leads
him to believe that his soul lives on in
some form after his death. From the
earliest times we have sought to explain
strange things by ascribing them to the
supernatural. We also have an in-built fascination for the occult and enjoy the sensation
of being frightened, particularly if we are
secure in our own homes or safely hidden
amongst a large cinema audience. Mike Ashley,
journalist and author of *Who's Who in Horror and
Fantasy Fiction*, threads his way through a literary
labyrinth of references to supernatural beings. He
begins with the Gothic novels of Horace Walpole
and looks at the traditional ghost stories of
Edgar Allen Poe and Dickens. It was a measure
of their skill and talent that they succeeded,
and so we can rightly regard the 1800s as the
flowering time of the ghost story. Evil or
malicious ghosts always chill the spine
more readily than benign apparitions
floating through convent courtyards;
this concept is explored and developed by 19th century writer
Sheridan Le Fanu in his novels and
short stories. Latterly, the supernatural powers have, at least for
the duration of an evenings'
film-viewing, become sheer
reality for thousands who
have seen *The Exorcist* and
many other films on a
similar theme on the
world's cinema screens.

Which of us, at one time or another, hasn't been thrilled by a ghost story? I know I have! Who hasn't had doubts about walking at night through an unlit cemetery, or laid awake in bed listening to the creaks and tappings that could not have been caused by any human agency? Fear is one of the basic instincts of all creatures, for it is fear that has helped us all to survive. But only man has imagination. Put these together and you have the ingredients for tales of horror.

The first narrative ghost stories were probably embellished accounts of true incidents, exaggerated with each recounting. This tradition will never die and is as popular today as ever. One such early account was in a letter from Pliny the Younger who lived in the 1st century AD. He told of a house in Athens haunted by the chain-rattling and 'hideous phantom of an old, old man, who seemed the very picture of abject filth and misery' (**Epistles 7:27**). The same is true in comparitively more recent times of 'The True Relation of the Apparition of one Mrs Veal' as set down by Daniel Defoe in 1706. Although once thought to be a story, it is now believed to be a direct report of an incident in Canterbury in September 1705.

Today there are literally hundreds of books reporting such true incidents. One researcher who wrote more on the subject than any other was Elliott O'Donnell (1872–1965), who collected information on psychic phenomena for over 60 years—he lived till he was 93—and published nearly 50 books. Some of the titles, alas now out of print, include **Ghostland** (1925), **Confessions of a Ghost Hunter** (1928), **Ghosts With a Purpose** (1951) and **Haunted Britain** (1963). His mantle has since been assumed by Peter Underwood who has carefully and systematically gazetteered ghosts throughout Britain.

The step from reputedly true hauntings to fabricated phantoms is a small one, but whoever took that first step is not known. The earliest easily accessible ghost story is 'The Nun's Priest's Tale' from Geoffrey Chaucer's **Canterbury Tales** (1388), in which the spirit of a pilgrim appears twice to a friend asking for help before he (the pilgrim) is murdered. When the spirit appears a third time, the foul crime has been committed.

'The Nun's Priest's Tale' is the exception rather than the rule. In most fiction before the 18th century, ghosts are not the central theme but merely a device to further the plot, Shakespeare's **Hamlet** (1602), **Julius Caesar** (1601) and **Macbeth** (1606) being prime examples. It is worth noting in passing, however, that in **Hamlet** the prince's mother points out that her son's vision of his father's ghost may be just 'the very coinage of your brain', thus demonstrating that Shakespeare was alert to the possibilities of what would be later dubbed the 'psychological' ghost story, in which the ghost may be more of mind than matter.

Ghosts seldom featured in fiction over the ensuing century, but the interest stimulated by the notorious case of the Cock Lane ghost in 1762 brought about a revival. Whether this helped create a market for the gothic novel or not, there is no denying that in 1765 a revolution occurred in supernatural fiction.

The Gothic Novel

It was in the last week of 1764 that Horace Walpole (1717–97) published **The Castle of Otranto** and unleashed the gothic novel on an apparently eagerly awaiting world. The book rapidly passed through several editions and to date has seen well over a hundred. Elements of the gothic novel had been evident in earlier works of fiction, in particular **Ferdinand, Count Fathom** (1753) by Tobias Smollett, but it was **Otranto** that contained all the essential ingredients of gothic horror: an ancient rambling castle, menacing and haunted, with trapdoors and long-forgotten passages and a

Below Called by Sir Arthur Conan Doyle 'the greatest medium of all time', William Hope was also one of the earliest exponents of psychic photography. This is a typical William Hope 'spirit photo' showing the appearance of the 'spirit extra'.

doomed hero and heroine propelled helplessly through events instigated by a villain hell-bent on revenge. It is stereotyped now, but was invigoratingly new to English readers in the decade before American Independence.

When Walpole first published the book he disguised it as a translation from a 16th-century Italian manuscript. He soon admitted its true authorship however, which should have come as no surprise. In 1747 Walpole had bought a cottage at Strawberry Hill, Twickenham, which over the years he elaborated into a gothic castle, thus contributing to a revival—not always appropriate—in that style of architecture.

The Castle of Otranto tells of the fate of Manfred, Prince of Otranto, who plans to divorce his wife in favour of Isabella, the betrothed of his dead son Conrad, who has been crushed to death by the mysterious fall of a giant helmet from the statue of Alfonso, founder of Otranto. Isabella seeks refuge in the castle vaults where she meets a peasant boy, Theodore, whom, it is later revealed, is the true heir to the towers of Otranto.

Ghosts, and people mistaken for ghosts, fill almost every page of the novel. They range from the archetype spook—'the fleshless jaws and empty sockets of a skeleton, wrapt in a hermit's cowl'—to this climactic evangelic vision:

> the form of Alfonso, dilated to an immense magnitude [which] accompanied by a clap of thunder ... ascended solemnly toward heaven, where the clouds parting asunder, the form of St Nicholas was seen, and receiving Alfonso's shade, they were soon wrapped from mortal eyes in a blaze of glory.

Despite the commercial success of the book the literary reception was mixed. Walter Scott later acclaimed it for its originality but others were less rapturous, showing a disdain for the overt and uncontrolled use of the supernatural. One such critic was Clara Reeve (1729–1807), the daughter of a Suffolk parson, who felt that the supernatural manifestations in **Otranto** 'destroyed the work of imagination and, instead of attention, excite laughter'. Her own work of gothic horror, nevertheless inspired by **Otranto**, was **The Champion of Virtue** (1777), later revised as **The Old English Baron**, which emphasized the historical aspect of the gothic novel, and any supernatural intervention was subsequently rationalized as the work of human hands. Consequently very early in its life the gothic novel divided between the less sensational, non-supernatural encouraged by Clara Reeve and Ann Radcliffe, and the supernatural which rapidly reached its most sensational peak in the hands of Matthew Gregory 'Monk' Lewis whose novel created a scandal.

Above left A scene from the movie Repulsion.

Left A moment of supernatural horror during the action of the horrifying movie Halloween.

Monk Lewis, Hardcore Supernaturalist

Lewis (1775–1818) had spent part of his youth in Germany where he had met Goethe. The supernatural fascinated Lewis and when in 1794 he read Ann Radcliffe's **The Mysteries of Udolpho** he would have none of its mundane explanations. His imagination fired, he wrote **Ambrosio, or The Monk** in the space of ten weeks. Published in 1796, when Lewis was not yet 21, it caused an uproar because of its provocative, licentious and blasphemous episodes and Lewis was forced to revise the text. **The Monk** concerns a monk who is led astray by the enticements of an evil spirit in the form of a beautiful woman in league with the Devil. Ambrosio thereafter commits every form of atrocity until his ultimate confrontation with the Devil himself!

The Monk was, if anything, more influential than Otranto, as it became the inspiration for countless Victorian melodramas and penny dreadfuls.

Lewis was the first committed writer of the supernatural, so The Monk was not an experimental one-shot. Apart from other books and plays, including The Castle Spectre (1798) and a collection Romantic Tales (1808), he edited two volumes of gothic stories, Tales of Terror (1799) and Tales of Wonder (1801). They were mostly adaptations and translations of German stories, but he also commissioned items from Walter Scott (1771–1832).

Scott was a close friend of Lewis and was influenced by the younger man. He adapted and refined the gothic style into the genuine historical novel, but he did not ignore the supernatural altogether and in 'Wandering Willie's Tale' (1824), 'My Aunt Margaret's Mirror' (1828), and especially 'The Tapestried Chamber' (1828), he showed his ability to write a gothic ghost story with the best of them.

By then, however, the gothic novel was past its prime and had been the subject of gentle parody by Jane Austen in Northanger Abbey (1818) published, ironically, in the year of Lewis's death. Thomas Peacock administered the coup de grâce with two devastating pastiches, Headlong Hall (1816) and Nightmare Abbey (1817). The 'gothic' tradition survives to this day only in the most basic of frameworks as epitomized by Daphne du Maurier's Rebecca, devoid of any supernatural element.

The Emergence of the Ghost Story Proper

It was time for the ghost story to go its own way. In the gothic novel, as in the earlier Elizabethan dramas, the ghost had merely been a plot device, a stock character. The fact that so many gothic novels rationalized their ghosts—and frequently thereby ruined the effect—showed that the supernatural was only present for effect and because a gothic novel without a ghost was as impotent as King Arthur without his sword. However authors found that it was both difficult and clumsy to sustain an effectively chilling and realistic supernatural atmosphere for the length of a novel and the reader's suspension of disbelief soon became unwilling. It was far easier to convince and involve the reader in a short story, and in such a small compass there was no room for any story thread other than that concerning the supernatural. So, in the death throes of the gothic novel the genuine ghost short story was born.

There was already evidence of its existence outside England. In Germany one of the master short story writers, Ernst Theodor Hoffman (1776–1822) was laying the groundwork.

Amongst his many stories is 'Das Majorat' ('The Legacy', 1817), set in a baronial castle where two visitors hear ghostly moans and scratchings at night. It transpires that the governor of the castle had pushed his new lord over a dangerous part of the battlements, but later toppled to his own death from the same spot when sleepwalking. It is his guilt-ridden spirit that haunts the castle.

Hoffman formulated many of the basic themes of the supernatural short story. 'Fraülein von Scuderi' (1819) is not only an early detective story but amongst the first to use the idea of a split personality; it was further developed by James Hogg in Confessions of a Justified Sinner (1824) and by Robert Louis Stevenson in his masterpiece, The Strange Case of Dr Jekyll and Mr Hyde (1886). 'The Magnetiser' (1813) adopted the idea of mesmerism, whilst 'The Cremona Violin' (1818) was the first of many stories that would concern spirit-haunted violins) of which the classic example is The Lost Stradivarius (1895) written by J. Meade Faulkner.

There was scarcely a writer whom Hoffman did not inspire. In Russia his influence was felt by Nikolai Gogol (1809–52) who was responsible for many fantasy tales and one supreme ghost story 'The Overcoat' (1842). It tells of a poor clerk who acquires a new overcoat which is promptly stolen. His pleas for help are ignored, but after his death his ghost returns to claim the overcoat of the man who could have helped him but didn't.

In America the supernatural story was thriving in the hands of such accomplished writers as Washington Irving and Nathaniel Hawthorne, but there was one writer whose genius and ability would eclipse not only these but most other writers in the field of the horror story, Edgar Allan Poe (1809–49).

Edgar Allan Poe

Poe was no ordinary writer. He suffered from frequent bouts of melancholia, lived in fear of being buried alive, and more than once attempted suicide. Yet so close is the dividing line between madness and genius that one cannot deny Poe his true calling. He had remarkable deductive powers and was an excellent cryptographer. When all this was channelled into his fiction the results were unique. Undeniably Poe was influenced both by the gothic vogue and by the works of Hoffman and Hawthorne, but he wove these threads into a cloth entirely of his own design. Ironically, Poe never wrote anything seriously concerning the supernatural, yet his technique and approach were vital to the development of the genre. One may read of Poe's horror stories and be affected in precisely

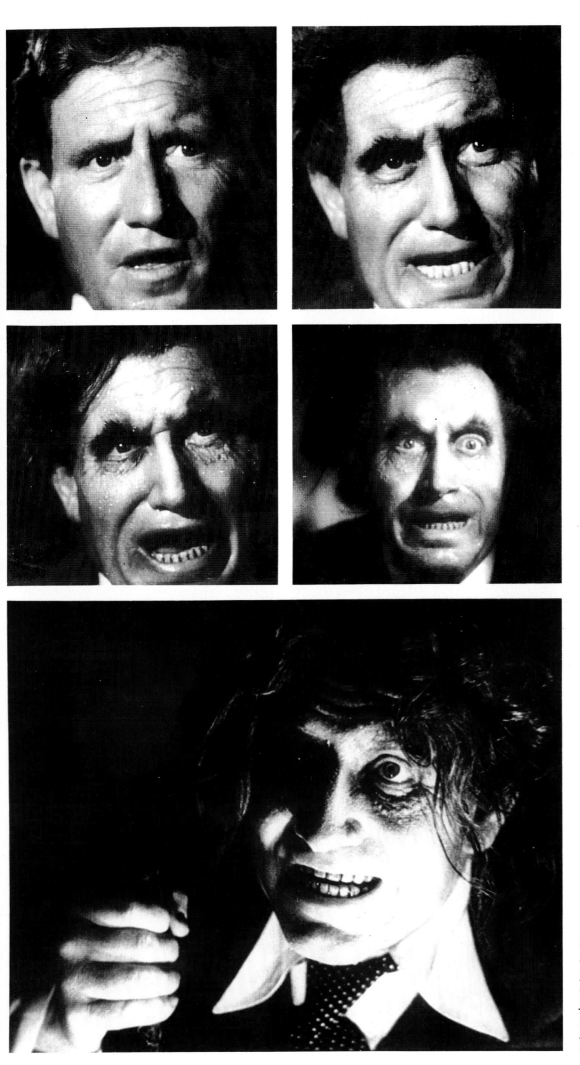

Captured on film in a very clever sequence of photography is the dramatic change from man to monster from the first of all supernatural stories Dr. Jekyll and Mr. Hyde. Spencer Tracey is the actor.

he same way as reading a psychological ghost story, because both reflect the fear and uncertainty of illusion or reality, madness or sanity. This is especially evident in Poe's stories where one of the characters has been mistaken for dead whilst in a state of catalepsy and later recovered from the tomb. Examples of this are 'Berenice' (1835). 'The Premature Burial' (1844), 'The Cask of Amontillado' (1846) and the heavily gothic 'The Fall of the House of Usher' (1839). Note from the dates of publication how this obsession remained throughout Poe's writing career.) Then there are the tales of a man haunted by the outward manifestation of his own conscience as in 'The Black Cat' and 'The Tell-Tale Heart' (both 1843), or of his own self, or doppelgänger, as in 'William Wilson' (1839).

Fear of a genuine ghost is something we could all conceivably reconcile, but the fear of not knowing whether the ghost was a reality or a sign of growing madness is something far more frightening, and it is this aspect of the supernatural that we shall see developing in the stories of Sheridan Le Fanu, Henry James and others in the coming years.

Dickens and his Circle

In Britain the future of the ghost story had passed into the hands of a man who was directly influenced by Poe, Charles Dickens (1812–70). Along with his close circle of friends he was responsible for popularizing the ghost story in the shorter form.

Dickens had always been attracted by the supernatural and, though he no longer believed in it, in later years he set down in **The Uncommercial Traveller** (1861) stories that he recalled had been told him by his nurse Mary Weller when he was but four or five years old, and had scared him witless; stories such as 'Captain Murderer' and 'The Rat Who Could Speak'. He incorporated several macabre stories in his early work but his first major attempt at the supernatural was **A Christmas Carol** published in (1843).

There is much of the gothic tradition in **A Christmas Carol**, although the rambling castle has been replaced by the frugal home of Ebenezer Scrooge. Furthermore the ghosts have become the major element of the story, and whilst it is true they are not essential to

Above An early interpretation of Mr. Hyde becoming acquainted with a young victim who doesn't seem that disturbed.

Left Christopher Lee becomes the evil Mr. Blake in Stephen Weeks' version of Dr. Jekyll and Mr. Hyde remade in 1970 as I, Monster.

advance the plot—Scrooge could have been subjected to a series of dreams—this would have lessened the effect upon both the reader and the miserly Ebenezer. What's more, Dickens appreciated the psychological angle. At first Scrooge regards Marley's ghost as the product of indigestion—'more of gravy than of grave'—but after the ghosts of Christmas Past and Christmas Present, Scrooge is faced with the most menacing spectre of all, the Ghost of Christmas Yet to Come, nothing but a spectral hand and one great heap of black.

A Christmas Carol was an instant success. Dickens's friend and biographer John Forster remarked that it did more to foster the Christmas spirit and to bring attention to the plight of the poor than a year's worth of Sunday sermons. Dickens was delighted with the reaction and for the next few years produced a series of Christmas books all of which employed the supernatural as a means to convey his moral message. However, the fifth book **The Haunted Man and the Ghost's Bargain** (1848), which took over a year to complete, caused so much personal anguish that he dropped the idea of an annual Christmas book. But he didn't drop the concept and, soon after he had established his magazine *Household Words* he published a special Christmas issue in which he included 'A Round of Stories by the Christmas Fire' with

contributions from several hands. For a ghost story he commissioned Mrs Gaskell, yet to be famous for her novels **Cranford** and **North and South**, and she produced a very effective gothic ghost tale, 'The Old Nurse's Story'.

For the remainder of Dickens's life, his magazine *Household Words* and its successor *All the Year Round* became the chief repository in Britain for stories of the supernatural, rivalled only by the Edinburgh-based *Blackwood's Magazine*. Most of Dickens's own contributions alas, whilst written in a deliberate mood of fantasy, seldom took recourse to the supernatural in preference to the moral. It would be nearly 20 years before he would write another ghost story, and this time purely as entertainment. 'No.1 Branch Line: The Signalman' (1866) tells of an apparition that appears to a signalman whose box is at the entrance to a dark cold railway tunnel. The ghost appears as a warning of impending disaster, its third and final appearance being the harbinger of the signalman's own fate. Gone are the gothic overtones and moralistic messages: an indication not only of Dickens's change of emphasis but of the shifting approach to the ghost story. By the latter half of the 19th century, it has acquired a mystique all its own and was moving towards its culmination as an art form.

One other ghost story by Dickens, 'The Tria

For Murder' (1865), was a collaboration with his son-in-law Charles Allston Collins, the brother of one of Dickens's closest acquaintances Wilkie Collins (1824–89), whom he met in 1851. Collins is best known for his two mystery novels **The Woman in White** (1860) and **The Moonstone** (1868) but he was equally accomplished at the supernatural. G. K. Chesterton later went so far as to say, concerning Dickens and Collins, '. . . there were no two men who could touch them at a ghost story', although there are many who would disagree. Collins's most enduring work in the field is 'The Dream-Woman' (1851), an early tale on the theme of premonitions. It is sometimes retitled 'The Ostler' as it tells of an ostler, Isaac Scatchard, who sleeping one night at an inn, awakes to see a woman stealthily advancing from the foot of his bed with an upraised carving knife. He evades the first two thrusts and the woman vanishes as the extinguished candle casts the room into darkness. Years later Isaac becomes enamoured of a young woman contemplating suicide only to realize that she is the woman of his vision, and fate inevitably draws to the moment when that vision comes true. Collins also attempted the supernatural novel, **The Haunted Hotel** (1877), a difficult task but one which Montague Summers praised as being 'wrought with consummate ability'.

Others who contributed regularly to Dickens's magazine included Amelia B. Edwards, Rosa Mulholland, Lord Bulwer-Lytton and Joseph Sheridan Le Fanu, but ironically the most important ghost story of the period appeared not in Dickens's pages, but in *Blackwood's Magazine*.

Bulwer-Lytton, Creator of the Evil Ghost

Until now it is evident that the ghosts have been instrumental in the stories as warnings or as bearers of news, and not as anything malevolent. All that was to change with 'The Haunted and the Haunters or, The House and the Brain' published in the August 1859 issue of *Blackwood's* and the work of Lord Bulwer-Lytton (1803–73).

In its original form this long story is in two distinct halves and most reprintings ignore the second half. The first deals with a night spent in a house in London's Oxford Street, a house seemingly haunted by every manifestation of the supernatural, from phantom footprints in the dust to ghostly knockings, from doors opening and closing of their own accord to a chilling description of an evil presence.

The narrator-investigator witnesses the phantom re-enactment of a murder that had happened at the house many years before but, as the second part of the story reveals, this is not the true reason for the hauntings, which turn out to be the machinations of a near-immortal black magician. Lytton, in the words of the narrator, firmly believed that behind every so called supernatural event there is a human agency, '. . . there may be a power akin to mesmerism, and superior to it—the power that in the old days was called magic . . .'

Lytton was not making up this explanation as he went along. He had been a devout student of the occult since his early years, and was a close friend of the French magician Eliphas Lévi whom he first met in 1854. This approach brought an authority and conviction to his stories that was absent from those of Dickens and Collins, quite simply because they did not believe in the occult. Moreover, Lytton had taken the next major step from the gothic approach. His spooks did not haunt at random. He rationalized their hauntings in supernatural terms which, if handled correctly, make the story utterly convincing. It was a technique that would be found in the later stories of Algernon Blackwood and Arthur Machen, and which in turn heralded a more scientific approach that in recent times has produced stories in which the ghosts are rationalized in technological terms.

Lytton's other major work was **A Strange Story** (1861–62), commissioned by Dickens, and a novel of outstanding stature. To some extent it used the theme of the second part of 'The Haunted and the Haunters' as a springboard to deliver a long novel of mystery, murder and the quest for immortality. Several times in the book the disembodied spirit of the evil immortal, Margrave, appears to others to force them to do his will. This powerful novel established Lytton as one of the foremost writers of supernatural fiction in Britain and his reputation would have continued had not he been overshadowed in retrospect by a contemporary Irish writer, Joseph Sheridan Le Fanu.

Below Sometimes, or perhaps, often, an element of classic horror stories is humour, as shown in this advertising poster for Fredric March in another version of Dr. Jekyll and Mr. Hyde.

Sheridan Le Fanu

Le Fanu (1814–73) started his career as a journalist, subsequently becoming the editor and proprietor of several magazines, in particular the *Dublin University Magazine* which published most of his early stories. It was first as a poet, and later a novelist, that Le Fanu achieved fame during his lifetime. Only posthumously was he recognized as one of the greatest of all writers of the short supernatural tale.

His first story, 'The Ghost and the Bone-Setter' (1838) was a brief, rather humorous encounter related mostly in dialect, which showed little promise of what was to come. Yet only one year later 'A Strange Event in the Life of Schalken the Painter', one of Le Fanu's most powerful stories, appeared. Gottfried Schalken was a historical figure, a Dutch painter who had lived some two centuries earlier. The story seeks to interpret one of his paintings and tells of events when Schalken was a student to Gerard Dou, and of the arranged marriage between Dou's niece, whom Schalken greatly admired, and the mysterious and very rich Vanderhausen, whose 'face was malignant, even satanic, to the last degree' and whose whole appearance was as the 'corpse of some atrocious malefactor which had long hung blackening upon the gibbet'. The significance of the story's dénouement was to become a trademark of Le Fanu's ghost stories: enough clues given to supply a supernatural explanation, but always the suspicion that it was an hallucination. Thus as early as 1839, Le Fanu was giving form to the psychological ghost story.

Le Fanu had a happy marriage but after his wife's death in 1858 he reputedly became a virtual recluse, living a secluded life, writing only in the early hours of the morning and being haunted by a recurrent nightmare of an old mansion which threatened to crush him. It was during this period that he wrote his string of memorable novels including **The House By the Churchyard** (1863), **Wylder's Hand** (1864) and the classic **Uncle Silas** (1864). These novels typify the gothic approach, and while they contain occasional supernatural episodes—frequently reworkings of earlier short stories—they betray no dramatic variation from the natural development of the macabre novel. His short stories, however, show that it was with this length that he was at his best and able to experiment with both technique and intent. He frequently reworked themes from earlier stories, developing them in various ways to achieve a desired result. Thus both 'An Account of Some Strange Disturbances in Aungier Street' (1853) and 'Mr Justice Harbottle' (1872) portray the ultimate retribution meted out to a cruel and corrupt judge. In the first story, Le Fanu used his original technique to give an alternate view on those who meet their deaths in the haunted house, either by supernatural means, or perhaps a fit, or even clumsiness under the influence of alcohol. In 'Mr Justice Harbottle' however, he is more definite, boldly stating the choice with regard to a phantom warrant, 'Was it a copy of an illusion, incident to brain disease?'

Le Fanu's masterpiece in this realm was 'Green Tea' (1869), published in Dickens's *All the Year Round*. It is important not because it introduced one of the earliest psychic investigators, Dr Martin Hesselius, but because it presents the ghost story at its best in terms of growing madness. The Reverend Jennings experiments with drinking green tea instead of his usual brew, and thereafter he begins to see a little monkey following him, a vision that only he can see and which finally drives him to suicide. 'Green Tea' heralded the concept of the use of drugs in fiction to open a character's awareness to the supernatural around him, thus echoing the views of the Swedish philospher Emanuel Swedenborg (1688–1772) who maintained that man is surrounded by supernatural powers that under certain conditions can be perceived by an 'inner eye'. This is a natural variant on the psychological ghost story, as it explains how one character could perceive a ghost which is not witnessed by another, but it still does not preclude the possibility that the heightened awareness might not be a step towards madness. After Le Fanu's death his work lapsed from favour.

Below Horror and fear of all subjects evil, ghostly or supernatural in this film still from the movie Food of the Gods.

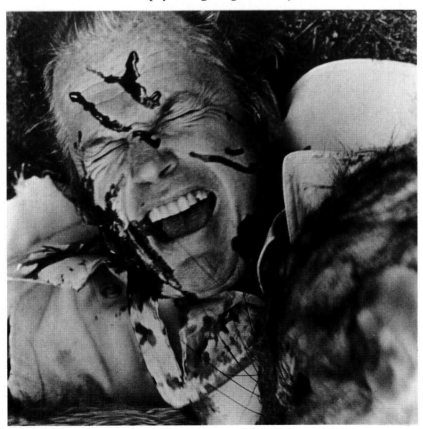

Henry James

In his introduction to the Penguin edition of **The Turn of the Screw**, S. Gorley Putt wrote that it is surprising to find 'how rarely Henry James employed the uncanny, or even a tang of other-worldliness, in his fiction.' This is an odd remark to make about an author whose **Collected Ghost Stories** (1948) contains 17 such stories and whose involvement with the genre spanned 40 years from 'The Romance of Certain Old Clothes' (1868), about the conflict between two sisters both enamoured of the same man, and which one has the last laugh, to 'The Jolly Corner' (1908) in which a soldier pursues the ghost of himself as he might have been, a twist to the doppelgänger idea.

There can be few, however, who would deny that **The Turn of the Screw** (1898), the model psychological ghost story, is one of the best short stories in any medium. Rather paradoxically for such a modern story, James set it in an old gothic country house. Furthermore he begins the tale as a story being told round a fire on Christmas Eve. Herein, of course, lies part of the story's strength, for the reader is lured falsely into believing he is reading an orthodox tale. Having ensnared the reader, James gradually tightens the screw.

The story told is found in a manuscript written by a governess in charge of two very beautiful children, Miles and Flora. Soon however she becomes aware of the presence of two others, Peter Quint, the master's former valet and the boy's constant companion, and Miss Jessel, the former governess, both of whom are now dead. The governess is also convinced that the children are aware of the ghosts, though neither will admit it, and it becomes a compulsion on the part of the governess to force the children into admitting that they can see Quint and Jessel. Throughout the story only the governess openly admits to seeing the ghosts. Thus she and therefore the reader are faced with the dilemma that either the ghosts are real and the children are possessed, or they are an hallucination and the governess is on the verge of insanity. Neither does the climax, which at first appears to resolve the problem, actually satisfy the dilemma. It is this that has given **The Turn of the Screw** its immortality for it can be read not only as a first class ghost story, but on a deeper level as a mystery into the workings of the minds of the governess and the children. James declared that his chief intent in the story was to make it 'reek with the air of evil', and his approach was to use the 'process of adumbration'. No one has ever doubted his success, a success that was repeated in the film adaptation scripted by Truman Capote, *The Innocents* (1961), starring Deborah Kerr as the governess.

Foreign Ghosts

An American contemporary of Henry James was Francis Marion Crawford (1854–1909), although he was born and finally settled in Italy. He wrote a number of novels but today is chiefly remembered for his collection of weird stories **Wandering Ghosts**. Although published posthumously in 1911 (with an English edition retitled **Uncanny Tales**) the stories were written mostly in the 1890s. Best known of all is 'The Upper Berth' with its 'clammy, oozy mass ... with supernatural strength' that nightly returns to sleep in stateroom 105 on the liner *Kamtschatka*. Other oft-reprinted tales from the collection are 'The Dead Smile' and 'The Screaming Skull', but one frequently overlooked though no less chilling is 'The Doll's Ghost' about a smashed doll that helps save a little lost girl.

Perhaps the most notorious American exponent of the supernatural story was Ambrose Bierce (1842–c1914). 'Bitter' Bierce as he became known, was renowned as a misanthrope and his pessimistic view of life is prevalent throughout his fiction. He sold his first story in 1871 but did not become generally accepted until publication of **Can Such Things Be?** in 1893. Bierce was an expert at the psychological and sardonic horror story, as in 'The Realm of the Unreal', 'John Bartine's Watch', and the now famous Civil War dream story of a man facing inevitable death, 'An Occurrence at Owl Creek Bridge'. Bierce seldom included the supernatural directly in his tales and even then left sufficient room for doubt, although 'The Night

Reaching out towards the evil forces in a scene from Dunwich Horror.

Doings at "Deadmans"' and 'The Middle Toe of the Right Foot' carry much conviction.

Other Americans who left a legacy of good supernatural fiction include Ralph Adams Cram (1863–1942) with **Black Spirits and White** (1895), W. C. Morrow (1853–1923) with **The Ape, the Idiot & Other People** (1897), and Robert W. Chambers (1865–1933) who was inspired to write by reading Bierce and produced a unique volume in **The King in Yellow** (1895), a series of loosely connected macabre tales that have as a common background a play of the same title which spreads evil over all who read it.

It would be wrong to think Britain and America had the lion's share of supernatural writers, as France could claim some of the best. Théophile Gautier (1811–72) was an especially gifted writer and his collection **One of Cleopatra's Nights** (1882) includes such ghost stories as 'The Mummy's Foot' (originally 1863) and 'Omphale' (1845). His novel, **Spirite** (1866) tells of a young man who falls in love with a ghost.

Guy de Maupassant (1850–93) ranks as one of the world's greatest short story writers, yet he lived his life in mortal fear of madness and he died insane aged only 42. His supernatural stories are, not surprisingly, of the psychological kind, such as the ghost story 'He?' where a man imagines another person in his empty room. His most famous weird tale is 'The Horla' (1886) which, like 'What Was It?' (1859) by the

Below Murders in the Rue Morgue *explictly gets across the feeling of the fear of evil.*

American Fitz-James O'Brien, and 'The Damned Thing' by Ambrose Bierce, concerns an invisible something that is definitely not of human origin.

Almost every country can claim at least one writer of note in the supernatural field. For instance Norway had Jonas Lie (1833–1908), Australia Gustav Meyrink (1868–1932) author of **The Golem** (1915), Poland Stefan Grabinski (1887–1936) and Russia Feodor Sologub (1863–1927) and Leonid Andreyev (1871–1919). But one writer who was effectively multi-national was Lafcadio Hearn (1850–1904). Hearn was born in Greece of a Greek mother and Irish father. He was raised in Ireland and England, spent 20 years in America; but found true contentment in his last 14 years in Japan. Hearn delighted in the grotesque and macabre, most of which will be found in **Fantastics** (1914), but his collections **In Ghostly Japan** (1899), **Some Chinese Ghosts** (1887) and **Kwaidan** (1904) will be enjoyed by those seeking some supernatural diversions from the traditional tale.

M. R. James and the Golden Age

Readers up till now may be excused the thought that the Victorian period produced all the best ghost stories, but the fact is that the 20 years from 1895 to 1914 saw the appearance of a canon of supernatural fiction superior to anything produced before or since. What other period could boast the talents of M. R. James, Arthur Machen, Algernon Blackwood, Rudyard Kipling, William Hope Hodgson, M. P. Shiel, A. C. Benson, E. F. Benson, Arthur Conan Doyle, Laurence Housman, Oliver Onions, W. W. Jacobs, Robert S. Hitchens, Barry Pain ... the list goes on and on. It is impossible to cover in depth this wealth of wonder, but a number of these authors are crucial to the development of the ghost story, and none more so than the master of them all, M. R. James (1862–1936).

James claimed as his inspiration Sheridan Le Fanu, though the connection can only be in the

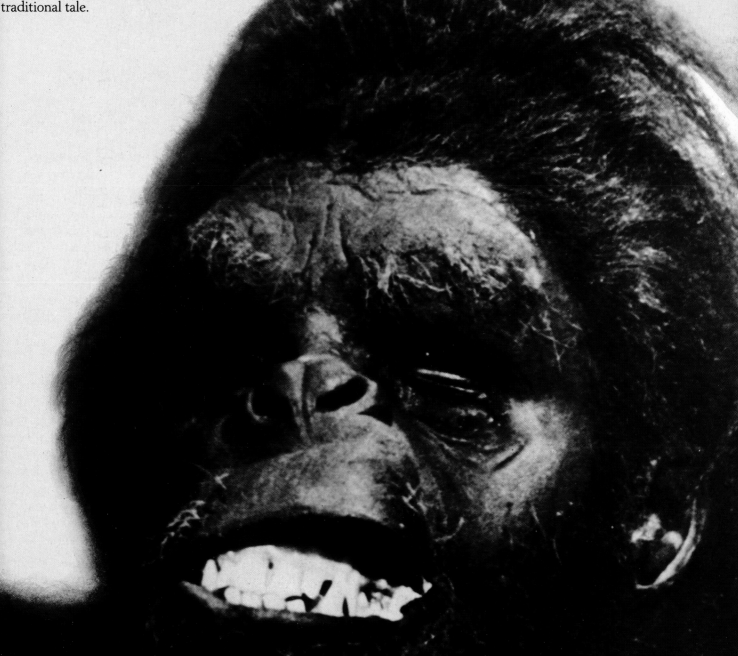

Above A masterpiece of horror and the supernatural, The Hunchback of Notre Dame *which occupies the centre of this illustration. Victor Hugo's* The Hunchback of Notre Dame *was first published as* Notre Dame de Paris *in 1831.*

two writers' development of the storyline and their interest in malevolent ghosts. To imagine any other connection between the Irish dream-haunted recluse and the antiquarian and Provost of King's College Cambridge (later Provost of Eton) is too much to believe. James assembled a collection of lost Le Fanu stories, **Madame Crowl's Ghost (1923)** and it was he who was chiefly responsible for the revival of interest in Le Fanu's work in the 1920s.

James later established a set of rules for writing ghost stories. First and foremost the ghosts had to be evil. Secondly he disliked any unnecessary occult verbiage by way of explanation, and finally the stories had to be set in everyday surroundings so that the reader could imagine that if he wasn't careful the same thing could happen to him. One could supplement this with two corollaries: that the ghosts should not be in the traditional forms of floating wraiths or disembodied voices, and that more should be implied than described. Add to that the simple factor that the stories must be above all entertainment, with no attempt at moralizing or lecturing, and you have the MRJ formula for success.

There was one tradition that James did not renounce. Just like Dickens, James began by recounting his ghost tales to his friends at Cambridge at Christmas. His first was 'Canon Alberic's Scrap Book' in 1894, but none was published in book form until **Ghost Stories of an Antiquary (1904)**. Three other collections appeared before his omnibus **Collected Ghost Stories** in 1931.

Part of James's power lay in his economy of words when it came to the climax. The shift from the normal to the abnormal could happen in the space of a single sentence as in 'The Treasure of Abbot Thomas' where the narrator is recovering a leather bag from its hiding place in a well. At last he has it—'It hung for an instant on the edge of the hole, then slipped forward on to my chest, and put its arms round my neck.'

Sometimes James allows a brief sentence or two to rouse the reader's suspicions as in 'The Diary of Mr Poynter' where Mr Denton, seated in his armchair, believes he is stroking his dog huddled on the floor. But the touch was unresponsive, and curious Mr Denton looked over the arm of his chair. 'What he had been touching rose to meet him. It was in the attitude of one that had crept along the floor on its belly, and it was, so far as could be recollected, a human figure.'

Seldom does James give a complete description of his ghosts, and even when he appears to do so, it is really the implication behind the description that is the most terrifying element in the story.

This is the trademark of an M. R. James ghost story. So masterly were his efforts that it was only natural that he should have his imitators. Not surprisingly many were also antiquarians, such as E. G. Swain, R. H. Malden, M. P. Dare, L. T. C. Rolt and, most successfully, A. N. L. Munby, but few could sustain the atmosphere beyond a certain number of stories. Perhaps the best tribute to M. R. James came from Kingsley Amis, who in **The Green Man** (1969) (discounting the sexual episodes) wrote a novel that James himself might have produced.

Algernon Blackwood and William Hope Hodgson

Blackwood's approach to the supernatural was vastly different from that of his colleague. He was not only the most prolific writer in the field, but the only writer of note whose total output was confined to it. But if one appreciates Blackwood's world view one will see that this was inevitable. Blackwood worshipped nature, he adored everything non-human about the world around him and this attitude is reflected in his best supernatural stories. For instance, in 'The Man Whom the Trees Loved' (1912), 'The Glamour of the Snow' (1911) and 'A Descent Into Egypt' (1914) we encounter characters whose inner spirit has become at one with nature or with the past. Blackwood possessed a Swedenborgian view. He believed it possible for a change in consciousness to make one aware of a new universe. He had studied religious beliefs far and wide and for some years had belonged to the occult Order of the Golden Dawn (as had Arthur Machen, Sax Rohmer and W. B. Yeats). Blackwood was therefore able to write with total conviction with the result that his stories are not fiction in the true sense of the word, but an outward expression of inner sentiments. Whilst he wrote a few traditional ghost stories, such as 'The Empty House', 'Keeping His Promise', 'The Listener' 'The Decoy' and 'A Psychical Invasion', his best stories are those which demonstrate the power of the hidden world ('The Willows',. 'The Wendigo' and his novel **The Centaur**), and no other writer has succeeded in capturing the world of nature so convincingly.

William Hope Hodgson's contribution to the field came from his eight years' experience as a merchant seaman. Like no other writer Hodg-

son was able to bring the terrors of the sea to the printed page. Supernatural sea stories had appeared earlier; perhaps the most effective was the long narrative poem 'The Rime of the Ancient Mariner' (1798) by Samuel Taylor Coleridge. A number of novels concentrated on the legend of the Flying Dutchman—the ship doomed to sail around the Cape of Good Hope forever—such as **The Phantom Ship** (1839) by Frederick Marryat and **The Death Ship** (1888) by W. Clark Russell. Hodgson penned his own Flying Dutchman variant, **The Ghost Pirates** (1909) but his special milieu was the seaweed-clogged Sargasso Sea where ships find themselves trapped for eternity. He used this setting in a number of stories, 'From the Tideless Sea' (1906), 'The Mystery of the Derelict' (1907) and the novel **The Boats of the 'Glen Carrig'** (1907). Hodgson's most enduring work however, **The House on the Borderland** (1908), was not set at sea, but in a derelict Irish house menaced by cosmic forces. More in the realms of SF than the supernatural, it nevertheless stands the test of time and is as frightening today as it was three-quarters of a century ago and has become a cult novel.

Above One of the best of any film interpretations of Poe's fiction was the Roger Corman's 1960 version of The House of Usher.

This is a film still from the 1920 version of Dr. Jekyll and Mr. Hyde *which starred the great profile himself, John Barrymore. He was already 40 when he made the movie, but looked years older. The audiences were thrilled to see his transformation to the hideous Hyde.*

Into the 20th Century

James, Blackwood and Hodgson created their own brand of the supernatural which made them unique. Others set about perfecting the more traditional tale, and the new century was greeted by three stories that will remain amongst the most outstanding psychological ghost tales.

The best known must be 'The Monkey's Paw' (1902) by William Wymark Jacobs (1863–1943) who, coincidentally, was also renowned for his sea stories. This short gem concerns a paw that will grant three wishes and what happens when a mother wishes her dead son alive again. Though no ghost appears in the story, the horror of the final paragraphs is as powerful as in any story of the supernatural.

The work of Robert S. Hitchens (1864–1950) is almost forgotten today with the possible exception of one story, 'How Love Came to Professor Gildea' (1900), which Robert Aickman calls 'one of the best ghost stories ever written'. It concerns Gildea, a man absorbed in his work to the exclusion of all romantic attachments, who finds himself subject to a presence that over the weeks falls in love with him. Hitchens shows with admirable originality how to create a supernatural atmosphere with the barest of tools in an episode where Gildea, and his friend Father Murchison, hide them-

Above left John Barrymore as Svengali in a silent version of Trilby.

selves in the room and watch the reactions of a parrot to the invisible presence, a reaction that becomes all the more disturbing when the parrot starts to imitate the voice of an idiot.

The third psychological ghost story is 'The Beckoning Fair One' (1911) by Oliver Onions, also praised by Robert Aickman as 'as almost perfect story'. In this instance the plot is the reverse of the Hitchens story. It concerns a novelist, Paul Oleron, who moves into an old house and finds himself in a room haunted by a young girl with whom he falls in love. Again no ghost appears, but Onions handles masterfully the hints and implications in the sound of hair being brushed, and the dripping of a tap that suggests the tune called 'The Beckoning Fair One'.

Faded Ghosts

Such a surfeit of good ghost stories appeared in the years before World War I, that it is easy to see the postwar years as something of a void. True the stories lacked some of the originality of the earlier years but writers like E. F. Benson, H. Russell Wakefield and A. M. Burrage were no less effective in their treatment of traditional themes. Other contributions at this time were W. F. Harvey, Saki (H. H. Munro), Margery Lawrence, Elizabeth Bowen, Marjorie Bowen and Margaret Irwin, but the one writer who

Left The concept of the invisible is always one to excite the devotees of the supernatural. Unfortunately the best, if not only, medium for this is through the cinema screen. A scene from the Invisible Man Returns with Cedric Hardwicke.

stands out from his colleagues is Walter de La Mare (1873–1956), equally famous for his poetry and children's books.

De La Mare mastered the psychological ghost story, pushing it to the extreme of inconclusiveness. In most of his stories, especially 'Seaton's Aunt', 'A Recluse', 'Out of the Deep' and 'The Guardian' the reader is never aware of the ghost yet knows there is something wrong. Thus, unlike the story with the explosive last line that has an immediate impact but spoils the story for any future reading, de la Mare's tales can be read time and again with the reader searching for those clues and impressions that will allow him access to the inner depths of meaning, just as in **The Turn of the Screw.**

Paradoxically, at this time of the low ebb in ghost stories, one such novel became a best seller, **Uneasy Freehold** (1942), retitled **The Uninvited** in America), a conventional haunted house tale by Irish writer Dorothy Macardle. The book was effectively filmed in 1944 underlining the point that the 1940s was a good decade for ghost films.

Most of them were played for laughs. Humorous ghost stories are seldom successful though Richard Barham had proved them a viable possibility in the 1840s with 'The Spectre of Tappington' and others in his **Ingoldsby Legends.** H. G. Wells also succeeded with 'The

Below William Marriott's fake photo of Doyle with cut out fairies from Night Light Adventure (1921) – The Cottingley Fairies case.

Inexperienced Ghost', Richard Middleton with 'The Ghost Ship' and, not surprisingly, Oscar Wilde with 'The Canterville Ghost' (1887). But the true master at this trick was Thorne Smith (1893–1934) who with **Topper** (1926) started a series of books, and subsequently films, about a meek little man haunted by the ghost of a mischievous girl. MGM made three Topper films between 1937 and 1941. Earlier, United Artists had made *The Ghost Goes West* (1935) about a Scottish ghost transported to America along with his castle and MGM were also responsible for *The Canterville Ghost* (1944) starring Charles Laughton.

Modern Masters

If a list were to be compiled of favourite haunted house novels, high on the list will be **The Haunting of Hill House** (1959) by Shirley Jackson and **Hell House** (1971) by Richard Matheson. Both rely to some extent on gothic techniques, although Shirley Jackson explores the psychological approach by examining the way a reputedly haunted house affects the four people who risk staying in it. Matheson takes over where Bulwer-Lytton left off to see how far a haunted house could be the product of a single powerful mind. Both novels were filmed: Shirley Jackson's as *The Haunting* (1963), directed by Robert Wise, and Matheson's as *The Legend of Hell House* (1973). Shirley Jackson (1919–65) wrote several other supernatural novels, including **We Have Always Lived in The Castle** (1962) an amusing tale about the spirits of three victims of poisoning.

From 1923–54 there existed a magazine in America called *Weird Tales*. From its pages emerged such writers as H. P. Lovecraft, Frank Belknap Long, Robert E. Howard, Clark Ashton Smith, Robert Bloch, Seabury Quinn, August Derleth, Henry Kuttner and Ray Bradbury, but despite that torrent of names only one contributor made any major contribution to the ghost story field, Fritz Leiber. Leiber's approach was to discover what the modern phantom would be like as opposed to the gothic spook and he came up with 'Smoke Ghost' (1941), a ghost that reflected 'all the tangled, sordid, vicious things. All the loose ends. And it would be very grimy.' Leiber's masterpiece in this field is **Our Lady of Darkness** (1977) set in modern San Francisco but seeking to discover the supernatural heart of the city that in the past had caused so many tragic deaths among its coterie of writers, such as Ambrose Bierce and Jack London.

Probably the most original of all ghost novels is **A Fine and Private Place** (1960) by Peter S. Beagle, set wholly in a New York cemetery where the only human resident has a rapport with the newly-arrived dead. Most fade into oblivion after a few weeks, but one new arrival struggles to fight, and remember life.

These books are all the work of Americans, and recent years have seen a revival of interest in the supernatural novel spurred by the success of films like *The Exorcist* and *The Omen* and by books from Stephen King and Peter Straub. The USA has never had a tradition in the supernatural field; its greatest exponents were either influenced directly by European writers, or wrote their best work in Europe. Today however the majority of good writers are American. Europe has few imitators and even fewer originators, though France's Claude Seignolle, author of **The Accursed** (1963) and Roland Topor, author of **The Tenant** (filmed so effectively by Roman Polanski) are particularly memorable.

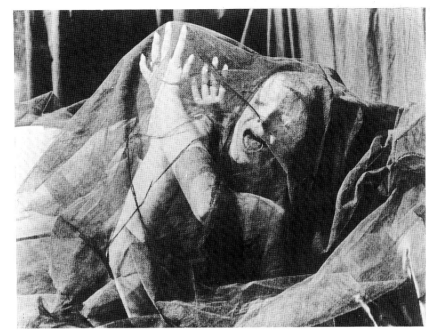

Above Elizabeth Shepherd struggles for air and her sanity in Roger Corman's film version of Edgar Allan Poe's The Tomb of Ligeia, *1964.*

Aickman, Campbell and the New School

However, in Britain, we are currently blessed with two of the greatest practitioners of supernatural fiction, Robert Aickman and Ramsey Campbell. Moreover, their talents are at their best on opposite sides of the ghostly coin; Aickman's psychological ghost stories and Campbell's Jamesian horrors.

Aickman prefers to call his fiction 'strange stories'. To a large extent he has inherited the mantle of Walter de La Mare by making many of his stories inconclusive and keeping his ghosts, as a rule, offstage. His first story, 'The Trains' appeared as long ago as 1951, but it was not until the 1960s that he began to acquire his due recognition, although it would be true to say that his work is still not appreciated by the major part of the reading public. Aickman does not seek the sensational that would make his books 'popular'. He is a master at his craft and will not be deterred from his intent, which is to portray the world as he sees it. Throughout his collections, such as **Sub Rosa** (1968), **Cold Hand in Mine** (1976) and **Tales of Love and Death** (1977) one will find stories that do not frighten, but rather unnerve, impinge on the mind, and remain hidden like some latent memory waiting for that moment to reawaken. His style is perhaps best displayed in the story 'The Waiting Room' (1956) where the main character has to spend a night at a remote railway station and his dreams are haunted by characters from a misty Victorian past. Thereafter the protagonist will be haunted by his visions, afflicted by a continuing uneasiness; such is the effect produced by reading any Robert Aickman story. Incidents will reawaken memories of parallels leaving the reader unsettled and cautious. His story 'Ringing the Changes' is perhaps his best known.

Ramsey Campbell, on the other hand, prefers the impact of M.R. James. He began writing in his early teens, inspired by the work of H.P. Lovecraft, but has since discarded that crutch and now writes highly individual stories blending the technique of M.R. James with certain aspects of the psychological story. One such example is his award-winning 'The Chimney' (1977), the story of a boy frightened by the belief that Santa Claus comes down the chimney and how one night he fancies something enters his room with a face 'like a charred turnip' a vision that was a warning had he known how to interpret it. Campbell's best stories will be found in his collections **Demons By Daylight** (1973), **The Height of the Scream** (1976) and the forthcoming **Dark Companions**.

Both Aickman and Campbell have turned their talents to editing. Aickman produced the first eight volumes of **The Fontana Book of Great Ghost Stories**, the single best series of supernatural stories available, while Campbell has concentrated on acquiring new fiction in **Superhorror** (1976) and **New Terrors** (1980).

The British tradition of the ghost story has a number of other admirable practitioners including Elizabeth Walters. R. Chetwynd-Hayes, John Blackburn, Rosemary Timperley and Basil Copper. From America can be added Russell Kirk, Manly Wade Wellman, Davis Grubb, C.L. Grant, Ray Russell, Joseph Payne Brennan and Dennis Etchison. Clearly the ghost story, despite its challenge from modern day technology, and despite the official view that nobody believes in ghosts any more, is alive and well. It has learned to adapt over the years to fit all and every situation. Because to know that thrill of horror in the security of your own home, and to recognize that phantom in your own mind is the simplest safety valve of all.

The Undead

Eerie legends of zombies and mummies have long been an inspiration to film-makers. Part of the fascination comes from the fact that, even today, on the island of Haiti, it is widely believed that zombies do exist. Tales of uncorrupted dead bodies possessed by evil and controlled by witchcraft are commonplace. Well-known radio and television script-writer, Richard Davis, has compiled a fascinating study of this cult of the Undead. He has explored the factual basis as well as the fictional creations of authors and film-makers. He looks at the making of zombies, the power of the voodoo cult together with accounts of zombie slaves seen working on plantations. The role of the zombie in the cinema has developed over the years. The fairy-tale *White Zombie* by the Halperin Brothers starring Bela Lugosi began the genre. Gradually, the persona of zombies has become increasingly aggressive until they are portrayed as killers and cannibals. While the cult of the zombie still attracts film makers and audiences, the subject of mummies seems to be currently out of favour. This is due, perhaps, to the static nature of the mummy who is rather unadaptable and exercises its evil mainly by curses. Richard Davis gives a fascinating insight into the secrets of the ancient Egyptian embalmers, however, and reviews the films of this genre.

Right *Famous voodoo priestess or mambo, Mamaloi posing for the camera with three assistants. She is holding a billy goat, destined for sacrifice to the loa, or gods of voodoo.*

Centre *This mambo has whitened her face for the start of the temple ceremonies. The white pigment is reputed to be made from graveyard earth and the ash of human bones. It is intended to send the dead against any enemy. Spreading the powder outside the victim's door or across a path that he takes regularly, is said to be enough to paralyse or kill him.*

Right *A sinister element is introduced into a street procession in Haiti; a man clad in a shroud whose face is whitened by ash represents a zombie. In Haiti no one smiles at the mention of zombies. The islanders are far too steeped in the voodoo legends to be sceptical about the existence of the Living Dead.*

The Undead stalk relentlessly through the pages of both literature and legend. Sometimes, as in the case of the vampire, their aim has been hostile; to harm mankind, to use us as a storehouse of sustenance, perhaps eventually to displace us as Earth's dominant species. But there are other sorts of Undead: those slaves who seek only instinctively, like animals, to survive; who have no will at all—the zombies.

Zombies in Fact

Zombies in fact are found mainly on the West Indian island of Haiti. Mainly, but not exclusively: while Haiti is generally regarded as their spawning-ground, they've been seen in the Amazon jungle, in the Far East, even in Europe.

A zombie is a corpse resuscitated by witchcraft, made to work usually at simple, routine and monotonous tasks, and usually by Haitian sugar plantation owners. In popular folklore, they are inextricably bound up with the practice of voodoo. So let's look at voodoo. Voodoo is a religion which owes its origins and derivation to a great many differing sources. It has taken elements from West Africa, where most of its practitioners came from originally, and mixed them with popular Catholicism, the official religion of Haiti. It also based some of its ceremonial on ritual magic found in the 18th-century *grimoires*, French volumes of sorcery. Its central religious rite is the invocation of the *loa*—voodoo gods—by drums, dance and sacrifice. These invocations end almost invariably in the entrancement and possession of one or more of those taking part.

African slaves brought the essence of voodoo with them when they were snatched from their homeland and brought to Haiti. The majority of slaves were imported from the Yoruba-speak-

ing areas of West Africa, and it was the Yoruba tribes who had the strongest traditional beliefs in possession by the gods. Voodoo, or *vaudoun*, to give it its Creole name, was the result of a blending, an adaptation, an assimilation. Catholic saints reappear in the guise of voodoo gods and, despite the disapproval of the established church, many voodoo adherents retain allegiance to Catholicism.

Voodoo Possession

It became a perfectly normal and accepted event to be possessed by a god. There was none of the unease surrounding the process which christians feel. You don't even have to be particularly psychic. It can happen to anyone. It happened to Maya Deren, a maker of avante-garde films, who first visited Haiti in 1947 and took part in several ceremonies. She left this description of what it felt like to become divinely possessed, in her case by Erzulie, the voodoo equivalent of Venus the love goddess. Her description is a valiant attempt to define and explain the indefinable and inexplicable:

> Resting. ... I felt a strange numbness. I say numbness, but that is inaccurate. To be precise I must call it a white darkness, its whiteness a glory and its darkness terror. It is the terror which has the greater force ... The white darkness starts to shoot up ... My skull is a drum ... This sound will drown me ... The white darkness moves up the veins of my leg like a swift tide rising, rising; it is a great force which I cannot sustain or contain, which surely will burst my skin. It is too much, too bright, too white for me. I hear it echoed by the voices, shrill and unearthly: 'Erzulie'. The bright darkness floods through my body, reaches my head, engulfs me. I am sucked down, and exploded upward at once.

Above A voodoo symbol or *vévé* is being drawn by a mambo to represent the attribute of the loa whom she wishes to invoke. These symbols can be drawn in maize, flour, ash, brick dust or even coffee grounds.

Left President Jean-Claude, son of the late 'Papa Doc' Duvalier (left). Papa Doc used the constant threat of voodoo reprisals to subdue both followers and opponents. Even today there is a permanent guard outside his tomb to prevent his remains from being stolen by sorcerers.

Could she be describing the effects of a drug?

Voodoo worshippers believe that the god cannot take over their bodies unless their souls are first displaced. The soul is believed to consist of two entities, the *gros-bon-ange*, and the *ti-bon-ange*, in Creole patois the large and the small good angels. The smaller is what we might call the conscience, and the larger is the essential soul, everything that makes a man what he is. It is the soul that is displaced during possession. Normally possession ends spontaneously as the gros-bon-ange is automatically restored. But sometimes the return can only be accomplished with the help of a priest—the *hungan*. If for some reason he chooses not to carry out the proper ceremony, the displaced soul may fall into evil hands, and the dispossessed body might become a zombie. For that is what zombies are: vacant bodies.

As we shall also see later when we discuss Egyptian mummies, great care is taken in most primitive religions to provide the disembodied soul with an alternative dwelling place. In voodoo, it spends some time at the bottom of a river, but during a special ceremony the hungan recalls it and places it in a sacred jar. It then becomes an ancestral spirit who will advise and protect the family. But its ultimate fate depends on the motivation of the officiating priest. There are good priests and bad priests. One man may conduct relatively orthodox voodoo ceremonies, and be a powerful sorcerer, or *bokor* on the side. If he is a sorcerer, he might have marked down the dispossessed body for his own purposes, including future work as a zombie.

Below Abbott and Costello meet the Mummy. Lon Chaney Jnr was reported to have said that if you met Abbott and Costello you were dead – in this case he happened to be right!

In the Power of the Bokor

To be fair, most voodoo priests are not sorcerers. They will use their position in the community for good, though of course at the same time they will need to understand the technique of sorcery in order to be able to combat it. And there are bokors who are not voodoo priests. Evil bokors run criminal secret societies, worship the Devil, and gather in cemeteries to practice sinister cults of the dead. But priests are human like the rest of us. They can be mixtures of good and evil. The danger is, the unwary may not realize that their bodies have been marked down for future zombie servitude. There are many motives for sorcerers to trap zombies. Revenge is one. Alfred Metraux in **Voodoo in Haiti** tells the story of a young girl who rejected the advances of a powerful priest. He stalked off muttering threats about her future. Sure enough the girl grew ill and died.

For some reason she was buried in a coffin too short for her, and her neck had to be bent to fit her in. While this neck-bending was going on, a candle near the coffin was overturned, burning the girl's foot. Years later people claimed to have seen her, clearly recognizable by her stoop and her burn. The jealous bokor had turned her into a zombie, and was keeping her as a servant until so much attention was drawn to the case that he was obliged to set her free.

A much more common motive is the provision of cheap labour. The owner of a neighbouring plantation might make a deal with the local bokor to rifle the cemetery, or a likely-looking body might be chosen before death. He would

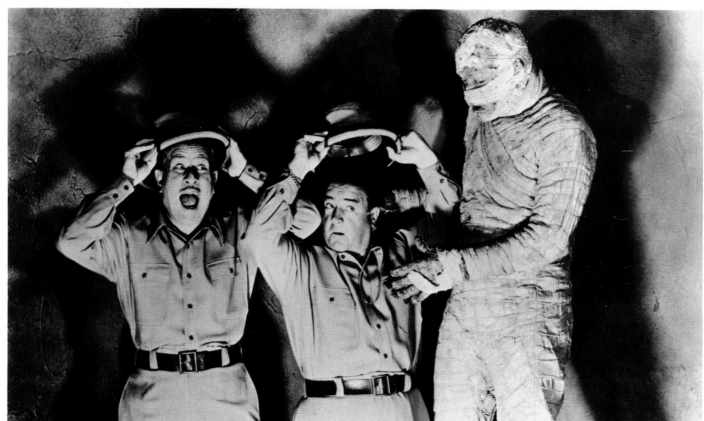

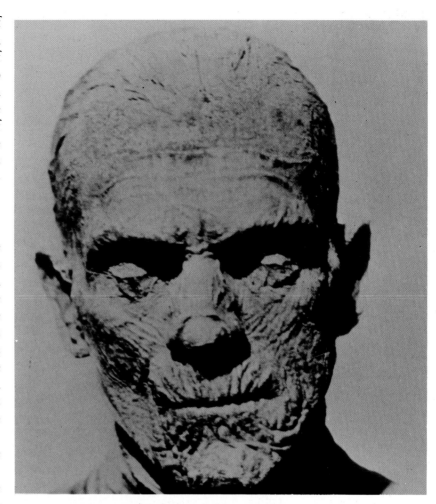

then, possibly by either the judicious use of poisons, or a really effective curse, be helped on his way. In still other cases, a kind of variation of the Faust legend tells of heads of families who make pacts with bokors for payment in human souls on account of services rendered. The client will then continue providing members of his family to work as zombies until supplies are exhausted. Like the hapless Faust who was finally carried off by Mephistopheles, ultimately the erstwhile client must take his turn.

Making a Zombie

Only the sorcerer can create zombies. There are various differing accounts of the actual process involved. One tells of what happens when a man is about to die and has been foreordained for the thrall of zombiedom. The bokor saddles a horse after dark, and rides, his head facing the horse's tail, to the victim's house. Placing his lips against a slit in the door, he sucks out the victim's soul, his gros-bon-ange, and traps it in a corked bottle. Shortly afterwards the victim falls ill and dies. At midnight on the day of burial, the bokor goes with his assistants to the grave, opens it and calls the victim's name. The untenanted body has no choice but to answer. As he lifts his head, the sorcerer passes the bottle with the corpse's soul under his nose, and the corpse is then reanimated. Dragging him from the tomb the bokor chains his wrists, and beats him about the head to revive him further. Then he carefully closes the tomb, making sure that nobody will notice that it has been disturbed.

Would-be cemetery raiders have to placate and gain permission from Baron Samedi, Baron Saturday, the spirit of the graveyard, lord of the dead, the equivalent of the god Osiris in Egyptian mythology, and it is to Baron Samedi that zombies are dedicated. He is normally a big black man with a long white beard, but perhaps as a result of his somewhat unlikely appearance, he usually chooses to remain invisible. He does however make his presence felt by signs. Without his consent it is dangerous to open a grave, and prayers are addressed for his appeasement over the consecration of black candles; 'Dormi pa fumé Baron Samedi', translated from the Creole as 'Sleep sweetly, Baron Samedi'.

Once out of the grave, the victim is led by the bokor and his associates, past his own house. This is said to ensure that he will never again recognize his home and try to return there. He is then taken to the bokor's house, or a voodoo temple, (a *tonelle* or a *peristyle*) and given a secret drug. Some say it's an extract of jimson weed or belladonna, ingredients that were sometimes used by the slaves of colonial days to kill their masters.

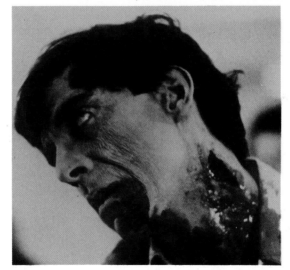

True Zombie Tales

Many writers quote stories of real-life zombies. Metraux (see above) tells of another zombie girl who escaped from the house where her parents left her locked up. Her behaviour so alarmed the neighbours that her zombiedom was confirmed. In **The Invisibles**, the well known anthropologist Francis Huxley passed on a story which had originally been recounted to him by a local magistrate. A catholic priest had gone blind after seeing a troupe of zombies in the hills. The magistrate remarked that one shouldn't laugh at such matters.

In some cases it's difficult not to. Another catholic priest, Father Sablon, told Huxley that

Above Boris Karloff's horrific make-up for the first version of The Mummy, *1932, directed by Karl Freund. When he 'goes for his little walk' to quote John Balderston's script, the professor who first uncovered him goes insane.*

Left A character from Zombies: Dawn of the Dead, *1979, directed by George Romero. This was the second in a 'zombie trilogy' and showed in macabre detail what happened when zombies overran New York. Most of the action takes place in a large supermarket which becomes awash with blood. The zombies apparently gravitate to the place which meant most to them when they were alive.*

he'd seen a zombie. The police wanted no part of a zombie. 'You found him first. You deal with him', the Inspector told the villagers. So the zombie sat outside, gnawing the rope which bound his wrists. By mid-afternoon somebody brought him salt water to drink. If you want to keep a zombie in your power, never give him salt. For salt is equated with blood, and if he drinks it or eats it he will find out he is a zombie and may well kill you—if he believes you were responsible for his present sad condition.

When the unfortunate zombie recovered his powers of speech he was able to give his name. His aunt was sent for and recognized him instantly. She said he had died and been buried four years before. When Father Sablon was brought in, he and the zombie had a talk together. He came from the house of a voodoo priest, he said, and indeed was one of a troupe of zombies who worked in the sorcerer's fields. The police were so scared they allowed the hungan to take his zombie if he paid them well, and so he did. Two days later, Huxley goes on, the zombie was dead. The sorcerer was arrested for murder and at the time the story was published, was still awaiting trial.

Tales of zombies aren't limited to the poorer classes. Metraux tells of a rich and well-educated landowner whose car broke down outside the door of a bokor. Assuring him that his breakdown was preordained, the priest invited him in and showed him a zombie. The landowner recognized him: he was a great

friend who had died some six months previously. Full of pity, he offered him a drink, but was stopped by the bokor who warned him of terrible dangers if he did so.

William Seabrook in **Magic Island** tells one of the most sensational of all zombie stories. Seabrook himself was quite a character. Before he finally committed suicide in 1945 he was said to have participated in many types of voodoo rites, and even eaten human flesh in Africa. Be that as it may, the story he tells concerns a number of zombies owned by a bokor called Joseph and looked after by his wife. One day she gave them salted biscuits by mistake. Awoken from their deathly trance, and knowing themselves for the walking corpses they were, they made straight for the cemetery, brushing aside all who would stop them. There they hurled themselves upon their graves and tried to dig themselves back into the earth, but turned into carrion as they did so.

Seabrook actually met and spoke to a zombie. He saw three men and a woman, not by night, with wraiths of mist rising from the fields, but in broad daylight. They were labourers, in a woman's charge, chopping the ground with

Below Tom Tyler, former cowboy star, changes roles to play Prince Kharis in Universal's first 'mummy' film, The Mummy's Hand, *1940.*

machetes, among straggling cotton stalks. Seabrook writes:

> As I clambered up from the trail, Polynice my guide was talking to the woman. She had stopped work; a big broad-boned, hard-faced black girl, who regarded us with surly unfriendliness. My first impression of the three supposed zombies, who continued dumbly at work, was that there was something about them unnatural and strange. They were plodding like brutes, like automatons. Without stooping down I could not fully see their faces which were expressionless.

When Polynice touched one on the shoulder and motioned him to get up he obeyed like an animal:

> What I saw then, despite what I had heard previously, came as a sickening shock. The eyes were the worst. They were in truth like the eyes of a dead man. Not blind, but staring, unfocussed, unseeing. The whole face, for that matter, was bad enough. It was vacant, as if there was nothing behind it. (This ties in with what we know of the untenanted body.)

It seemed not so much expressionless as incapable of expression. I had seen so much in Haiti that was beyond normal experience that for the flash of a second I had a sickening, almost panicky lapse in which I thought or rather felt, 'Great God, maybe this stuff is really true, and if it is true, it is rather awful, for it upsets everything'. I recovered from my mental panic. I reached out and grasped one of the dangling hands. Holding it I said 'Bonjour compère'. The zombie stared without responding.

Zora Hurston, another American writer who also took part in many voodoo ceremonies, went one better than Seabrook. She not only met a zombie, but also photographed it. She writes:

> I had the rare opportunity of seeing and touching an authentic case. I listened to the broken noises in its throat and then I did what noone else has done. I photographed it. If I had not experienced all this in strong sunlight, in a hospital yard, I might have come away from Haiti interested but doubtful. But I saw the case, and I know that there are zombies in Haiti.

Below Prince Kharis again, this time played by horror expert Christopher Lee in Hammer's The Mummy, 1959. *The Egyptologist who disturbs his tomb is played by another famous master of the macabre.*

Above Hammer's Plague of the Zombies, *1966 directed by John Gilling contains a graphic decapitation sequence. The story is set in England with a sorcerer, played by John Carson arousing the Living Dead from Cornish tin mines.*

The zombie's name was Felicia Felix-Mentor and her story was fairly typical of zombie cases on record. She had died of a sudden illness in 1907. In 1936 she was found wandering naked on the road near her brother's farm. Both her brother and her husband identified her as the woman they had buried 29 years before; she was in such a wretched condition that she was taken to the hospital in Port-au-Prince, Haiti's capital, and it was there, a few weeks later, that Miss Hurston saw her. 'The sight was dreadful', she went on. 'That blank face with the dead eyes. The eyelids were white all around the eyes as if they had been burned with acid. There was nothing that you could say to her, or get from her except by looking at her, and the sight of this wreckage was too much to endure for long.'

Miss Hurston also quotes one of the most famous of all zombie cases, still recounted in Haiti today. It concerns Marie, a lovely young society girl who died in 1909. Five years after her death Marie was seen by some former school friends at the window of a house in Port-au-Prince and to satisfy public opinion her grave was opened. Inside was a skeleton, too long for the coffin and plainly not Marie's. People say she had been dug up and used as a zombie until the bokor died who had held her captive. His widow then turned her over to a Catholic priest.

After her schoolmates had seen her, her family smuggled her out of Haiti and sent her to a convent in France, where she was later visited by her brother. 'No-one', says Miss Hurston, 'can stay in Haiti long without hearing zombies mentioned. The fear of this thing and all it means seeps over the country like a grand current of cold air.'

The late President, François 'Papa Doc' Duvalier, used this fear of zombies as a political threat both to his enemies and subjects, to enforce total subjugation and obedience from his own party and to deter any opposition from the others. Before becoming president, he had published articles in erudite university journals about voodoo, and was well versed in both its mythology and psychology. His élite body-guard was known by its nickname, the 'Ton Ton Macoute', the term for travelling sorcerers, and the threat of witchcraft—applied for purposes of personal vendetta—underlay his orders and pronouncements. His grave, ironically, now has a permanent guard over it to ensure that his body is not removed by sorcerers.

What is Zombiedom?

So do zombies really exist? And if so, what are they? Discounting the theory that they really are walking corpses, despite the assertions of those who say they are, it is obvious that they are in some sort of deep trance, blindly obeying those who give them orders.

Edgar Allan Poe, who used the theme of catalepsy in so many of his stories, was mortally afraid of being 'prematurely interred within the tomb' and biographers declare that he always carried papers on him, begging the doctor who should attend him after some accident, to make sure that he was really dead before signing a certificate. It seems that his fears may have been justified. Some years ago a newspaper report was published regarding a cemetery in France. It was decided to resite it, which meant that the graves had to be dug up. An uncomfortably high proportion of skeletons were discovered in positions in which they were not originally buried. We know that catalepsy is not an infectious disease, but could it be that it is more widespread than is popularly supposed, and doctors more easily fooled into signing premature certificates? Of course they will deny this strenuously, but doctors have been known to make mistakes quite often. It's an uncomfortable thought.

Suppose that in Haiti, and other places where zombies are found, sorcerers, magicians—whatever name you give them—are able to induce catalepsy in their victims, so convincingly that they are declared dead, and buried, and then continue this catatonic state by the careful application of indigenous herbs or drugs. And suppose this state can continue indefinitely. Nearly 30 years were involved in the case of Felicia Felix-Mentor.

The other theory is that zombies are really mental defectives, and some alleged cases of zombies merely describe conventional insanity. Perhaps, it is said, the families of these unfortunates carefully conceal them, pretending that they are dead until they have the bad luck to be seen again. This might explain some cases, but not all. While it is not unprecedented for a small confined society prone to much intermarriage to produce a higher proportion of congenital idiocy than a large, mobile society, Haiti does seem to have more than its fair share of 'defectives'. And what about the official testimony, supported by evidence, to the death, burial and reappearance of so many cases? Are Haitian officials really that corrupt? Article 246 of the Haitian Criminal Code, quoted so often, perhaps sums up the arguments best:

> Also to be termed intention to kill is the use of substances whereby a person is not killed but reduced to a state of lethargy, more or less prolonged, and this without regard to the manner in which the substances were used or what was their later result. If following the state of lethargy the person is buried then the attempt will be deemed murder.

Zombies in Fiction

If real-life zombies present us with a great question mark, no such enigma lies at the heart of the fictional variety. They return from the dead with no ambiguity at all, and if George Romero has his way will probably conquer the world in the 1980s.

Film producers have certainly made up for the neglect of novelists and short story writers in exploring the theme of zombieism. Zombies have proliferated in the cinema, after a fairly late start, and shambled through many tales of genuine terror. Perhaps one reason for their celluloid success may be the comparative lack of make-up required to create the desired effect. The audience does most of the work. As Denis Gifford remarks, of all the B-movie monsters the zombie soon became favourite.

> The walking dead looked pretty much like the walking quick, particularly if you used less expressive, hence less expensive, actors. Besides in cinema convention zombies can't talk, and the Union scale was lower for a non-speaking part.

While Frankenstein monsters, vampires and the rest remain fairly anchored to fantasy, it's an incontravertible fact that we will all share the attributes of a zombie when the end comes. We

may prefer not to promenade out of our graves, but even stationary, we all take on the characteristics on which the film zombie has traded for his horrific effect: the white, blood-drained face, the protuberant, staring yet sightless eyes are our inescapable inheritance.

The popular stance and movement adopted by zombies—unseeing eyes fixed straight ahead, wooden, robotic movements, arms pressed straight down to sides—has been employed and parodied as a sterotyped convention by most film monsters. How zombies really move and walk we don't know. None of the eye witness accounts mention this aspect of their behaviour. Perhaps without the trimmings they wouldn't be as effective. In any event the cinema's first truly imaginative attempt to present them on the screen didn't take place till 1932 with White Zombie.

Zombies in Hollywood

White Zombie was produced and directed by the Halperin Brothers and starred Bela Lugosi in the only part of stature comparable to Dracula he ever achieved in his subsequent career. William Seabrook published his **Magic Island** in 1929, and the study of voodoo and zombies only became newsworthy at that time. White Zombie however is concerned with voodooism

Above Bela Lugosi as satanic 'Murder Legendre', the evil zombie-master in White Zombie, 1932 by the Halperin brothers. One of the best zombie movies, this film showed Lugosi at the height of his career bringing a rare authority to the role.

Following pages Peter Cushing's face is truly fearsome as he emerges from the grave to revenge himself on his tormentor in Tales from the Crypt, 1971. This successful film, directed by Freddie Francis for Amicus Films, comprised a number of short stories.

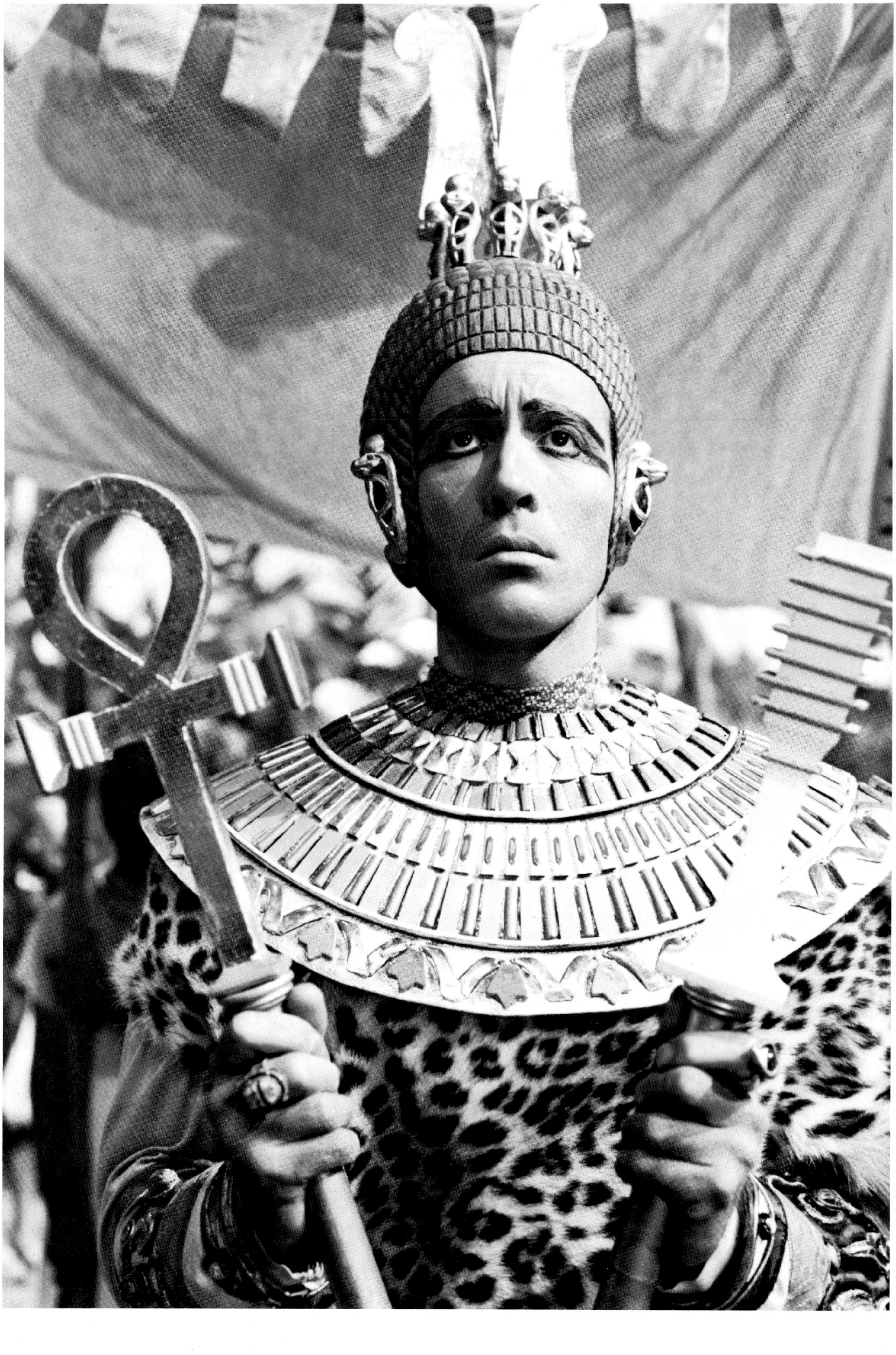

only superficially. Its story is really an amalgam of fairy tale, being more akin to Cocteau's 'La Belle et La Bête' or 'The Sleeping Beauty' with its narcoleptic princess, evil necromancer and benign wizard. Madge Bellamy plays Madeline, the New York *ingénue* who arrives to marry a bank clerk in Port-au-Prince. On the boat she is noticed by a plantation owner (Robert Frazer) who falls in love with her and determines to stop the marriage. On his return to the island he visits Murder Legendre (Lugosi) the evil sorcerer and zombie master, and together they conspire to bewitch the girl and turn her into a zombie. Presumably Frazer's plan is to marry a passive wife, but Lugosi wants the girl for himself, and he turns Frazer into a zombie. All is resolved when as an act of redemption and a momentary return of willpower Frazer himself kills Lugosi and the girl is released from the evil spell to marry her young man.

The film is withal a cop-out. The girl isn't really dead, and as Lugosi falls to his death she is magically released. Whether this is closer to the truth of the real-life variety as we discussed above, is beside the point as the fictional zombie is, less ambiguously a walking corpse. Lugosi's other staff are unarguably dead: but in 1932 the heroine's life—and honour—had to be jealously preserved intact.

Contemporary reviewers found *White Zombie* old fashioned and melodramatic. But they misunderstood the genre: they might have

allowed that it was a gothic fairy tale filled with traditional symbols. The heroine's name is Madeline: her resemblance to the sonambulistic Madeline Usher is enhanced by her white-gowned appearance. She is white sartorially as well as physically. Today the film's stylized atmosphere is only enhanced by the passage of time.

Three years later the Halperins tried to repeat their initial success with *Revolt of the Zombies*, but failed. Its zombies were not the walking dead of Haiti, but a regiment of defunct Indo-Chinese soldiers, killed and revived to perform some bloody feats for the greater glory of France during World War I. The idea for a resurgence of a paramilitary zombie force was worked again in the 1960s with two Italian pieces, *Tombs of the Blind Dead* and *Return of the Blind Dead*. In this saga the zombies were the Knights Templar.

A very bright comedy featuring Bob Hope appeared at Paramount in 1940. It was called *Ghost Breakers* and one scene had Paulette Goddard chased round a haunted castle by a real zombie (Noble Johnson) whose convincing presence managed to instil some genuine chills among the laughs. But in 1941, zombies invaded Monogram, the quota-quickie studio. They made *King of the Zombies*, and the zombies moved back from Cambodia to Haiti. In 1943 they followed with *Revenge of the Zombies* featuring John Carradine, an actor of superb

Far left Christopher Lee impressive in his regalia as Prince Kharis from The Mummy, 1959. *This character was to appear and reappear in both Universal's and Hammer's 'mummy' series. In the story Kharis is tortured before he is buried alive (above) and his tongue is extracted as a punishment for crimes against the gods of Ancient Egypt.*

presence but mostly given shoddy vehicles, as a Nazi scientist, operating to the greater glory of the Führer from a Louisiana manse.

Yet the same year saw another work to compare in imaginative quality with *White Zombie*. Val Lewton, a producer of great subtlety and taste, qualities in short supply in 1930s and 1940s Hollywood, left his mark on many distinguished fantasies around this time, and one of the best was *I Walked with a Zombie* directed by Jacques Tourneur.

Tourneur is on record as saying that he prefers this to all his other films, and its derivation was unlikely, to say the least. The title was borrowed, according to Denis Gifford, from a series of newspaper articles written by Inez Wallace for the Hearst Sunday supplements and dealing with Haitian witchcraft and voodoo. Although billed as an original screenplay by Ardel Wray and Curt Siodmak (later to write 'Donovan's Brain', a story about a brain kept alive artificially, and filmed several times), *I Walked with a Zombie* had its real spiritual home at Haworth Parsonage on the Yorkshire Moors of England, where lived Charlotte Brontë. Val Lewton called it 'Jane Eyre in the West Indies', and that is really what it was. The mad wife whom Rochester kept in his attic has here been transferred to Haiti as a zombie. Rochester's wife was in fact a Creole, and her early life leading to the onset of her insanity was ingeniously chronicled by Jean Rhys in her novel **The Wide Sargasso Sea**. The film has since bcome something of a cult, though not on account of its literary roots.

A young nurse (Frances Dee) is retained by a wealthy planter—who does *not* keep zombies—(Tom Conway) to care for his sick wife Jessica (Christine Gordon), victim of a mysterious malady which has left her a walking catatonic, speechless and mindless, To the superstitious islanders she is indeed a zombie, and the nurse decides to take her to a voodoo priest. The nocturnal walk through the canefields, while the approaching drums drown out the rustling of the wind, constitutes the core of the film, as well as one of the great set pieces of screen terror.

Bela Lugosi returned to Monogram and the manipulation of the Undead in 1944 in *Voodoo Man*. He kept his wife alive, although she had died 22 years before, by kidnapping girls, instilling their souls into her living corpse. Finally he resorted to voodoo, accompanied by John Carradine on drums!

After this, zombies appeared in various forms: created by atomic power in Edward L. Cath's *Creature with the Atomic Brain* (1955) and by the use of gamma rays on local children in *The Gamma People* (1956).

Killer Zombies

When zombies crossed over into the realms of SF, there was, of course, no stopping them. They became fairly obvious symbols of political propaganda as soon as their relationship with the practice of brain-washing became cystallized for film-makers of the 1950s, 1960s and early 1970s. It culminated in the overt political statement of John Frankenheimer's *The Manchurian Candidate* (1962) where Laurence Harvey, newly returned from Korea, was issued with post-hypnotic orders aimed at political subversion by the Red Chinese, and thus became a kind of zombie. Significantly, in this brilliant and witty film, it was Harvey's evil old mother , terrifyingly well played by Angela Lansbury, who was ultimately revealed as a communist agent who carried responsibility for the destruction of her son's mind.

The more obvious kind of zombie couldn't be left out of the great Hammer horror revival of the 1950s and 1960s, and John Gilling made *Plague of the Zombies* in 1966. John Carson was the zombie master, and the zombies emerged, in excellent colour, from the Cornish tin mines.

But now new problems arose. Zombies were inherently harmless. Because they had no will of their own, the evil had to be directed from a Lugosi-type sorcerer figure. So in order to imbue them with evil potential, they had to be invested with some new propensity, conforming to the public demand for ever more explicit horror. The evil puppetmaster became superfluous. And in 1968 *Night of the Living Dead* perhaps the greatest zombie film ever made, arrived. Made in black and white, on a shoestring budget, it came nearer to genuine nightmare than any other movie in the genre.

It has of course been copied since, but never equalled. A Spanish-Italian coproduction, shot on location in Britain, *The Living Dead of the Manchester Morgue*, which arrived in 1974, had its share of cannibalistic zombies and effective moments. Baron Samedi himself appeared in *Voodoo Girl* (1973), to disinter Guinea slaves from the 17th century; but the accolade for sheer technique went to Mr Romero's piece. From the moment the first zombie lumbers unheralded into frame as the young couple have stopped their car to visit a country graveyard, to their final desperate siege in the lonely house while zombies clammer to get in, the tension never slackens.

It was George Romero's first horror film, and he skates very lightly over the SF reasons for the zombies' return—artificial stimulation of genes caused by excessive radiation in the Earth's polluted ground. This has brought about not only widespread reanimation, but a desperate craving for blood from the living. This however doesn't really matter. For Romero, reanimated zombies are symbols of man's misuse of his own potential and amenities. The seeds of his own destruction lie within himself, and he is more than halfway there. The menace comes from no alien monster, no prehistoric survival.

He has borrowed elements from the vampire and werewolf myths. Those killed by zombies become zombies themselves—unless they have the misfortune to be eaten first. That is how the contagion spreads. In one terrifying sequence a child slaughters and eats its own parents. And you can't get more symbolic than that! The film is the first of a projected trilogy. The second appeared in 1979, first shown in London at the London Film Festival.

In *Dawn of the Dead*, or *Zombies: Dawn of the Dead* to give it the title with which it was distributed in the UK—the zombies have overrun New York. Most of the action takes place in a huge and glossy supermarket (we are told that zombies will gravitate after death to the places that meant most to them in life). Mr. Romero now has colour, and blood is gorier in colour. Mr Romero has never been one to eschew physical grue. Characters have the tops of their heads blown off in graphic closeup. Bolstered by larger budgets, Mr Romero doesn't always resist the temptation to indulge himself, and is in danger of overstatement as far as his moral message is concerned. In the third episode of the trilogy, now in production, the rumours are that zombies conquer the world.

So we can only say to producers of future zombie movies, 'Follow that'. Where they will go is anyone's guess. But it's a cinch that the silent, reticent zombies of Val Lewton's film will never reappear. Or will they?

There will of course be many more rip-offs of the Romero cycle. In 1979 the latest one appeared. *Zombie Flesh Eaters* had Richard Johnson carrying out some rather vague experiments on a Pacific island, but he is as surprised as anyone when graves start opening up all over the place. These zombies overrun New York too. Directed by Lucio Fulci, *Zombie Flesh Eaters* is obviously intended as the beginning of a series.

Literature has remained oddly reticent about zombies. We still await the great zombie novel, although Romero has produced paperback tie-ins. A character called Simon Garth, 'The Zombie' appeared in a comic called *Tales of Terror*. The cover of the third issue exclaimed that he was 'seeking out the only man who can help him, a mysterious hungan who is known as Doc Kabel'. One wonders if he ever found him. The use of the word Hungan indicates that the writer is conversant with the terminology of voodoo.

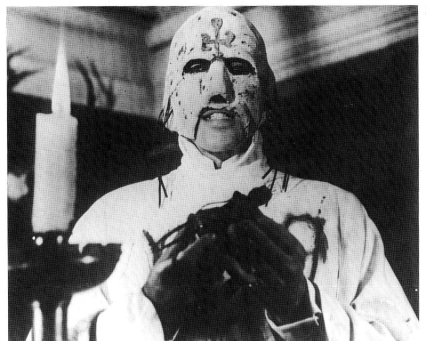

Mummies in Fact

Unlike the zombie cycle, that of the mummy seems to have come to a temporary standstill. As a member of the Undead Club, the mummy labours under a strict disadvantage. Nobody has claimed to have met a mobile mummy in real life. Mummies stay dead, preferring to work to the discomfiture of mankind vicariously, through curses.

The curse that everyone has heard about is of course the one attached to Tutankhamen's tomb. In 1922, an expedition led by Howard Carter and Lord Carnarvon uncovered the largest hoard of treasure ever excavated, as well as the intact mummy of the boy king. Both were placed on public view. Most of those who had gone to the Valley of the Kings suffered personal tragedy of one kind or another. It is of course fatally easy to ascribe natural disaster to the workings of a supernatural agency. Egyp-

Top Behind the demonic mask lies a powerful and terrible mind about to engage in a horrific ritual.

Above Nazis on ice! A cinematographic attempt at preserving horrors for the future.

150

tian curses—like voodoo or any other kind of curses—probably work only when the victims believe that they will. Faith, we are told, moves mountains. Perhaps it causes avalanches as well.

Certainly the Ancient Egyptians believed in magic. Their dead, like those of the Haitians, had to be protected at all costs, and the fate of the soul in the afterlife was bound up closely with that of the physical body. Mummification was really a ritual re-enactment on behalf of the deceased of the acts that were supposed to have raised the god Osiris from the dead. If he followed the prescribed drill, the corpse too would rise. Like Christ, Osiris was believed to have risen from the dead. The difference was that in his case his body was kept intact and free to receive his soul by processes of embalming carried out by his wife Isis. Osiris—the 'Mighty One'—came to preside as Judge of the Dead— the equivalent of Baron Samedi in Haitian folklore. Originally an Egyptian king, his consort Isis was also his sister. He was murdered by his brother Seth, whose own wife Nephthys was also Isis' sister. After his restoration from the dead, Osiris didn't resume his earthly throne. First he presided over the trial of Seth, who was found guilty of fratricide, and then he became Lord of the Underworld, Lord of the Dead. Various prayers dedicated to Osiris have been discovered on excavated papyri and tomb inscriptions and scrolls.

Certainly the custom of mummification goes back a stupendously long way. It was already well established in 2400 BC when the Pyramid Texts were composed, and lasted till around the 4th century AD when christian influence led to its abandonment.

Making a Mummy

The Greek historian, Herodotus, left a detailed description of the embalming process, gruesome as it was, and accompanied by suitable prayers to Osiris and the other gods. His account is confirmed in most details by mummy examination. Professional embalmers carried out the process. They operated more or less as taxidermists do today. There were cheap ones and better-class more expensive ones. Here is the account of one around the middle bracket:

They take first a crooked piece of iron, and with it draw the brain through the nostrils, thus getting rid of a portion, while the skull is cleared of the rest by rinsing with drugs. Next, they make a cut along the flank with a sharp Ethiopian stone, and take out the whole contents of the abdomen, which they then cleanse, washing it thoroughly with palm wine, and again frequently with an infusion of pounded aromatics. After this they fill the cavity with the purest bruised myrrh, with

cassia, and every sort of spicery except frankincense, and sew up the opening. Then the body is placed in natron [hydrated carbonate of sodium] for 70 days and covered entirely over. After the expiration of that space of time, which must not be exceeded, the body is washed, and wrapped round, from head to feet, with bandages of fine linen cloth, smeared over with gum, and in this state is given back to the relations who enclose it in a wooden case which they have made for the purpose, shaped into the figure of a man.

Herodotus then describes other methods, the first of which consisted of injecting cedar wood by syringe, which dissolved the stomach and intestines, and was drained out through the anus. The body then had its natron soak, which dissolved the flesh, leaving only skin and bones.

Far left Kharis again, this time an earlier version played by Lon Chaney in The Mummy's Ghost, 1944. The cinema has always depicted mummies as having great strength. This idea is possibly based on the embalming method, using bitumen, which renders the body practically indestructible.

Above Not a mummy this time but the Living Dead. In the 1970s cannibalistic zombies became a popular theme with horror film-makers. This Spanish-Italian film with the unlikely title of The Living Dead of the Manchester Morgue, 1974 had some very chilling moments.

Left An old image of a mummy conveying the daunting atmosphere of horror.

Above A scene from Vault of Horror, *1972, follow-up to* Tales from the Crypt *directed by Roy Ward Baker. This collection of scary episodes used stories taken from American horror comics. Totally unrecognisable under their decaying features are Tom Baker, Michael Craig, Curt Jurgens, Daniel Massey and Terry Thomas.*

Centre right Christine Gordon, Frances Dee and Darby Jones as the zombie in Val Lewton's I Walked with a Zombie, *1943. Directed by Jacques Tourneur for RKO, this is regarded as one of the best zombie movies. Frances Dee plays a nurse searching for the sorcerer who, she hopes, will free her patient from her catatonic trance.*

Right One of the corpses emerging from the grave in Hammer's Plague of the Zombies, *1966, with characteristic mouldering earth and evil mist.*

He doesn't mention bitumen, an essential ingredient which was used for packing the cavities from which the organs had been removed. This had the effect of blackening the body, and added to its weight, but made it practically indestructible. So the cliché used by cinema and television in which mummies invariably show the physical strength of the Hulk plus sundry assorted oxes seems to have had a basis in fact. It was the bitumen stain that made so many mummies dark-coloured when they were found, and the word 'mummy' is itself derived from an Arabic term meaning bitumen.

The second method, used only by the poorer classes, describes how the intestines were removed by clyster, a process involving the injection of a liquid—he doesn't say what—followed by the 70-day natron soak.

The organs that had been removed, Herodotus tells us were separately embalmed bitumen and wrapped in bandages. They were then placed in canopic jars, of which four were used for each person, and the jars were then interred in a special chest together with the mummified body.

The tomb in which the mummy was finally laid was furnished with a variety of goods according to the dead man's rank, and it became his 'eternal house', at which food offerings were regularly made. Your social class was often

indicated by the number of coffins in which you were buried. Tutankhamen (1354–1345 BC) was enclosed in three, the inner one being of pure gold. The coffins were normally placed in a massive stone sarcophagus for maximum protection. Coffins were brightly painted both inside and out, with images of protective deities, magical symbols and texts from **The Book of the Dead**, a sort of guide book to the Underworld. As well as household goods, amulets and charms were scattered round the mummies. They were placed either on the body or in the wrappings, and the one most highly favoured to give the maximum magical protection was that of the scarab beetle which was placed in the breast cavity.

The whole process was an elaborate attempt to cheat death. It is ironic that in the Middle Ages embalmed bodies were often pounded up and sold as drugs.

Non-Egyptian Mummies

Of course mummies have been found elsewhere than in the tombs of Egypt. In England, in Blandford, Dorset, a mummified cat was found in the foundations of a demolished shop. Sometimes the mummification process is a natural one. In Pompeii and Herculaneum, bodies were discovered miraculously preserved among the rocks after the final holocaust. In

Above A horrible moment from Zombies: Dawn of the Dead, *1979. In the 1970s, horror movies with their surfeit of blood and special effects were becoming almost too gruesome and frightening for the average horror fan.*

Centre left A rare example of a successful zombie comedy. Bob Hope and Willie Best are on a guided tour around the haunted castle in Paramount's Ghost Breakers, *1940, directed by George Marshall.*

Left The mummy (Dickie Owen) catches up with the latest news during the filming of Curse of the Mummy's Tomb, *1964 directed by Michael Carreras.*

sulphur caves in many parts of the world corpses have been preserved by natural conditions; when taken out of the caves they may crumble to dust. In parts of South America and Brazil the dead are still embalmed in the catacombs.

Peter Haining, in **The Monster Trap** (1976) tells a particularly interesting tale of a strange survival. In 1932, two gold prospectors in Wyoming, USA discovered the body of a strange mummified man.

> The figure seated there seemed to be perfectly formed, a little man about 14 inches high. He was sitting cross-legged and with his arms folded in his lap. His skin was a deep bronze colour, and he was very wrinkled all over. One of his eyes seemed to droop lower than the other, and the prospectors couldn't help getting the impression that the figure was almost winking at them.

Scientists from the Smithsonian institute in Washington came to examine him, expecting to find a fake. They were baffled: X-rays revealed that the mummy had been a genuine human being. The skeleton showed up quite clearly, albeit in miniature. A scientist from the American Museum of Natural History named him a 'Hesperopithicus', after a form of anthropoid which supposedly roamed the North American continent during the middle of the Pliocene period. Representatives from various universities agreed that he was 'the most perfect prehistoric mummy ever discovered.' His teeth showed him to have been not a child but an adult of 65 when he died. Later the mummy was placed on exhibition but soon disappeared. His only memorial is a marker indicating the cave where he was found. It was christened 'The Little Man Mine.'

Below Another mummy lying in state.

Below right A painted voodoo face.

Mummies in Fiction

While mummies have never been known to come back from the dead in fact, despite their rifled tombs, they have made up for it amply in fiction. In real life all their elaborate precautions have come to nought: the remnants of their grandiose schemes on view in museums all over the world are the pathetic memorials of their frustrated hopes.

We should pause briefly, very briefly, at the public library, on our way to the cinema. Literary mummies aren't quite as thin on the ground as literary zombies but the scene is desolate enough: Théophile Gautier, in his short story 'The Foot of the Mummy' shows an imaginative sense of the unreal; Conan Doyle, in two short stories 'Lot 249' and 'The Ring of Thoth', Algernon Blackwood in 'A Descent into Egypt' and Richard Marsh in his novel **The Beetle** explored themes of Ancient Egyptian survival; and Bram Stoker's novel **Jewel of the Seven Stars** was filmed by Hammer and is currently being filmed again. It is sporadically exciting, and has the distinction of being the only novel in the English language to be published simultaneously with two different endings. Presumably Mr Stoker couldn't decide which was the best. The diligent bibliophile can still find copies of each if he is prepared to rake second-hand bookshops. *Aida* has its operatic mummies of course, but they appear very little in the theatre. It is, as always, up to the cinema; and in this case movie-makers started on the subject very early.

After all, in the theatre there's not a lot you can do with a mummy. In the convention of the times not only his appearance, but also his intelligence, is securely covered by his bandages.

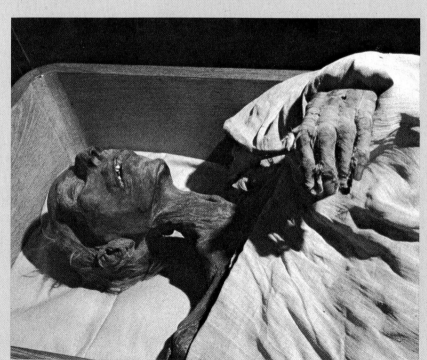

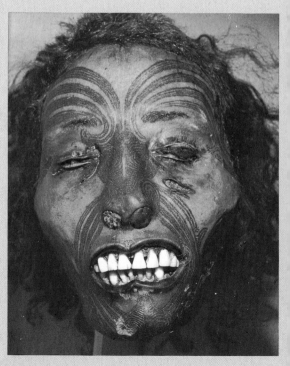

Immortality in Celluloid

The French were early contenders with *The Vengeance of Egypt* (1912), the first feature sold purely on its horror value. Napoleon himself was one of the characters, digging up a mummy case. A French lieutenant steals the scarab ring and sends it to his sweetheart. When she puts it on she dreams of a mummy, and is promptly murdered by a burglar. Various people handle the ring and die, and only when an Egyptologist finally returns it to its rightful place do the killings stop.

As early as 1901, in *The Haunted Curiosity Shop*, the cinema was trying to convince its audience that mummies return. An antiquarian is confronted with a living mummy. Before he can recover from his surprise the wrappings fall away and the living Egyptian stands before him. The flesh melts away till only the skeleton remains. The first feature-length British attempt was *The Avenging Hand* (1915), in which the ghost of an Egyptian princess comes to London looking for her severed member! Another spectral immigrant (Leah Douglas) brought vengeance upon an MP in *The Beetle* (1919), an adaptation of Richard Marsh's novel.

But it wasn't till 1932, the year of *White Zombie*, that the first classic of the genre was produced. 1932 was a vintage year. This time they found a vintage monster: who else but Karloff? He had the skill of arousing sympathy for the most bizarre creation, and now he added a new monster to his portfolio. *The Mummy* had a screenplay by John L. Balderston, who had already worked on the best of the Universal horror cycle, *Frankenstein*, *Dracula*, and *Bride of Frankenstein*, perhaps the best of all. Balderston had originally been London correspondent of the *New York World*.

Brilliantly directed by Karl Freund (his first directional assignment), Karloff plays Imhotep, buried alive after stealing the sacred scroll of Thoth in order to bring his love to life again. An archaeologist opens the tomb some 3000 years later, reads the words on the scroll aloud, and inadvertently brings the mummy to life again. The mummy 'goes for a little walk', promptly driving the archaeologist insane. Ten years pass and Karloff reappears, face incredibly wrinkled and deathlike but minus bandages, to lead another British expedition to his tomb so that they can bring out the mummified body of his love. The second mummy is taken to the Cairo Museum, but when reanimation is unsuccessful, Imhotep turns his attention to Helen Grosvenor (Zita Johann) the modern-day reincarnation of his love. This is a favourite plot device of mummy movies: the audience has, willy-nilly, to accept not only the mummy

Left This example of trick photography from the 1860s could be an appropriate illustration for William Seabrook's traditional tale **Magic Island**. *The story tells of a young girl in Haiti who discovers on her wedding night that she is married to a voodoo sorcerer. He tells her that he is giving a special wedding banquet for her. On opening the door of the banqueting hall she finds that her guests are all mouldering corpses.*

Below left A portrait of the author William Seabrook.

Below Fact or fake? A pair of supposedly mummified corpses of ju-jus or Devil Men found in a cave on the island of Haiti. The legend on the box-lid tells the story.

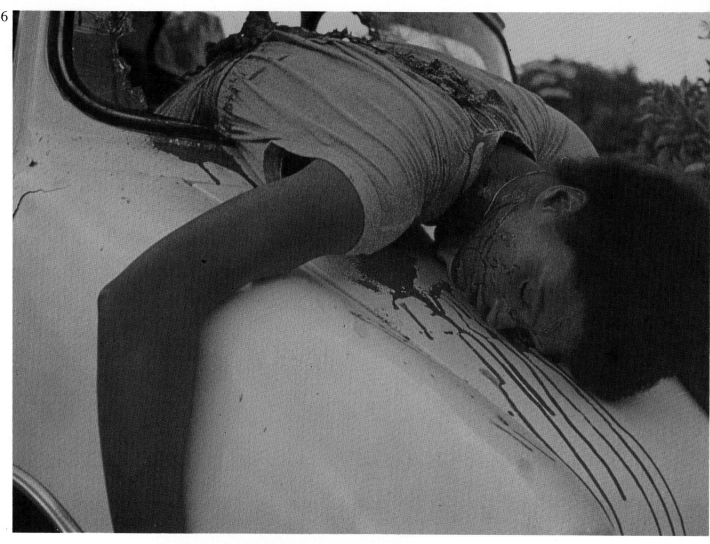

Above and far right *The* Hammer House of Horror *series produced for Thames Television by Roy Skeggs, featured 13 teleplays.* Charlie Boy *featured a voodoo fetish doll with murderous powers. Two of its victims are seen here.*

Right *The cat was considered to be a sacred animal by the Ancient Egyptians. Their corpses were accorded ritual mummification in the same fashion as humans.*

survival, but reincarnation as well. All is finally sorted out when the statue of Isis comes to life and saves Miss Grosvenor, whom Karloff is trying to murder in the museum.

While *The Mummy* was made in the USA, Gaumont-British borrowed Karloff and, playing it safe, also used Ancient Egypt as a background for his first British horror release. In *The Ghoul* (1933) he returns from the dead to avenge the theft of the jewel 'The Eternal Light'. In 1940 Universal brought their own bandages back into service, and Tom Tyler, former cowboy star, stepped into them. He was chosen because of his resemblance to how Karloff had looked in 1932, so that shots from the previous film could be incorporated into the new one. *The Mummy's Hand* marked the first appearance of Prince Kharis, who was to figure in every one of Universal's future films in the cycle. He would even be reanimated by Hammer in the 1950s.

Prince Kharis, the Boss Mummy

The stories were more or less routine. Kharis was brought to life, pursued various reincarnations of his lost love, and was brought to a temporary halt at the end of the picture. The same formula—with the exception of the reincarnation element—was used by Universal for their *Frankenstein*, *Dracula*, and *Wolfman* cycles; though oddly the Mummy never intermingled, or 'met' any of the others.

Tom Tyler was reawakened by George Zucco in *The Mummy's Hand*, and a year later in *The Mummy's Tomb* it was the turn of Lon Chaney Jnr. In this one the scene shifts to America, where it was to stay. This time the Mummy is destroyed by fire—spliced in from *Frankenstein*, according to Denis Gifford. But Kharis wouldn't stay dead, and turned up again in 1944 for *The Mummy's Ghost*. Zucco was back, and John Carradine reported for duty as the High Priest. Chaney again played Kharis, and this time ended in a swamp. But he was out of it again later the same year in *The Mummy's Curse*, although the action was said to begin '25 years later'! The swamp has been drained, and Kharis, with the girl friend he had taken with him, now holes up in an abandoned monastery, which he brings down on everyone's head. With the end of the monastery came the end of this particular cycle.

Abbott and Costello 'met the Mummy' at the beginning of the 1950s, and in 1956 Bel-Air produced *The Pharaoh's Curse*, but these were only sporadic revivals. Chaney once complained that if you met Abbott and Costello you were dead. He met them in his best-known persona as Lawrence Talbot, the Wolfman, and this ended the Lawrence Talbot cycle. And it ended the Mummy cycle too. What Chaney really meant was that after the slapstick treatment typified by the two comics, no-one could take the character seriously ever again. Perhaps the most blatant example of comedy killing was when Old Mother Riley met the Vampire—and it happened in a British film. This nearly finished Bela Lugosi's career.

Hammer meets the Mummy

When in the 1950s Hammer decided to revive all the old horror figures, in full colour, they didn't forget the Mummy, or, more specifically, Prince Kharis.

In 1958 Jimmy Sangster wrote a new script for *The Mummy*, basing it on John Balderston's 1932 original. Christopher Lee (who else?) revived Kharis in the Victorian England of Peter Cushing's John Banning. Yvonne Furneaux played the dual role of the Princess Ananka, for whom Kharis had had his tongue cut out and been mummified alive, and her reincarnation Isobel, carried off at the instigation of the mummy's modern-day master. Terence Fisher, and the expertise of Cushing and Lee ensured the 'classic' status of the remake.

Lee has always brought great integrity to everything he does, and is well-known in the profession for doing his own stunts. But it was Dickie Owen who went down in the swamp for him, and Dickie Owen who took over the role in *Curse of the Mummy's Tomb* in 1964, with a script both written and directed by Michael Carreras. Kharis was rested at last; he hasn't appeared since 1958. In the latest opus, Terence Morgan played a hero-turned-villain, condemned to eternal life for his brother's murder.

In the same year Christopher Lee went to Italy and as a 19th-century count, began filling his castle with mummified corpses in *Castle of the Living Dead*. Hoist with his own petard, he himself joined the merry throng, when he was nicked by a scalpel dipped in his own embalming fluid. Back at Hammer, John Gilling had a go with *The Mummy's Shroud* in 1967. The plot was very loosely based on the Tutankhamen story, concerning as it did a boy king taken from a defiled tomb, and the defiance of an ancient and deathly curse.

But by far the most distinguished of this little Hammer group was their next and last, *Blood from the Mummy's Tomb*, made in 1971, and adapted from Bram Stoker's **Jewel of the Seven Stars** which it followed pretty closely. It was the only script based on a novel, the others having been original screenplays. Seth Holt died halfway through production, and his work as director was completed by Michael Carreras.

For the time being mummies have retreated back into their tombs, and their bandages have stopped unrolling—while their cousins the zombies are marching forward to conquer the world. But it will be only a temporary setback. already we're promised a new version of *Jewel*.

Travelling Beyond

Science fiction is an area which some
purists might argue was not truly of the
horror genre. Audiences of the film of
H.G. Wells' **War of the Worlds**, however, know well that horror can be created
in futuristic themes. There have been many
notable horror stories arising from distant
galaxies which rival even **Count Dracula** for
suspense and almost unendurable terror. Douglas Hill is well-qualified to tackle a review of this
subject as editor of numerous SF collections and
author of a number of books and articles on the
topic. He shows how themes from horror stories
have been used to illustrate SF ideas and explores
how one genre relates to the other. Beginning
with classic SF author Ray Bradbury and his
terrifying **Fahrenheit 451**, he traces the
development of science fantasy in the complex worlds of Fritz Leiber and Michael
Moorcock. John Wyndham has a special
slot in the science/horror fiction category; his themes of innocent infants
manifesting themselves as alien super-
beings in **The Midwich Cuckoos** is
very convincing. **The Day of the
Triffids** makes even the keenest
gardener temporarily regard
climbing plants with suspicion.
SF presents a different element of horror: that in
which the imagination
knows no bounds and
where we see terror
in a futuristic setting.

'Science fiction was born from the Gothic mode, is hardly free of it now.' That assertion comes from Brian Aldiss's masterful history of science fiction, **Billion Year Spree** (1973). The book remains the finest available account of science fiction's origins and evolution; and of course Aldiss himself stands among the giants as a creator of high-quality modern SF. Yet despite his credentials there was some widespread outrage and dissent when the book first appeared over Aldiss's location of a central taproot of SF in the same fecund soil that nurtured the exotic growth of the 19th-century gothic novel. And the firm assertion quoted above (and necessarily wrenched out of a carefully orchestrated context) will probably still raise a few eyebrows.

Gothic fiction has far more to it, as Aldiss makes absorbingly clear, than its outward garb of atmospheric settings. And science fiction has much more to *it* than bits of incidental gimmickry.

The fact that SF suffers still from the burden of its 'spaceships and guns' image is not entirely a condemnation of the genre. It is more a condemnation of those (especially media persons, who are given to snap judgements based on limited exposure) who feel a need to force things into ill-fitting pigeon holes, slap on misleading labels, and then dismiss the contents

out of hand. But by doing so they can get into terrible difficulties. Healthy living organisms (like fiction, or human beings) often tend to burst through the walls of these labelled compartments, like seedlings under asphalt. Then they engage in riotous interaction, and produce fascinating hybrid offspring—much to the despair of people who believe that sensible civilization depends on proper labelling. For instance: does a librarian shelve Poe's 'Murders in the Rue Morgue' under horror fiction or detective fiction? Does a film archivist store a print of *Alien* under horror or SF? and where do we put **Frankenstein**?

The only answer, again, is that we must leave our labels, our misleading assumptions and inaccurate preconceptions, to one side when we enter the teeming, sprawling world of imaginative fiction. It is more of a Megalopolis than the east coast of America. You can be fairly sure of where you are when you're in the urban heart of one city or another—but certainty vanishes when you move into the shadowy areas between, where two or more modes flow and blend into one another. Reading Le Fanu's **Carmilla**? You're in one of the older but still grand sections of Horrorville. Reading Verne's **From the Earth to the Moon**? You're in the crumbling original centre of SF city. But where are you when you're reading **Frankenstein**?

Below The last normal man on earth (Charlton Heston) searching for his enemies, the living dead, in a scene from the film Omega Man, *1971 based on Richard Matheson's novel* I Am Legend.

The Frankenstein Connection

Mary Shelley's novel (first published 1818) is sadly but undoubtedly not widely read today, except in 'modernized abridgements'. The slow, heavy prose—the unfamiliar narrative conventions—the drawn-out longueurs of philosophical discourse and scenic description—all these elements impose barriers that balk any but the most determined, or specialist, of modern readers. Yet literally millions of people know, or think they know, the essentials of the story—because of the many diluted, debased, misinterpreted versions offered by the cinema. And the filmic Frankenstein, those millions would say, is a dominant figure of modern horror.

After all, in the films the obsessional scientist has created a monster, and monsters are creatures of horror. He has done so, usually, inside an eerie castle during a thunderstorm, and those are notorious clichés in the outward trappings of horror. The monster is a grisly revenant, composed of stitched-together bits of dead bodies brought uncannily back to life as parts of a new whole, so he has much in common with the golem and the zombie—creatures of horror. The monster does ghastly and fearsome things, including threatening the life and virtue of assorted *deshabillées* actresses, even if he does so at the behest of whatever evildoer may be manning the electrical switches. And his aspects of supernatural horror are magnified by the apparent fact that he cannot be killed—not in Hollywood, anyway. No matter what happens at the end of one film, he remains intact, waiting only for a shot of high voltage to be revived for the next film.

But Frankenstein is a *scientist*, driven in large part by scientific curiosity and a desire to extend the boundaries of human knowledge. These basic urges, well-known traits in the fictitional prototype of the scientist, would seem to be worthy and laudable. But they can also be a short road to disaster—when they go hand in hand with an indifference to effect, a disregard of what certain scientific advances might do to ordinary human beings and their society, an unworldly ignorance of how some new developments or discoveries can be misused and corrupted, by venal men, to the detriment of mankind. When Frankenstein flees in horror from the monster he has created, modern readers might recall Einstein's gloomy wish, after the nuclear bomb had become a reality, that he had been a violinist instead of a physicist.

And this is the most central and greatest theme of science fiction—the revelation of all the ways in which scientific progress and technological advance can turn sour, because of

the inherent weaknesses, criminalities and evils, in human beings. It is true that in SF's earlier days it tried to offer assurances that modern science and the age of technology would assuredly usher in a Golden Age. But as SF matured, utopias went out of fashion. The greatest works of the genre today all contain, to some degree, this element of social criticism—disturbing reflections of the ultimate truth that man's nature cannot cope with the products of his scientific intelligence and inventiveness.

SF writers may take us to outer space and alien planets, into alternative histories or parallel worlds, but always, somewhere, we must confront the fatal flaws in our human nature. This confrontation occurs most explicitly when SF takes us into future societies on our own planet, most of which are convincing extrapolations from elements already visible in the 20th century—and few of which allow us to feel hopeful about humanity's future.

Equally, this has been a major theme in modern mainstream literature, beyond SF. It is a theme that appeared with and kept step with the progress of the Industrial Revolution—from Blake's unsettling image of the effects of technology ('God took the spinning jenny/out of His side') to Arnold's bleak view of industrial humanity as ignorant armies clashing by night.

Above *Magazine illustration portraying H.P. Lovecraft and a montage of the monstrous horrors he created, dominated by the ghastly Cthulhu.*

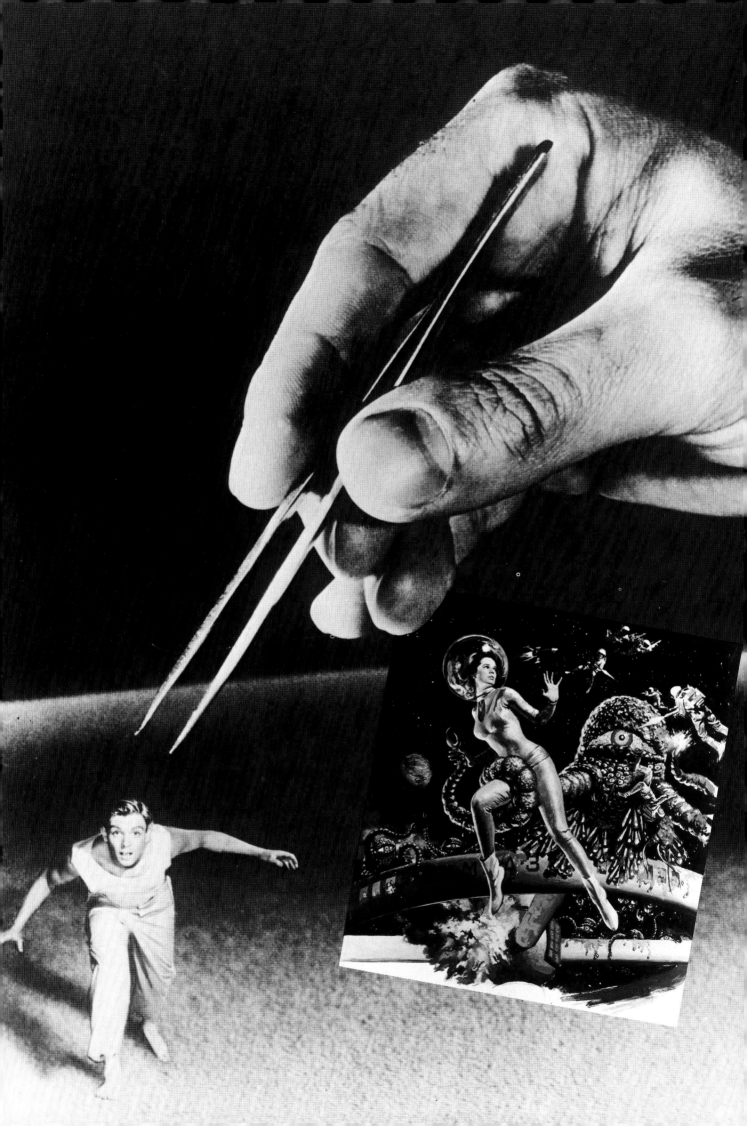

It is no accident that mainstream writers like Orwell and Huxley turned to the SF mode to create their appalling futures as grim warnings of where we may presently be going. So Frankenstein's Monster reappears time and again in many guises, inside SF and out of it, confirming Brian Aldiss's view that it is the 'first great myth of the industrial age'.

The Thrill of the Fantastic

There is a further connection to be found in the reasons why we read imaginative fiction. It is a complex psychological area. Only a fool would rush in, but we can skirt safely round the edges with the general consensus that such fiction is exhilaratingly liberating in a very special way—not an ingrown escapism from the constraints of the day-to-day, but an extension and expansion of the everyday world, gained through letting the imagination off its leash for a little healthful exercise. And within that liberating effect, horror fiction has a special function of its own, engendering a 'profound emotional response', in the words of the late Dr Christopher Evans. We read horror fiction because we enjoy feeling terror in safety. We enjoy the special stimulus of

eerie mystery and blood-freezing ghastliness, when we're in control and can stop it simply by closing the book. And so we go to horror fiction for that liberating, stimulating effect of being placed in the presence of the inexplicable, the unforeseeable, the (almost) unendurable.

But the fact is that science fiction provides precisely those effects, too, in its own ways. It can even do so, sometimes, with as much poetry as science—notably in the work of one of the best-loved artists of modern SF, who has made his own extended contribution to the 'myth of the industrial age'.

The Illustrative Man

Ray Bradbury is one of those few SF writers whose name is known even to those who do not read the stuff. Today his fame may be partly due to the fact that his best novel, **Fahrenheit 451** (1953) became a major film, and the short-story collection that established his early reputation, **The Martian Chronicles** (1951), has at last reached the television screen. But during the 1950s and 1960s, it was his writing alone that spread his fame beyond the bounds of the SF ghetto. And a case could be made for the idea

__Above__ When technology runs amok, fiction writers find a fruitful theme. This still from the film The Cars That Ate Paris *shows a deadly Volkswagen.*

__Far Left__ Scientific experiments gone awry, with horrifying results, including The Incredible Shrinking Man, *1957.*

__Inset__ This is possibly the prototype of popular SF's favourite horror, the bug-eyed monster. Alien, tentacled being grabs lissom space traveller in a magazine illustration for Green Slime.

Right Deadly plant life features prominently among the threatening monsters of science fiction. Here Krynoids, alien vegetable pods, menace The Doctor (Tom Baker) and Sarah (Elizabeth Selden) in The Seeds of Doom *an episode of the long-running BBC Television series* Dr Who.

that he attained his stature because many people believed he was *not* an SF writer.

But we must avoid the pigeonhole syndrome. Bradbury was always an SF writer, in his own eyes and in those of the SF world. The two books mentioned could be nothing else: the novel pictures a particularly repellent future society, and the stories are manifestly about Mars, and human approaches to that planet. Yet at the same time Bradbury is a freeman to that imaginative-fiction Megalopolis, fully at home in all of its thoroughfares, suburbs, alleyways and parks. That is what makes him a near-perfect encapsulation, for our purposes, of the close family links and resemblances between SF and horror.

For Bradbury, what matters is what a story can be made to do to the reader. In other words, as with his great predecessor in American fantasy, Edgar Allan Poe, it is effect that counts—before plot line, narrative structure, characterization and other considerations. And much of his effect, comes through his unique prose style—that delicate, melodic onrush of echoing words, resonant phrases, evocative images. With that style, Bradbury can be describing the most familiar, everyday scenes—and there builds up a terrible atmosphere of mystery, chilling menace, shadowy glimpses of Things crossing the border between the ordinary world and the darkness beyond. . . .

Because of that prose style, his admirers (including Christopher Isherwood) have called Ray Bradbury a poet. Because, partly, of that style, his detractors have called him whimsical, sentimental. And we may see why, when we see how Bradbury is impelled by the emotions of

nostalgia. He longs for, and sings the praises of, the lost innocence and peace of childhood and of small-town America. He mourns the passing of imagination, romance, beauty, magic, all of which have been ground to dust by the rationalist bulldozer of technological progress, destroyed by the Frankenstein Monster of the Industrial Age.

So with his atmospheric 'prose of effect' and his yearning for things devalued or uprooted by the materialist, mechanist present, we might expect Bradbury to be a writer of the most pure, unadulterated fantasy. And so he is, often enough—among the supernatural beings of his stories in **October Country** (1955), in the spooky terrors of his novel **Something Wicked This Way Comes** (1963) and in many of the stories in collections like **The Illustrated Man** (1951). He can even use a fantasy story to make his nostalgia message blatantly clear, as in 'Usher II' (1950), when the rationalist members of the Society for the Prevention of Fantasy are systematically, horribly killed by fantasy's defenders, using all the best methods of the great practitioners of horror fiction. And he used the same idea in 'The Exiles' (1950), when the creators and creations of fantasy or horror fiction make their last stand against men of the technological world coming to erase them finally from the imagination.

But in both stories the fantasy exiles have taken refuge on Mars, and the rationalists are coming by rocketship. Bradbury has moved sideways into science fiction—and nothing is changed. In short, what he can make a story do to us remains the same even when it features rockets or robots, when the ghosts are in the machine and not in haunted houses. Fahrenheit 451, again, depicts a society seeking to erase those things which Bradbury holds most dear, and does so by burning books—which are sniffed out by a robot hound, a creature of pure horror, far more chilling than that of the Baskervilles. Magic and horror are there again in 'The Veldt' (1950), representing a high technology future in which the nursery belonging to two children contains a perfectly reproduced three-dimensional image of an African scene, complete with lions. The children make grisly use of that scene, as if somehow breaking through into it from reality, when their parents try to take the nursery away from them.

No less symbolic of the fightback by fantasy against the rational world is the superb story 'Zero Hour' (1947), in which a little girl called Mink and her small friends are playing some zany, faddish game known as 'Invasion'. Older children scoff, parents smile indulgently or worry about the kids being over-imaginative. But the little ones go on making their weird contraptions—which turn out to be gateways to other dimensions, and intended for the inhabitants of those other dimensions. The story ends with the vague, unspecified entry of these visitors. And we can call the invaders aliens, if we want a good, solid SF label. But they are no more or less than creatures from the unknown, from beyond, and so are creatures of horror as much as any demon conjured into a pentagram.

The key word is beyond, which sums up the fraternal connections between SF and horror.

Going Beyond

Beyond the confines of our limited awareness of reality; beyond our blinkered belief that the here and now and everyday is all there is; beyond our inadequate conceptions of what is true or possible: it doesn't matter if going beyond takes you into outer space or inner nightmare; to a hellish future or a satanic past; to the moons of

Below While horror fiction has deadly dolls and grisly golems, SF has robots gone out of control – as in the film Westworld, 1973. *Here Yul Brynner as the gun-fighting robot with heat-seeking vision undergoes repair.*

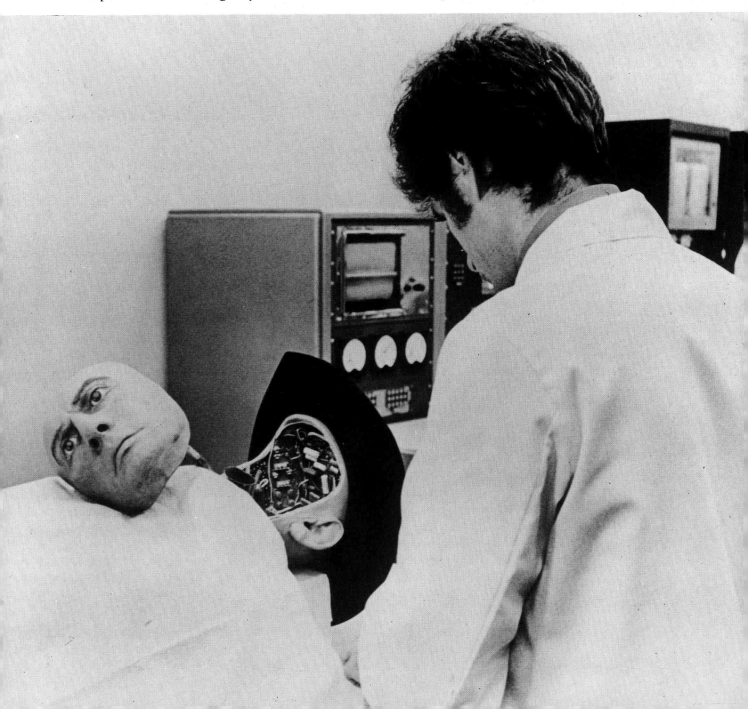

Above Green Slime again, this time a still from the screen version where the victim of the alien tentacled monster makes a last dash for safety.

Jupiter or to Transylvania. Nor does it matter if you go by flying saucer or broomstick, by time machine or magical spell. It doesn't even matter if the pleasure of going is solely in the delicious frissons of pure effect, or in the extra perception of some truth about our human nature. When it comes to going beyond, as Mary Shelley and Ray Bradbury prove, science fiction and horror fiction can coexist, sometimes indistinguishably. It's all the same trip.

Space and sorcery

One stretch of that route into the beyond, where SF and horror are one, may look at first like a diversion—some would say even a dead end. It is the special form of adventure fiction that is usually lumped together under the expressive generic name of 'sword and sorcery'. Most commonly, such stories feature a mighty-thewed, virile and violent warrior-hero bestriding fantasy land where evil magicians, powerful demons, nightmarish monsters and hot-blooded damsels variously await his attentions. The plots often tend to be variations of the quest motif, in which the hero must carve his gory way through hosts of armed opponents and supernatural enemies in order to confront the dark forces who are causing all the trouble.

Some proponents of sword and sorcery have come to prefer to call it by the less disparaging

general name of 'heroic fantasy', and to trace its genealogy back to ancient myth and legend, classical epic, medieval romance and the like. No doubt this can lead us by way of some rewarding later fantasy writers like Lord Dunsany or Walter de La Mare to some of the finer heroic fantasy being written today. In this context of course the list is rather dominated by J. R. R Tolkien's awesome **Lord of the Rings** (1954–55), which trails a horde of lesser but hopeful imitators in its wake. But the same context also includes Ursula K. Le Guin's haunting **Earthsea** trilogy (1968–73) and perhaps also, for children, C. S. Lewis's **Narnia** books (1950–56). But if such works are heroic fantasy, they can be seen to differ in many significant ways (primarily in the far smaller importance they give to swashbuckling deeds and violent combat) from what is more properly known as sword and sorcery. And for that kind of fantasy fiction, the essential roots are more recent—to be found among that lively assortment of pulp magazines that sprang to life in America during the 1930s and 1940s.

One of the writers who churned out the material that filled the columns of the pulps was a young man named Robert E. Howard. His fertile imagination and flair for actionful story-telling were noticeably greater than his literary craftmanship, but in those marketplaces that was not a severe handicap. Howard poured out many dozens of stories for the pulps—westerns, conventional horror and more—before he died (by his own hand) in his early thirties. And he might have been entirely forgotten, just another of a host of hacks, if he had not contributed to that uniquely fruitful magazine *Weird Tales*, where an astonishing number of very successful fantasy and horror writers got their start. There Howard began to create his tales of sword-wielding heroes embattled with darkly magical powers—like King Kull and Bran mak Morn, but above all the brooding and fearless barbarian hero whom Howard named Conan the Cimmerian. Today Conan remains still the first and greatest of the sword and sorcery warriors, and his saga is continued in stories and novels by other writers, as well as in comic books and other spin-offs.

Now the sword-and-sorcery subgenre, of which Howard was virtually the 'onlie begetter', makes abundant and vivid use of every one of the conventions of horror fiction that it can possibly manage. The supernatural in all its forms crowds into the pages (sometimes indeed in forms that would make Poe wince and Blackwood blanche), queuing up to have a crack at the beleaguered hero. But the point is that plainly recognizable elements of SF are often there too, comfortably cheek by jowl with all the werewolves and elementals, the black magicians and hideous demons.

Oddly enough, even outside the stories, the SF and horror coexistence in sword and sorcery is apparent. In any specialist SF bookshop, racks and racks of sword and sorcery are displayed prominently among the space hardware and future-city SF covers. At any of the proliferating SF conventions where fans love to gather, the sword-and-sorcery subcult again stands out (especially in the costumed capers of the fancy dress competitions). More importantly, a surprising number of leading sword-and-sorcery writers are also (though Robert Howard was not) leading SF writers.

Leiber and Moorcock

One of them, the American writer Fritz Leiber, did nearly as much as Howard in the days of the pulps to establish the sword-and-sorcery genre, and with much better written stories. Leiber too appeared in the treasury that was the magazine *Weird Tales*, and has a considerable parallel reputation as a writer of 'pure' horror: it would be a sorely incomplete collection of horror fiction that did not include Leiber's **Conjure Wife** (1952) and **Gather, Darkness!** (1950). Equally, he is recognized as a major figure in 'pure' SF, with novels like **The Big Time** (1961), **The Wanderer** (1964, winner of the ultimate SF accolade, the Hugo award) and **A Spectre Is Haunting Texas** (1969), along with numerous SF story collections. But it is likely that his most fervent fans are those who cannot get enough of the adventures of his fantasy heroes Fafhrd and the Gray Mouser. They first appeared in print in 1942, and new stories about them were still coming from Leiber's pen in the 1970s. And in all the adventures of this swashbuckling pair, Leiber extended and refined the nature of sword and sorcery (indeed, he coined that generic term), introducing new dimensions of magic and devilry, also introducing elements of humour, style and adult appeal which the genre sorely needed.

No less productive, and certainly no less influential in more recent years, is the younger British writer Michael Moorcock. His prodigious sword-and-sorcery output began with the unique hero Elric of Melnibonë, something of an antihero with a chaotic and unstable nature, taking his strength from his vampiric sword which gives its name to the best novel **Stormbringer** (1965). Moorcock followed his Elric stories with tales of other heroes, in his **Runestaff** books (1967–69), the various books about the hero Corum, others about Erekosë including **The Eternal Champion** (1970) and many more. Yet during the same years, as both an

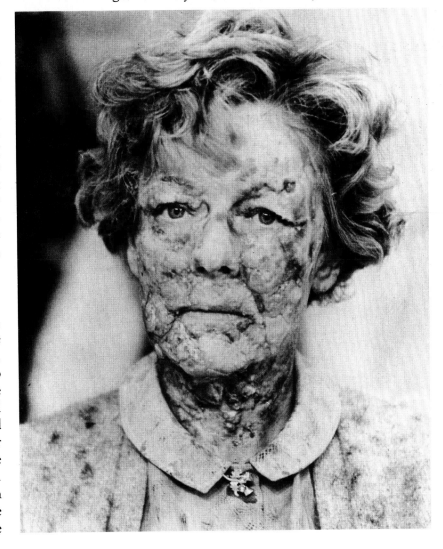

Below The gruesome results of an attack by The Deadly Bees. *The perennial horror theme of scientists tampering with nature, provoking retaliation in fearsome ways.*

author and an editor in the controversial heyday of the magazine *New Worlds*, he was almost singlehandedly wrenching SF out of its own doldrum conventions, launching the sadly mis-named 'New Wave' of SF which proved that SF could be a vehicle for modern fiction that could hold its head up in any literary company. Above all, Moorcock proved it in his own tetralogy about the multifaceted future hero Jerry Cornelius, beginning with **The Final Programme** (1968)—four unforgettably original books that manage simultaneously to contain and to mock all the central myths and obsessions of the late 20th century.

Changing Hats

Beyond Leiber and Moorcock, there is a legion of other well-known SF authors who have often and regularly stepped aside to dally in the magical lands of swords and sorcery. L. Sprague de Camp, for one, who has continued the Conan series; Edmond Hamilton: Henry Kuttner: Poul Anderson; Jack Vance; Roger Zelazny; John Brunner, in his own way; and a great many more, even including the old master of hard-edge SF, Robert Heinlein. However, the list is endless.

And it is surely the very fact that the same writers can move so effortlessly from one mode to the other that is most relevant here: the easy and frequent mingling of elements of the two modes within the same story. One common formula for this coexistence occurs where the hero is a man of the technological 20th-century, somehow transported (across the dimensions, into parallel universes or whatever) to a realm where technology is limited or unknown, and where magic and dark forces hold sway. Moorcock uses this technique to get his hero Erekosë into action (carrying, it should be added, a uniquely 'radioactive' sword). Heinlein's tough-guy American hero travels in a similar way to pursue his quest on the **Glory Road** (1963). And in a very recent fantasy, **Tetrarch** (1980) by Alex Comfort, a scientist with a head full of neuropsychological metaphysics and quantum logic enters a fantasy world where he is both warrior and adept sorcerer.

On other occasions, the hero must travel through space in true Flash Gordon fashion to reach a world where, to his technologist's astonishment, the sword-bearing folk are much given to sorcery. That introductory gimmick was almost the special property of Edgar Rice Burroughs, who flung his 'modern' heroes on to Mars and Venus to indulge in swordplay, monster-slaying, damsel-rescuing and so on (though of course there wasn't much sorcery in evidence). The SF writer Leigh Brackett simi-larly chose Mars and Venus for some rollicking tales in the true 's-and-s' vein, like **The Sword of Rhiannon** (1953), A newer writer, Christopher Stasheff, has found a rich vein of comedy in the idea of a space pilot marooned on a sorcerous planet, in **The Warlock In Spite of Himself** (1974). And of course the hugely popular **Darkover** books of Marion Zimmer Bradley are all set on a planet where high-technology visitors from other worlds have to be careful of all the swords and sorcery, as in **The Spell Sword** (1974). But Lin Carter, a noted scholar as well as author of fantasy, prefers the old Burroughs path when he transports his modern hero to the magic and monster-strewn surface of the world Callisto.

Likewise, the sword-and-sorcery authors have no compunction about introducing, when they care to, hardcore SF elements into the midst of their fantasy hero's adventurings, along the lines of the 'radiation' in the sword that Moorcock gives to Erekosë. Though most of the

Below Again no theme has seemed more fruitful for film-makers seeking terror effects than that of nature striking back at technological man – as in the onslaught of desert ants in the film Phase IV, 1973.

standard works of the subgenre are set in worlds of a Bronze or Iron Age barbarism, others have taken a cue from Michael Moorcock, who set his four **Runestaff** books in the distant future, where many of the monstrosities that confront Dorian Hawkmoon are leftover mutations from the nuclear holocaust of the Tragic Millennium. And the sorcerers are as likely to work in laboratories as in dank caves, while the evil warriors of the Dark Empire (called, it must be added, Granbretan) carry flame lances as well as broadswords.

Jack Vance's 'Mazirian the Magician' (1950) is a denizen of a far future when Earth is dying, and is as much scientist as sorcerer. Roger Zelazny's hero Dilvish the Damned rides a horse that is a combination of robot and demon, and more than either, in stories like 'The Bells of Shoredan' (1966). And other writers happily weave the same odd combination, sometimes giving us rationalizations akin to that of Poul Anderson in an introduction to his classic novel of elves and trolls, warlocks and warriors, **The Broken Sword** (1971 edition):

> It seemed only natural that the dwellers in Faerie would be technologically advanced beyond their human contemporaries. Assume, if you will, that there really were races once that could do magic. . . . Assume that they could live indefinitely, change their shapes and so on. Such an alien metabolism might have its own penalties, in an inability to endure the glare and actinic light of the sun or in disastrous electrochemical reactions induced by contact with iron. Why should these handicapped immortals not compensate by discovering non-ferrous metals and the properties of their alloys? Might the elven ships sail "on the wings of the wind" because of having virtually frictionless hulls? . . . In the same way, other apparent anachronisms would be simply the achievements of races older than man.

That is a clear example of the ready ease with which sword-and-sorcery writers will interweave their horror and SF elements—because they know, as do their hordes of loyal readers who are probably also avid collectors of SF, that there is no need for segregation when you take the imaginative journey to beyond.

Outer Darkness

The same non-exclusive interweaving happens all the time in terms of SF and outright horror or supernatural fiction. And again there is a host of writers such as Ray Bradbury and Fritz Leiber who have moved smoothly and readily between the two modes. Other writers, whose reputations were also first established in the 1930s

and 1940s, have moved back and forth in the same way. Jack Williamson wrote classic space operas like the series he developed from **The Legion of Space** (1947), and the important robot novel **The Humanoids** (1949) among the abundant SF of a long and fruitful career. But he also wrote an equally classic treatment of the werewolf theme, **Darker Than You Think** (1949), which is all the more frightening because of the scientific strands—anthropology, palaeontology and the like—that are woven through the horror. And a near-contemporary, Henry Kuttner, another alumnus of the *Weird Tales* proving ground, authored a flood of short stories in both modes, as well as novels of eerie horror like **The Dark World** (1965) and books sitting solidly in the central traditions of SF, like **Mutant** (1953).

Towering even among these giants are SF masters like Theodore Sturgeon, about whom it can be said that he has never written a poor story. Novels like **The Dreaming Jewels** (1950) or **Venus Plus X** (1960) are certainly SF of high quality and originality, but he too can shift effortlessly into the pure terror of stories in collections like **Not Without Sorcery** (1948) or in the unsettling but non-supernatural novel of psychological warping, **Some of Your Blood** (1961). And in just the same way the late, great James Blish could tear himself away from his space-faring novels about 'cities in flight', like **A Life for the Stars** (1957) and its continuations, to write **Black Easter** (1968) and a sequel, **The Day After Judgment** (1971), unsurpassable treatments of high occultism, satanism and the coming of Armageddon.

The catalogue could go on almost indefinitely to include fine writers like Richard Matheson and Charles Beaumont, Jack Finney and Kate Wilhelm, Clifford Simak and Fredric Brown, all the way along to younger writers like Keith Roberts and Robert Holdstock. But naturally there is much more to the SF/horror interconnections than merely the admirable flexibility of the authors.

Some Recurring Themes

More importantly, in its long history horror fiction has developed certain central and recurring themes, plot lines, motifs, to which writers return again and again—often because, as with any traditional literary themes, they illuminate or focus some fundamental factor within the human condition, which is the stuff of fiction. And, interestingly, the very same themes and motifs occur in SF, doing the same job, instantly recognizable despite their altered costumes and settings, props and details.

Foremost among such themes must be the tradition of 'dire forces released by foolish,

meddling men'. It informs the Frankenstein story, and in another way Stevenson's **Dr Jekyll and Mr Hyde** (1886). It is also at the heart of all the stories about demons conjured up by magicians but found to be beyond the conjuror's control, which stories take us back one way or another to the Faust legend and beyond, to the Pandora myth. More specifically, it is the primary (almost the only) plot-line of that unique giant among modern horror writers, the mighty H. P. Lovecraft.

H. P. Lovecraft

Of course Lovecraft wrote a great many kinds of stories, and there is no space here even to begin commenting on the extent of his strange *oeuvre*. But above all he is remembered for those stories in which the creatures of horror are not ghosts or vampires or other stock nightmares, but unimaginably monstrous things of evil that once existed on earth and seek to do so again, to reimpose their unspeakable, hellish rule. Yet they need help to get through certain barriers, which means they need the help of dabblers in dark mysticism, meddlers in deeper occultism—anyone single-minded or insane enough to speak the spells in the ghastly, forbidden book **Necronomicon** and open the portals to what Lovecraft calls this 'Babylon of elder

demons'. Cthulhu is the name of the most prominent of the ancient monstrosities, and the stories that Lovecraft wrote around the theme of their return came to be grouped together as the 'Cthulhu Mythos'. Indeed, it caught the imagination of many other writers (from the old *Weird Tales* days, again) such as August Derleth, Donald Wandrei and Robert Bloch, all of whom added fine stories of their own to the Cthulhu canon.

And there is no doubt that these 'elder demons' blend in their nature (at least as much as does, say, the Frankenstein Monster) elements of SF along with the horror. They are beings who have conquered space, time and death—and they are poised not merely to wander around at night frightening people but to invade Earth and enslave it, exactly as many an aggressive race of super-aliens has sought to do in SF, from H. G. Wells's **War of the Worlds** (1898) onwards. A Lovecraft character (in 'The Dunwich Horror', 1929) quotes from a version of the **Necronomicon**:

The Old Ones were, the Old Ones are, and the Old Ones shall be. Not in the spaces we know, but *between* them, They walk serene and primal, undimensioned and to us unseen. ... Man rules now where They ruled once: They shall soon rule where man rules now.

Above *Flashing swords in the superb fantasy film* The Golden Voyage of Sinbad, *especially rich in supernatural monsters and evil sorceries. Here an adversary has an unfair advantage having multiple sword-arms, showing brilliant animation and editing.*

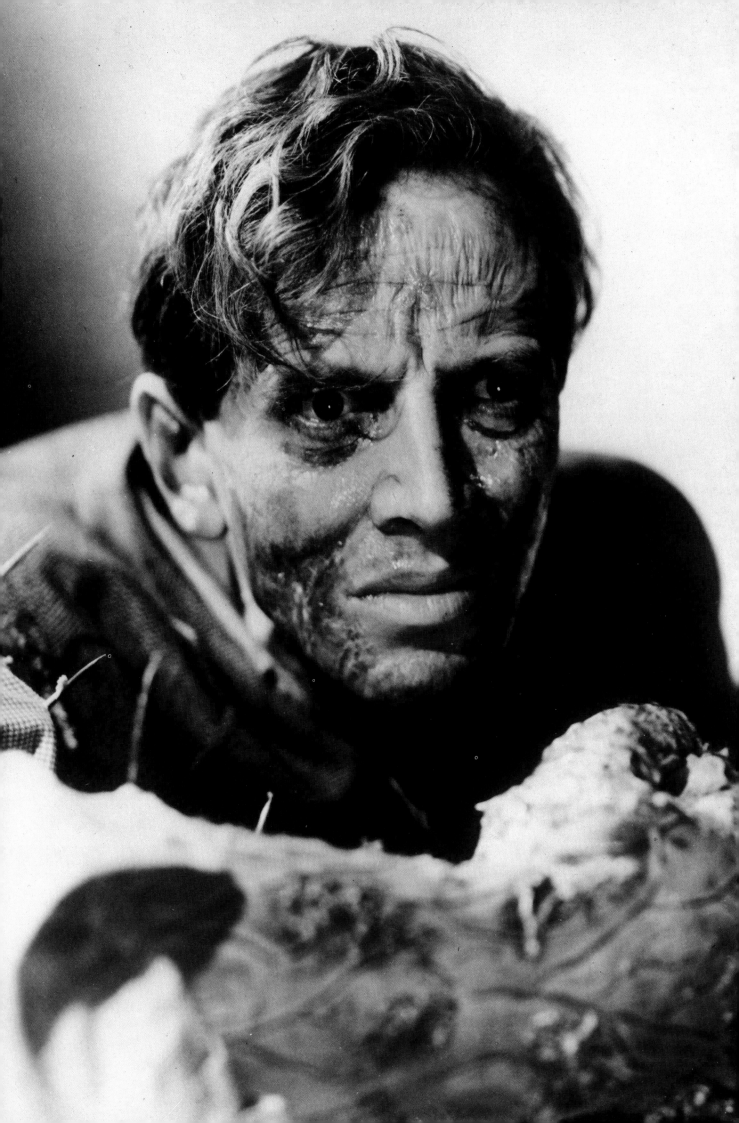

Then again, even outside the Cthulhu stories Lovecraft never hesitated to make use of SF elements when he wished to. One of his most disturbing stories is 'The Colour Out of Space' (1927), in which a meteorite brings an evil essence, perceived as a colour, to haunt and horrify a rural community. And similar borrowings can be found in other leading modern horror writers, such as August Derleth, who was also an SF writer and a tireless anthologist.

The Sins of the Fathers

So in reverse but precisely the same way, have SF writers made free and unashamed use of that traditional horror theme, evil released by meddlers—although the evil may not be overtly supernatural, nor the meddlers interested in occultism. Every one of the major classics of SF that deal somehow with catastrophe, manmade, overcoming the world is directly rooted in this theme—of man's technological reach exceeding his moral or intellectual grasp. All the nuclear holocaust stories belong here, including the borderline 'near-future' novels like Nevil Shute's **On the Beach** (1957). Man has destroyed civilization with nuclear war before the story begins in Walter M. Miller's marvellous, ironic 'Canticle for Leibowitz' (1960), and destroys it again before the book ends. Advanced computers grow into a new kind of uncontrollable monster in D. F. Jones's **Colossus** (1966) and David Gerrold's **When Harlie Was One** (1972). Similarly, robots created to serve mankind come to threaten his existence in a huge array of stories, beginning with the one that gave the world the term robot, Karel Capek's 'R.U.R.' (1923). And scientific experiments inadequately thought through, or the accelerating and greedy overuse of re-sources, or new strains of deadly disease, or all the other fatal examples of human venality and shortsightedness, bring us SF novels like **The Death of Grass** (John Christopher, 1956), or **The Drowned World** (J. G. Ballard, 1962), or **The Genocides** (Thomas M. Disch, 1965).

All of the foregoing, on the theme of dire forces released, in fact grows no less directly from the even more fundamental and classic theme of sin and retribution, which takes us back at least as far as the Oresteiad of Aeschylus in the 1st century BC. And just as the horror writers relish that theme, bringing the sins of the fathers out of their graves to haunt the sons, so the SF writers thrive on it too. Except that these are our present-day sins, which will be visited upon our descendants in the future, who have to lie—or die—on the technological bed we are making. So future generations live in their misery, as if accursed, because of our tendency to thoughtless overpopulation, in John Brunner's **Stand on Zanzibar** (1968) and Harry Harrison's **Make Room, Make Room** (1966). To the future, a chilling level of violence is the norm, in Damon Knight's **Analogue Men** (1955) or John Brunner's **Jagged Orbit** (1969)—and they also know inhuman levels of racism in Christopher Priest's **Fugue for a Darkening Island** (1972) and sexism in Suzy McKee Charnas' **Walk to the End of the World** (1974). Generations to come will live in societies undermined by drugs—Philip Dick's **A Scanner Darkly** (1977), or mind-softening media—C.M. Kornbluth's 'The Marching Morons' (1952), or extremism and corruption of many sorts— Norman Spinrad's **Bug Jack Barron** (1969), or of course ultimate forms of totalitarianism, a favourite theme in the shadow of Orwell's **1984** (1949).

Horrors in Disguise

When SF writers produce their purer strains of terror, often as not they will ring the changes on another basic theme or motif—which states that there are dire forces and dark presences already among us, through no particular fault of our own, except perhaps the persistent 'common sense' refusal to believe in them.

This theme, too, is recognizably a favourite in the horror field, when ordinary folk scoff at the idea that the harmless folk next door like to bite people's throats at night (see Richard Matheson's 'No Such Thing as a Vampire' (1959). In the same way, people always refuse to accept that there could be a giant ape on a faraway island, a Yeti in the mountains, a Creature in the black lagoon, or a Thing under the stairs. And much the same sort of people laugh at the thought that there might be alien invaders among us, carefully disguised—as

there are in Keith Laumer's **A Plague of Demons** (1965) not to mention Jack Finney's **The Body Snatchers** (1955), or indeed the American television series of the 1960s, *The Invaders*. Other variations on this theme of evil among us even include special sorts of SF 'hauntings'—a favourite plot of John Lymington's SF thrillers, like **The Night of the Big Heat** (1959), and found in different form in Murray Leinster's **War with the Gizmos** (1958), Frederic Brown's **The Mind Thing** (1961) and even in a special way the ghostly time-stopped tableaux of Christopher Priest's 'An Infinite Summer' (1976).

One more vein must be traced within this quick glimpse of shared SF and horror themes, and it is one that indicates conclusively how

Below Captain Kirk of starship Enterprise *grapples with an alien being discovered on his travels through space. This 1960s American television series* Star Trek *has become an international cult amongst fans of popular science fiction.*

non-exclusive the writers are. Many a good SF novel has been based on the idea that the old folklore of the supernatural might have some rational, scientific explanation, some believable original cause that started people off, long ago, believing in ghosts and magic and the rest. It's much the same principle as von Daniken's determined efforts to show that humanity's religious impulses stem from our primeval ancestors having actual 'close encounters' with alien spacemen who were passing through. We have already seen something of this SF idea in Poul Anderson, before, and in the plot of Jack Williamson's **Darker Than You Think**. Clifford Simak's **The Werewolf Principle** (1967) runs a variation on the theme, introducing alien presences to decorate it further. Simak again, in **The Goblin Reservation** (1968) brings in time travel to prove that many of the creatures of myth and horror did have actual existence, once upon a time, and can be brought back to today to exist again. And Richard Matheson's terrifying **I Am Legend** (1954) projects a future world after the holocaust in which scientifically produced vampires have become real.

Tomorrow's Monsters

With the people and creatures of imaginative fiction we are perhaps on the safest ground of all if we seek to show the family resemblances between SF and horror. Horror fiction is populated with magicians, sorcerers, necromancers, witches and their ilk who have 'Power'. So is SF, coming to the same destinations by the more 'scientific' route that begins in modern experiments with parapsychology and ESP. Not that the SF possessors of the Power are always glad of it—as can be seen in Arthur Sellings' frightened **Silent Speakers** (1962), John Brunner's disturbed **Telepathist** (1964), Bob Shaw's painful **Dagger of the Mind** (1979) or John Wyndham's maligned **Chrysalids** (1955).

A recurring strain in these psi novels of SF is the view that the people with the Power are the next stage in man's evolution: they are homo superior, and so they are much hated and reviled by nervously envious ordinary folk. Sometimes the ordinary folk have good cause, as when the powerful people are dangerous (Phyllis Gotlieb's **Sunburst**), or 'possessed'—by aliens rather than devils—as in John Wyndham's **The Midwich Cuckoos** (1957). Sometimes the beleaguered Power people fight back, as in A. E. van Vogt's classic **Slan** (1947); at other times they merely learn to band together, in super-Powerful gestalts as in Theodore Sturgeon's matchless **More Than Human** (1953) or in areas of separate development like Henry Kuttner's **Mutant**.

Mutants of many sorts are naturally popular with SF writers, and return us briefly again to the theme of sin and retribution, with all those experiments that go wrong and produce ghastly monsters— giant insects (**Them**, 1954), demonic children (**The Brood**, 1980) and a great many more. Sometimes it is the experimenter himself who suffers the most, as it should be— like the over-confident necromancer who calls up a demon that destroys him, or the unwise occultist who wants to see if the old spell for changing into a werewolf really works. Similarly in SF there are all the ultimately self-destructive scientists who develop X-ray eyes, or who shrink, or melt, or become invisible, or whose creations like those on H. G. Wells's **Island of Dr Moreau**, (1896) turn and rend them. And whenever a scientist goes too far in these ways and does deadly harm to himself and the world around him, we hear again the echo of **Frankenstein** and **Dr Jekyll and Mr Hyde** where SF and horror have always coexisted in perfect harmony.

The only important difference, perhaps, between the creatures of horror and those of SF is that horror tends to summon its monsters from the past, while SF generally looks to those from a technological future. Horror likes to awaken ancient sea-monsters or Krakens, to revive prehistoric terrors in dinosaurs and Godzillas, to summon rejuvenated mummies or gorgons from the long-dead darkness of myth and legend. But for every one of these, SF can offer at least its equal in the squelching, tentacled, ravening Bug-Eyed Monsters of alien worlds. The BEMs make their hideous, destructive progress through almost every page of the grand old pulp space operas (Edgar Rice Burroughs was particularly fond of them, as was Alex Raymond, the creator of Flash Gordon), and have found a new lease of life in today's

Below Rock Hudson is about to see the results of rejuvenation in the film Seconds, 1966, a chilling variation of the Frankenstein theme, with equally unpleasant results for the subjects.

media equivalents of the pulps, from *Star Trek* to *Star Wars*. But writers with higher brows are also not averse to a BEM or two: consider the sandworms in Frank Herbert's superb **Dune** (1965), the specialized 'monsters' of Isaac Asimov's **Fantastic Voyage** (1966) or the entire planetful of increasingly horrific monsters dedicated to the destruction of the inhabitants in Harry Harrison's **Deathworld** (1960).

So could a full account of another top favourite among SF monsters be discerned among the shapes of things to come—the intelligent alien beings, the extraterrestrials, who can freeze the blood at least as successfully as any werewolf or succubus. As often as not they do so unintentionally, having no evil purpose, but merely frightening people whose reflexes cause them to scream in the face of the Unknown. Many an alien visitor receives unpleasant first-hand experience of man's xenophobia, expressing itself in hostility and aggression. It happened to the godlike alien in the film *The Day the Earth Stood Still* (1951), not to mention Walter Teris's *The Man Who Fell to Earth* (1963). But SF writers have never let us down in the realms of pure terror opened to them by the idea of initially aggressive, deadly aliens coming to threaten Earth. They do so in armies, as in **The War of the Worlds**, or as lone outriders, like the eponymous monster in Clifford Simak's **The Night of the Puudly** (1962). They can come as parasites Heinlein's (**The Puppet Masters** 1951), as sentient mists (Fred Hoyle's **The Black Cloud** 1957), as plants (Wyndham's **Day of the Triffids**, 1951), as

mental forces (Theodore Sturgeon's **To Marry Medusa**, 1958). And best of all, for the effect of sheer terror, is when they are so super-powerful that man seems to have no hope against them, as is certainly the case in one of the best-known of the recent variations, the highly successful film *Alien* (1979).

That film necessarily brings us full circle, especially if we remember how so many people (mostly film reviewers) seemed seriously disturbed by the difficulty of pinpointing the film as either horror or SF. They had not perceived that it's all the same trip when you go beyond, whether you get to a haunted castle or a spooky spaceship, or whether it's spectral chains or computer hardware that you hear rattling. Certainly readers know it well, even if critics don't, and are just as happy to get their adrenalin-jolt from the 'profound emotional response' to fictional terror within a futuristic, SF setting. And of all the writers who are happy to provide the means to that response, and who can move freely and non-conclusively within the modes, it may be fitting to let H. P. Lovecraft have the last word (from his essay on 'Supernatural Horror in Literature', 1945):

The oldest and strongest emotion of mankind is fear, and the oldest and strongest kind of fear is fear of the unknown. . . .
When to this sense of fear and evil the inevitable fascination of wonder and curiosity is superadded, there is born a composite body of keen emotion and imaginative provocation whose vitality must of necessity endure as long as the human race itself.

Far right *A surrealist book jacket by artist Chris Moore for the classic science fiction story* **Quatermass**.

Below *The rebellious hero is under duress in the film* THX 1138, *1971, a vision of a technocratic totalitarian future that makes 1984 seem attractive by comparison.*

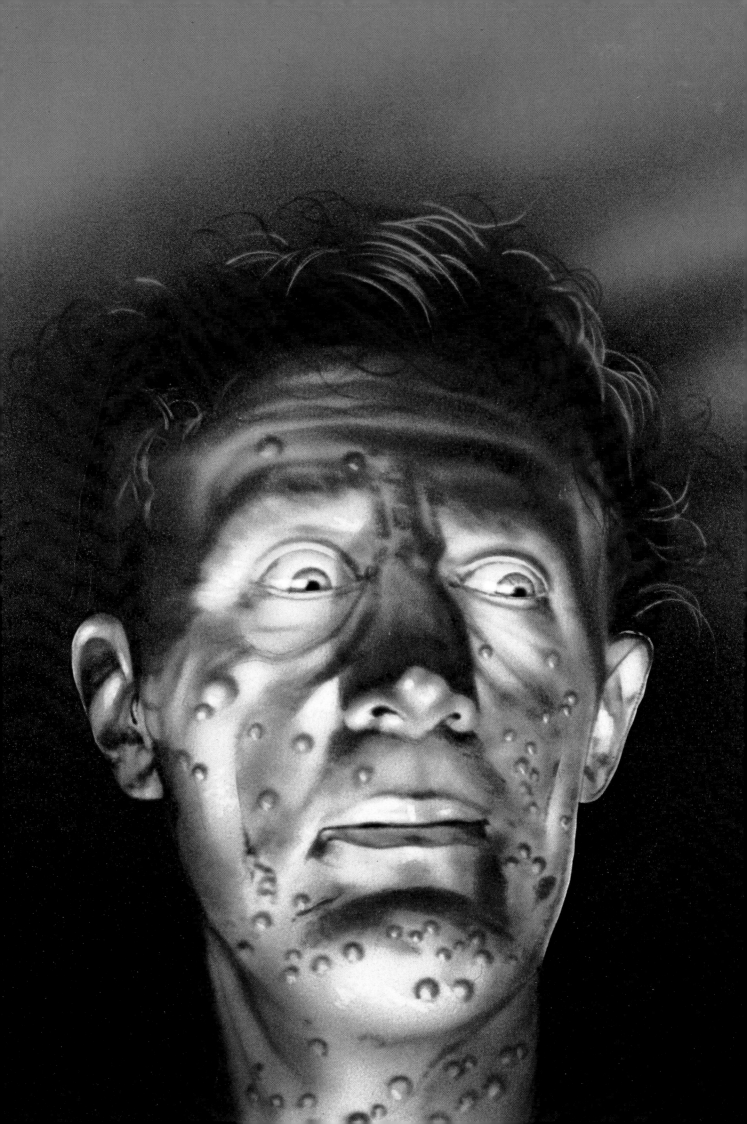

Year	Month	Title	Publisher	Run
1948	Fall	Adventures into the Unknown	A.C.G.	174
	Nov	Mysterious Traveler Comics	Transworld	4
1949	Aug	Marvel Tales	Atlas	57
	Dec	Suspense Comics	Atlas	29
1950	Jan	Captain America's Weird Tales	Atlas	2
	Apr	Crypt of Terror	E.C.	3
	Apr	Vault of Horror	E.C.	29
	Apr	The Black Tarantula	Fox	1
	May	Weird Fantasy	E.C.	22
	May	Haunt Of Fear	E.C.	28
	Sep	Journey into Unknown Worlds	Atlas	59
	Oct	Tales from the Crypt	E.C.	27
	Oct	Black Magic	Prize	49
	Nov	Adventures into Terror	Atlas	31
	Nov	Beyond	Ace	33
	Nov	Strange Worlds	Avon	22
	Win	Ghost Comics	Fiction	11
1951	Jan	Adventures into Weird Worlds	Atlas	30
	Jan	Witches Tales	Harvey	28
	Feb	Web of Mystery	Ace	29
	Mar	Mysterious Adventures	Story	25
	Mar	Mystic	Atlas	61
	Apr	Astonishing	Atlas	61
	May	Eerie	Avon	17
	May	Journey into Fear	Superior	21
	May	Weird Adventures	P.L.	3
	Jun	Black Cat Mystery	Harvey	37
	Jun	Chamber of Chills	Harvey	6
	Jun	Dark Mysteries	Master	30
	Jun	Forbidden Worlds	A.C.G.	145
	Jun	Strange Tales	Atlas	168
	Sep	Mister Mystery	Media	19
	Sep	Strange Mysteries	Superior	21
	Sep	Weird Thrillers	Ziff-Davis	5
	Oct	This Magazine is Haunted	Fawcett	21
	Nov	Baffling Mysteries	Ace	24
	Dec	Hand of Fate	Ace	19
	Dec	House of Mystery	National	
1952	Jan	Worlds of Fear	Fawcett	9
	Feb	Out of the Night	S.C.G.	17
	Feb	The Thing	Capitol	17
	Mar	Mystery Tales	Atlas	54
	Mar	Witchcraft	Avon	6
	Mar	Tales/Stories to hold you Spellbound	Atlas	34
	May	Beware Terror Tales	Fawcett	11
	May	Frankenstein Comics	Prize	16
	May	Voodoo	Ajax	19
	May	Startling Terror Tales	star	14
	Jun	Beware	Youthful	3
	Jun	Haunted Thrills	Ajax	21
	Jun	Journey into Mystery	Atlas	125
	Jun	Uncanny Tales	Atlas	57
	Jun	Tomb of Terror	Harvey	16
	Jun	Strange Suspense Stories	Fawcett	71
	Jun	Strange Terrors	St John	7
	Jun	Tales of Horror	Toby	13
	Jun	Tales of Terror	Toby	6
	Jul	Sensation Mystery Comics	National	7
	Jul	Out of the Shadows	Standard	10
	Sum	Nightmare	Ziff-Davis	4
	Aug	Phantom Stranger	National	6
	Aug	Weird Horrors	St John	9
	Aug	Strange Fantasy	Harvey	14
	Aug	Strange Stories from Another World	Fawcett	4
	Aug	Strange World of your Dreams	Prize	4
	Sep	Horrific	Media	13

M. C. Gaines (christened Max Charles), haberdasher and creator of that popular Prohibition favourite, the 'We Want Beer Necktie', is credited with creating the comicbook by assembling 32 pages of reduced-size Sunday supplement strips, putting them in a specially drawn cover entitled *Funnies on Parade*, and giving 10,000 of them away through Proctor and Gamble's store in 1933. The next year he bundled up 64 pages of reprints, called them *Famous Funnies* and sold 35,000 through Woolworth's for 10 cents apiece. The comicbook industry was born, and there was no horror in it. There couldn't be—the books were 100 per cent newspaper strip reprints, and syndicates like King Features, United and N.E.A. kept eagle editorial eyes on artists and writers. No trace of horror or the supernatural was allowed, lest it offended the eye of some small-town subscriber who might cancel the strip and lose the syndicate its two dollars.

The door to horror was opened by one Major Malcolm Wheeler-Nicholson. In February 1935 he published the first issue of *New Fun*, a tabloid-sized comicbook of all new artwork, originally planned for his National Allied syndicate, a Sunday supplement scheme that seems not to have come off. Among the serialized secret agents, cowboys and cavemen was 'Don Drake on the Planet Saro', a science-fiction saga by Clemens Gretter which soon set its hero against outsize ants and, on the front page of No. 3, an alien with 6 legs, 11 tentacles, and countless teeth, described by the artist as 'a foul and pitiless creature'. Earthbound horror began in issue No. 6 (October 1935) with the introduction of a new character, 'Dr Occult the Ghost Detective'. Assisted by the attractive and aptly-named Rose Psychic, Doc, as he is known by his intimates, does battle with an archfiend from the shadows, the Vampire Master.

Hot on the heels of Major Wheeler-Nicholson came the Comic Magazine Company, who launched *Funny Picture Stories* in 1936. This was the first all-adventure strip comicbook and in No. 2 (December) appeared a six-page strip called 'The Monster Man'.

Dick Briefer, a cartoonist much obsessed by horror movies, began to serialize a strip version of Victor Hugo's classic **Hunchback of Notre Dame** in the weekly *Wags*, a comic produced for export only sales in the United Kingdom.

Atmospheric but slapdash, the serial started in *Wags* No. 17 (23 April 1937). The Universal film, *Son of Frankenstein*, was adapted into strip format in the first edition of *Movie Comics* (April 1939), a new venture for M. C. Gaines. This innovative comicbook was advertised as 'A Full Movie Show for Ten Cents, printed in the New Natural-Color Photographic Process'—which turned out to be coarse-screened photographs overprinted in the usual red/blue/yellow, with hand-lettered speech balloons pasted on each picture. It is worth noting that the Frankenstein Monster in his first appearance in colour was tinted green!

With the outbreak of World War II in 1939, the importation of 'Yankee Comics', as the American comicbooks were called, into the United Kingdom ceased. There were more important items to be shipped across the U-boated waters. Gerald G. Swan, one of the leading importers, saw his opportunity: with no more comicbooks coming across, the answer was to publish his own. January 1940 saw No 1 of Swan's *New Funnies,* a sixpenny 68-page comicbook, the first all-British effort in straight imitation of the Yankee variety. It sold out, and other titles quickly followed. In April, *Thrill Comics* No. 1 hit the comic-hungry kids, the first 100 per cent adventure strip book, 36 pages of action for threepence.

Swan's *Slick Fun* No. 1 arrived in June, bringing with it 'Master of Sin', a hideous dwarf hunchback and master criminal, who was shortly replaced by the first true horror strip in British comics, 'Horror Island'. This grim tale took its two submariner heroes into a lagoon within an iceberg on a hunt for vampires.

Fresh Fun No. 1 (June 1940) introduced Swan's longest-running horror strip, 'Dene Vernon, Ghost Investigator', drawn by Jock McCail, and probably inspired by 'Dr Occult'. Vernon's first case featured the graphic horror of a gigantic black strangler, chained by the neck, who turned out to be the ghost of a deformed heir born in 1785! Jock's brother, William McCail, drew 'Professor Mennock', an insane animal-enlarger, in *New Funnies* (1941), and another long-running series starring a perambulating corpse, 'Back From the Dead', in *War Comics* (1940). Amazingly, there was no outcry from the authorities: but perhaps eager young readers snapped up all available copies before the authorities could see them.

When American comicbooks were once again allowed into the UK after the war, Swan changed his policy. Unable to compete with the full-colour funnies he converted his titles into imitation of the traditional British juvenile formats in the hope that these would be successful.

Year	Month	Title	Publisher	Run
	Sep	Weird Terrors	Media	13
	Sep	Shocking Mystery Cases	Star	11
	Oct	Weird Mysteries	Gilmore	14
	Nov	Web of Evil	Quality	21
	Dec	Chilling Tales	Youthful	5
		City of the Living Dead	Avon	1
		Adventures into Darkness	Standard	10
		The Unseen	Standard	15
1953	Jan	Beware	Trojan	15
	Jan	The Purple Claw	Toby	3
	Jan	Spook	Star	8
	Jan	Terrifying Tales	Star	5
	May	Fantastic Fears	Ajax	3
	May	Mysteries	Superior	11
	Sep	Chilling Weird Stories	Star	5
	Dec	Nightmare	St John	4
		Monster	Fiction	2
		Terrors of the Universe	Star	2
1954	Mar	Secret Mysteries	Merit	4
	Jul	Weird Chills	Key	3
	Oct	Amazing Ghost Stories	St John	3
	Nov	Fantastic	Ajax	2
1955	Feb	This is Suspense	Charlton	4
	Feb	Witches Western Tales	Harvey	2
	May	Terrific comics	Ajax	5
	May	Prize Mystery	Key	5
	Oct	Strange Stories of Suspense	Atlas	12
	Nov	Unusual Tales	Charlton	49
	Nov	Adult Tales of Terror Illustrated(*)	E.C.	2
	Dec	Strange Tales of the Unusual	Atlas	11
1956	Feb	Tales of the Unexpected	National	104
	Apr	Mysteries of Unexplored Worlds	Charlton	48
	Apr	World of Suspense	Atlas	6
	May	Adventure into Mystery	Atlas	8
	Jun	Mystical Tales	Atlas	8
	Jun	World of Mystery	Atlas	7
	Aug	Tales of the Mysterious Traveler	Charlton	13
	Nov	House of Secrets	National	154
1957	Mar	Strange	Ajax	6
	July	This Magazine is Haunted	Charlton	5
	Aug	Midnight	Ajax	6
	Sep	Alarming Tales	Harvey	6
	Sep	The Man in Black	Harvey	5
	Sep	Strange Journey	Ajax	4
	Oct	Dark Shadows	Ajax	3
	Nov	Do You Believe in Nightmares?	St John	2
1958	Apr	Challengers of the Unknown	National	
	Dec	Strange Worlds	Marvel	5
1959	Jan	Tales to Astonish	Atlas	101
1960	Aug	Unknown Worlds	A.C.G.	57
1961	Jan	Midnight Mystery	A.G.G.	7
	May	Gorgo	Charlton	23
	Jun	Konga	Charlton	23
	Jun	Amazing Adventures	Marvel	6
	Aug	Reptilicus	Charlton	2
	Nov	Tales Calculated to Drive you Bats	Archie	7
	Dec	Amazing Adult Fantasy	Marvel	8
		The Twilight Zone	Dell	91
1962	Jan	Reptisaurus the Terrible	Charlton	7
	Sep	Ghost Stories	Dell	37
	Oct	Tales from the Tomb	Dell	2
	Oct	Boris Karloff Thriller	Gold Key	2
	Apr	Boris Karloff Tales of Mystery	Gold Key	
	Aug	Little Archie Mystery Comics	Archie	2
		Strange Mysteries	I.W.	13
1964	Aug	Frankenstein	Dell	4
	Aug	Masque of the Red Death: Movie Classic	Dell	5
		Eerie	I.W.	5
		Eerie Tales	Super	5
		Mystery Tales	Super	3
		Creepy(*)	Warren	
1965	Sep	Eerie(*)	Warren	
1966	Jan	Weird(*)	Eerie	
	Apr	Ghostly Tales	Charlton	
	Sep	Dracula	Dell	8
	Nov	True Weird(*)	Ripley	2

Year	Month	Title	Publisher	Run
	Dec	Werewolf	Dell	3
1967	May	The Many Ghosts of Dr Graves	Charlton	65
	Oct	Strange Suspense Stories	Charlton	12
1968	Feb	The Unexpected	National	
	Jul	Ghost Manor	Charlton	19
	Nov	Tales of Voodoo(*)	Eerie	35
1969	Feb	The Witching Hour	National	85
	May	Shock(*)	Stanley	18
	May	Dark Shadows	Gold Key	35
	May	Phantom Stranger	National	41
	Jun	Chilling Tales of Horror(*)	Stanley	12
	Jun	Horror Tales(*)	Eerie	
	Jul	Tales from the Tomb(*)	Eerie	36
	Jul	Witches Tales(*)	Eerie	34
	Sep	Vampirella(*)	Warren	
	Sep	Tower of Shadows	Marvel	9
	Oct	Chamber of Darkness	Marvel	8
	Oct	From Beyond the Unknown	National	23
	Dec	Web of Horror(*)	Major	3
1970	Jan	Where Monsters Dwell	Marvel	38
	Jul	Where Creatures Roam	Marvel	7
	Aug	Weird Worlds(*)	Eerie	5
	Sep	Ghosts	National	
	Nov	Adventures into Fear	Marvel	31
	Nov	Ghoul Tales(*)	Stanley	5
	Dec	Nightmare(*)	Skyward	23
	Dec	Stark Terror(*)	Stanley	5
1971	Jan	Psycho(*)	Skyward	24
	Feb	Monsters on the Prowl	Marvel	22
	Mar	Creatures on the Loose	Marvel	28
	Sep	Weird War Tales	National	
	Sep	Dark Mansion of Forbidden Love	National	4
	Sep	Ghostly Haunts	Charlton	39
	Sep	Haunted	Charlton	30
	Oct	Sinister House of Secret Love	National	4
	Oct	Ghost Manor	Charalton	
1972	Jan	Grimm's Ghost Stories	Gold Key	
	Mar	Mystery Comics Digest	Gold Key	26
	Apr	Tomb of Dracula	Marvel	70
	May	Forbidden Tales of Dark Mansion	National	11
	Jun	Weird Western Tales	National	
	Jun	Secrets of Sinister House	National	13
	Jul	Weird Mystery Tales	National	24
	Aug	Weird Worlds	National	10
	Aug	The Demon	National	16
	Sep	Chilling Adventures in Sorcery	Archie	5
	Sep	Werewolf by Night	Marvel	43
	Oct	Journey into Mystery	Marvel	19
	Oct	Swamp Thing	National	24
	Nov	Chamber of Chills	Marvel	25
	Dec	Midnight Tales	Charlton	18
	Dec	Supernatural Thrillers	Marvel	15
1973	Jan	Crypt of Shadows	Marvel	21
	Jan	Monster of Frankenstein	Marvel	18
	Feb	Vault of Evil	Marvel	23
	Mar	Beware	Marvel	8
	Apr	Haunted Love	Charlton	11
	Arp	Worlds Unknown	Marvel	8
	May	Occult Files of Dr Spektor	Gold Key	24
	Jul	Monsters Unleashed(*)	Marvel	11
	Aug	Scream(*)	Skyward	11
	Aug	Tales of the Zombie(*)	Marvel	10
	Aug	Vampire Tales(*)	Marvel	11
		Dracula Lives(*)	Marvel	14
	Oct	Black Magic	National	9
	Dec	Dead of Night	Marvel	11
	Dec	Uncanny Tales	Marvel	11
	Dec	Weird Wonder Tales	Marvel	22
1974	Jan	The man-thing	Marvel	22
	Apr	Red Circle Sorcery	Archie	6
	May	Haunt of Horror(*)	Marvel	5
	Jul	Tomb of Darkness	Marvel	15
	Sep	Giant Size Dracula	Marvel	4
	Sep	Madhouse	Archie	3
1975	Jan	Grim Ghost	Atlas	3
	Jan	Weird Tales of the Macabre(*)	Atlas	2

Graduate horror

As far as British comics were concerned, horror was dead. But in America the seeds, planted prewar, were beginning to grow. The comic-book had grown too, in sales and in stature. It had become the favourite recreational reading of the GI, and millions of copies were shipped every month to service Post Exchanges around the world. With adult readers outnumbering the original kid market, content was upgraded to suit young soldiers' tastes. Cartoon girls found their bosoms expanding as their skirts shortened, while crime and bloodshed, bondage and torture, catered to shadier tastes.

The first horror cover was drawn by L. B. Cole for the first issue of *Mask Comics* (February 1945): a fierce, fanged face frowns out from behind a green candle, stuck in a blood-red holder inscribed 'Evil', while naked girls with butterfly wings singe themselves at the flame. The contents, however, were no more gruesome than the average crime comic of the time. It was a start, however, and hot on its heels came a trio of titles from the Gilberton Company's hitherto impeccable educational outfit, *Classic Comics*. These were *Dr Jekyll and Mr Hyde*, the cover of which showed R. L. Stevenson's evil entity striding like a giant over a screaming girl; *The Hunchback of Notre Dame*, the crude cartoons of Hugo's hero more hideous than Briefer's prewar caricature; and *Frankenstein*, which was pictorially closer to the Universal–Karloff movie than the Mary Shelley novel.

1946 brought the first attempts at regular comics on horror themes. Harvey Comics published *Strange Story* which starred 'The Man in Black', Bob Powell's personification of Fate modelled on such radio hosts of the supernatural as Raymond, the narrator of *The Inner Sanctum*. Avon published *Eerie Comics* at the close of the year, the cover depicting a leggy girl in bondage about to be slashed by a bald-headed moon maniac. Neither comic reached a No. 2. The American Comics Group had more luck with their *Adventures into the Unknown*. First published in the Fall of 1948, this reached issue No. 174 by the time it was closed in August 1967. Longest completed run of any horror comic. Although the stories ranged through the spectrum of the supernatural, including a serial 'Spirit of Frankenstein', the artwork was always neat, clean, and straightforward 'comicbook', never lapsing into the excesses of gruesome detail that would eventually end the era.

Marvel Comics, always quick to sense a new trend, converted their long-running *Marvel Mystery Comics*, a super-hero title, to *Marvel Tales* with issue No. 93 (August 1949). Under the headline 'The Strangest Stories Ever Told' (accent on the word 'Strangest'), editor/writer

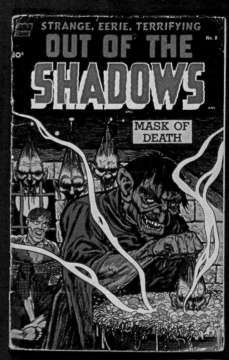

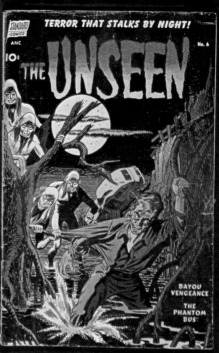

Year	Month	Title	Publisher	Run
	Feb	Weird Suspense Tales	Atlas	3
	Feb	Tales of Evil	Atlas	3
	Apr	Secrets of Haunted House	National	14
	May	Spine Tingling Tales	Gold Key	4
	May	Tales Of Ghost Castle	National	3
	Jun	Kong The Untamed	National	5
	Jul	Creepy Things	Charlton	6
	Jul	Beyond the Grave	Charlton	6
	Jul	Masters of Terror(*)	Marvel	2
	Aug	Scary Tales	Charlton	20
	Oct	Marvel Chillers	Marvel	7
1977	Jan	The Rampaging Hulk(*)	Marvel	16
	Aug	Godzilla	Marvel	24
1978	Jan	Doorway into Nightmare	National	5
1979	Nov	Man-Thing	Marvel	
	Nov	Tomb of Dracula	Marvel	
	Dec	Tales to Astonish	Marvel	

(*): magazine format (b/w not colour), rather than comicbook
where no figure shown under run, the title is still in publication

Stan Lee began a long series of unconnected horror strips, short-story style. Despite the lack of regular characters, hitherto a comicbook prerequisite, the new format was such a success that Marvel quickly switched *Suspense Comics* (1949), based on a radio series, to horror, and followed up with the ultimate degradation for a hitherto hero: *Captain America* became *Captain America's Weird Tales* from issue No. 74.

Shock horror

In 1945 M. C. Gaines sold out his interests in his All-American Comics Group to his partner, Harry Donenfield of D. C. Comics (National Periodical Publications). With his half a million dollars, Gaines set up Educational Comics and published *Picture Stories from the Bible*, with artwork as crude as the Gilberton *Classics* he was imitating. Two years later he was dead, killed in a motorboat accident. His son William took over the company. Soon, everything was changed except the logo: E.C. now meant Entertaining Comics, not Educational Comics. *International Comics*, launched in 1947 to stimulate young America's interest in the world outside, became *International Crime Patrol*, then *Crime Patrol* starring 'Captain Crime'. In No. 15 (December 1949) a new strip was introduced. 'The Crypt of Terror' hosted by one of those radio-inspired characters who were becoming increasingly popular in comicbooks. This white-maned skeleton called himself 'The Crypt Keeper' and told a tale entitled 'Return from the Grave'. The artist/writer was Al Feldstein. In the same month's issue of a companion comic, *War Against Crime*, No. 10, a shrouded cackler called 'The Vault-Keeper' introduced himself, his abode 'The Vault of Horror', and a tale entitled 'Buried Alive'. The artist/writer was the same Al Feldstein. At the close of each strip readers were asked to write and tell the editor if they liked this type of story. Evidently they did, for just two editions later, *Crime Patrol* had changed its title to *The Crypt of Terror*, *War Against Crime* had become *The Vault of Horror*, and range-ridin' fans of another E.C. favourite, *Gunfighter*, were confused to discover their cowboy comicbook had turned into *The Haunt of Fear* (May 1950).

The new Gaines promoted his 'New Trend' as 'Illustrated Suspenstories We Dare You to Read', and comicbook fans everywhere took up his challenge. That Gaines and his team tried to upgrade comicbooks is unarguable: the switch from 'comics' to 'illustrated suspenstories' is evidence enough. What they forgot, or chose to ignore, was the hard fact that the majority of comicbook readers were young children, the adult market of the early 1940s having virtually disappeared with the end of the war. Newsdealers' racking and packing systems allowed no differential between adult-orientated comicbooks and the regular juvenile titles, even assuming they could take time or trouble to sort them out. As New Trend E.C.s fell into parents' and teachers' hands, the concern over comicbooks began, *The Crypt of Terror* had only run three issues before Gaines, sensitive to trade pressures, changed its title to *Tales from the Crypt* (October 1950). It was a small gesture, and his only one. As rival comicbook publishers became aware of E.C.'s sudden success, imitations began to creep onto the market. Fox Features put out a couple of classic-type one-shots, *The Black Tarantula* (April 1950) starring Count Rorret who was not backward when it came to terrorizing women, and a startlingly stylish version of *Dr Jekyll and Mr Hyde* (May 1950) by the tyro Wallace Wood. The top comicbook team of the time, Joe Simon and Joe Kirby, produced *Black Magic* for Prize Publications (October 1950).

By the end of 1950 there were 18 horror comics in publication; one year later another 25 titles had been added, and 41 more were introduced during 1952. With only four titles, including *Shock Suspenstories* plus two which mixed science-fiction themes with occasional horrors, *Weird Science* and *Weird Fantasy*, E.C. Comics found their much-vaunted 'New Trend' was indeed a new trend. Perhaps then it is no wonder that, as pioneers in the field, they considered themselves pacemakers, having to outdo their rivals and imitators at all costs. Thus a snowball effect began, with money-chasing publishers attempting to grab the market by outdoing the originators in sensational graphics. Classical vampires, werewolves, and mummies were no longer enough to stimulate the reader into parting with his pocket money; ever greater horrors had to be devised and gloatingly illustrated. An apex, or nadir, was reached in *Mount of Fear* No. 19, when a baseball team took revenge on one of their number by dismembering and disemboweling him alive, using his parts for a last macabre game: his heart as the home plate, his scalp as a brush, his leg as a bat, his torso as a chest-protector, his hands as gloves.

The backlash begins

Agitation against American comicbooks began in England in 1949 with 'Comics that Take Horror into the Nursery', an attack against sex and crime comics published in the *Sunday Dispatch*. The author was a worried churchman, Hon. Sec. for the Society of Christian Publicity. Within a year he had launched his own comic; he was the Rev. Marcus Morris and the comic was *Eagle*, perhaps the finest children's publication of modern times. In 1952 the Authors' World Peace Appeal established a Children's Literature Committee who published a graded list of 76 British and American comics: 26 American titles were condemned as Objectionable and Very Objectionable. Also in England the Comics Campaign Council was formed, and in 1952 the member of parliament for Coventry raised the matter in the House. His quotation from *Eerie Comics* is in *Hansard*: 'The Thing picked up the body of the unfortunate girl and threw it into an underground pit filled with sulphurous smoke and a strange flickering blue fire that did not burn like an ordinary flame. From out of that pit rose corpse after corpse, shrunken, withered . . .' For although the importation of American comicbooks was limited under an earlier parliamentary decision with an eye to the dollar drain, many minor British publishers like L. Miller & Son and Thorpe & Porter were buying papier-maché matrixes of the original line blocks and producing British editions in hundred thousand runs.

Parallel with British agitation, the Americans set up the Joint Legislative Committee to Study the Publication of Comics. In 1950 the *New York Times* published the pleas of a psychiatrist, Dr Frederic Wertham, that the public health laws should be used to ban the sale of horror comics to children under 15. Nothing was done until three years later, when in June 1953 a Senate Sub-Commmttee was formed under the chairmanship of Robert C. Hendrickson. Another year passed before publisher/editor William C. Gaines was called before the Committee.

Democrat Senator Estes Kefauver of Tennessee held up the current number of *Shock Suspenstories*, following Gaines' statement that there was no limit to what he would publish in a comic, other than the bounds of good taste.

'Here is your May issue', said Kefauver. 'This seems to be a man with a bloody axe holding a woman's head up, which has been severed from her body. Do you think that's in good taste?' 'Yes, sir, I do', replied Gaines. 'For the cover of a horror comic. A cover in bad taste might be defined as holding the head a little higher so that the blood could be seen dripping from it, and moving the body over a little further so that the neck of the body could be seen to be bloody.' Kefauver: 'You've got blood coming out of her mouth'. Gaines: 'A little.'

Out of his own mouth, Gaines was destroyed, and with him horror comics and very nearly the industry his own father had created. Publishers, following the precedent of the film producers in the 1930s, set up their own self-censoring body, the Comics Code Authority, and on 17 September 1954 Judge Charles F. Murphy published their 40-point code. Among the rules:

> No comics magazine shall use the word horror or terror in its title; All scenes of horror, excessive bloodshed, gory or gruesome crimes, depravity, lust, sadism, masochism, shall not be permitted; Scenes dealing with, or instruments associated with, walking dead, torture, vampires, and vampirism, ghouls, cannibalism, and werewolfism are prohibited.

In July 1955 the annual Comics issue of *Newsdealer* reported no fewer than 95 horror and crime titles had been discontinued. The same year, in England, the Childrens' and Young Persons' Act (1955) was passed, putting an end to the reprints.

Son of the horror comic

The horror comic was dead; but as with the monsters, vampires, and zombies of its subject matter, it would rise again. First, as magazines in a higher-priced, larger-paged format, a style which enabled them to escape the stigma of the Code. James Warren was the pioneer here, with his well-drawn *Creepy* (1964) and *Eerie* (1965). An outfit called Eerie Publications revived *Tales from the Crypt* (1968) as a title, and began reprinting vintage horror strips with added tones. Marvel Comics started a successful magazine line with *Tomb of Dracula* (1972). Then a whole new slew of horror comics glutted the market as the Code was relaxed to permit vampires, ghouls and werewolves 'when handled in the classic tradition such as **Frankenstein, Dracula,** and other high calibre literary works.' Thus the *Marvel Classics* series of 1976 which issued new strip adaptations of **Dr Jekyll and Mr Hyde, The Hunchback of Notre Dame,** and **Frankenstein**: the trio that had been published 31 years before!

THE VAULT OF HORROR

NO. 26 $1

FEATURING

THE VAULT-KEEPER

THE OLD WITCH

THE CRYPT-KEEPER

GHOSTLY TALES OF SPINE-CHILLING HORROR

WEIRD TERROR

HERE ARE TALES THAT WILL USHER YOU INTO

THE HAUNT OF FEAR

NO. 12 $1

FEATURING

THE OLD WITCH

THE VAULT-KEEPER

THE CRYPT-KEEPER

WE DARE YOU TO READ THESE EERIE TALES OF SUPERNATURAL HORROR!

WITCHES TALES

WITCHES TALES MAGAZINE

No. 21 OCT. 10¢

WEIRD YARNS OF UNSEEN TERRORS

THEY CAME ON AND ON... WAS THERE NO END TO THE INVASION?

GIANT 52-PAGE SIZE! BUY NO LESS!

ADVENTURES INTO THE UNKNOWN!

No. 11 JUNE-JULY

10¢

CLASSICS Illustrated

FEATURING STORIES BY THE WORLD'S GREATEST AUTHORS

FRANKENSTEIN by MARY W. SHELLEY

No. 26

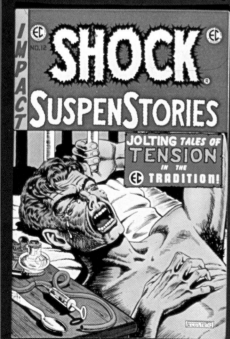

IMPACT

SHOCK SuspenStories

NO. 12

JOLTING TALES OF TENSION IN THE EC TRADITION!

TALES OF TERROR AND SUSPENSE!

CHAMBER OF CHILLS

No. 19 SEPT.

MAGAZINE   10¢

HERE'S LOOKING AT YOU DARLING ON OUR HAPPY ANNIVERSARY!

DARING the SUPERNATURAL

OUT OF the NIGHT

No. 12 JAN.

10¢

THE MUSIC OF THE DEAD CALLS! WE RISE AT YOUR COMMAND!

MUSIC for DEAD!

Films

Year	Title	Directors/Principals	Distribution
1910	Frankenstein	starring Charles Ogle	Edison one-reeler, USA
1913	The Student of Prague	dir. D. Stellan Rye, Paul Wegener	Bioscop, Germany
1913	The Vampire	dir. Robert Vignola	USA
1914	The Golem	dir. Paul Wegener; starring Henrick Galeen	Germany
1919	The Cabinet of Dr Caligari	dir. Robert Wiene; starring Conrad Veight	Decla-Bioscop, Germany
1920	The Golem:	dir. and starring Paul Wegener	Union/Ufa, Germany
1920	The Phantom Carriage	dir. Victor Sjostrom	Sweden
1920	Dr Jekyll and Mr Hyde	dir. John S. Robertson; starring John Barrymore	Paramount, USA
1922	Nosferatu	dir. F. W. Murnau; starring Max Schreck	Prana Co, Germany
1922	Witchcraft Through the Ages (Haxan)	dir. Benjamin Christensen,	Svenska, Sweden
1922	Dr Mabuse	dir. Fritz Lang	Ullstein UCO/Ufa, Germany
1923	The Hunchback of Notre Dame	starring Lon Chaney	USA
1923	Greed	dir. Erich von Stroheim	USA
1923	Der Nibelungen	dir. Fritz Lang	Ufa, Germany
1924	The Hands of Orlac	dir. Robert Wiene; starring Conrad Veight	Pan-film, Austria
1924	Waxworks	dir. Paul Leni; starring Werner Krausse	Neptun Films, Germany
1925	The Phantom of the Opera	dir. Rupert Julian; starring Lon Chaney	Universal, USA
1925	The Lost World	dir. Harry D. Hoyt; starring Wallace Beery, Bessie Love	First National, USA
1926	The Bells	dir. Terence Young; starring Lionel Barrymore, with Boris Karloff	USA
1926	Metropolis	dir. Fritz Lang	Ufa, Germany
1926	Secrets of a Soul	dir. G. W. Pabst	Ufa, Germany
1927	The Cat and the Canary	dir. Paul Leni	Germany
1927	London after Midnight	dir. Tod Browning; starring Lon Chaney	Universal USA
1928	Fall of the House of Usher	dir. Jean Epstein	
1930	Dracula	dir. Tod Browning; starring Bela Lugosi	Universal, USA
1931	Frankenstein	dir. James Whale; starring Boris Karloff	Universal, USA
1931	Vampyr	dir. Carl Dreyer	CD Prods, France
1931	Murders in the Rue Morgue	dir. Robert Florey; starring Bela Lugosi	Universal, USA
1932	Dr Jekyll and Mr Hyde	dir. Rouben Mamoulian; starring Frederic March	Paramount, USA
1932	The Old Dark House	dir. James Whale; starring Boris Karloff	Universal, USA
1932	Freaks	dir. Tod Browning	MGM, USA
1932	Mystery of the Wax Museum	dir. Michael Curtiz	Warner Bros, USA
1932	The Most Dangerous Game	dir. Ernest B. Schodesack, Irving Pichel	USA
1932	The Island of Lost Souls	dir. Erle C. Kenton	Paramount, USA
1932	The Mummy	dir. Karl Freund	Universal, USA
1932	White Zombie	dir. Victor Halperin	Amusement Securities, USA
1933	The Ghoul	dir. T. Hayes Hunter; starring Boris Karloff	Gaumont British, UK
1933	King Kong	dir. Ernest B. Schoedsack, Merian C. Cooper	RKO, USA
1933	The Invisible Man	dir. James Whale	Universal, USA
1933	The Last of Dr Mabuse	dir. Fritz Lang	Nero Filmgesellschaft, Germany
1933	The Sphinx	dir. Phil Rosen	Monogram, USA
1933	Son of Kong	dir. Ernest B. Schoedsack	RKO, USA
1933	Supernatural	dir. Victor Halperin; starring Carole Lombard, Randolph Scott	USA
1934	The Black Cat	dir. Edgar G. Ulmer; starring Boris Karloff, Bela Lugosi	Universal, USA
1934	The Hands of Orlac	dir. Karl Freund	USA
1935	The Bride of Frankenstein	dir. James Whale	Universal, USA
1935	Mark of the Vampire	dir. Tod Browning	MGM, USA
1935	Werewolf of London	dir. Stuart Walker	Universal, USA
1936	Devil Doll	dir. Tod Browning	USA
1936	The Golem	dir. Julien Duvivier	AB Film/Metropolitan Pictures, Czech/France
1936	The Walking Dead	dir. Michael Curtiz	Warner Bros, USA
1936	Revolt of the Zombies	dir. Victor Halperin	Halperin Pictures, USA
1936	Dracula's Daughter	dir. Lambert Hillyer	Universal, USA
1939	The Cat and the Canary	dir. Elliot Nugent	Paramount USA
1939	Son of Frankenstein	dir. Rowland V. Lee	Universal, USA
1939	Hunchback of Notre Dame	starring Charles Laughton	USA
1940	Dr Cyclops	dir. Ernest B. Schoedsack	Paramount, USA
1940	The Invisible Man Returns	dir. Joe May	Universal, USA
1940	The Mummy's Hand	dir. Christy Cabanne	Universal, USA
1941	Dr Jekyll and Mr Hyde	dir. Victor Fleming; starring Spencer Tracy	MGM, USA
1941	The Invisible Woman	dir. A. E. Sutherland	USA
1941	The Wolfman	dir. George Waggner	Universal, USA

Year	Title	Directors/Principals	Distribution
1941	King of the Zombies		Monogram USA
1942	The Mummy's Tomb	dir. Harold Young;	Universal, USA
1942	The Ghost of Frankenstein	dir. Erle C. Kenton	Universal, USA
1942	Son of Dracula	dir. Robert Siodmak	Universal, USA
1943	Phantom of the Opera	dir. Arthur Lubin; starring Claude Rains	Universal, USA
1943	Revenge of the Zombies		Monogram, USA
1943	I Walked with a Zombie	dir. Jacques Tourneur; Val Lewton	RKO, USA
1943	The Uninvited	dir. Lewis Allen	Paramount, USA
1943	The Cat People	dir. Jacques Tourneur; Val Lewton	RKO, USA
1943	Day of Wrath	dir. Carl Dreyer	Palladium Films, Denmark
1943	The Return of the Vampire	dir. Lew Landers	Universal, USA
1943	Frankenstein Meets the Wolfman	dir. Roy W. Neill	Universal, USA
1944	Voodoo Man		Monogram, USA
1944	The Mummy's Ghost	dir. Reginald le Borg	Universal, USA
1944	The Mummy's Curse	dir. Leslie Goodwins	Universal, USA
1944	The Curse of the Cat People	dir. Robert Wise; Val Lewton	RKO, USA
1944	The House of Frankenstein	dir. Erle C. Kenton	Universal, USA
1944	The Cry of the Werewolf	dir. Henry Levin	Universal, USA
1945	Dead of Night	various directors	Michael Balcon Prods, UK
1945	Isle of the Dead	dir. Mark Robson	USA
1945	The Body Snatcher	dir. Robert Wise; Val Lewton	RKO, USA
1945	The House of Dracula	dir. Erle C. Kenton	Universal, USA
1945	A Game of Death	dir. Robert Wise	
1945	The Picture of Dorian Gray	dir. Albert Lewin	USA
1946	La Belle et la Bête	dir. Jean Cocteau	Andre Pavlé Prods, France
1946	Bedlam	dir. Mark Robson; Val Lewton	RKO, USA
1946	The Valley of the Zombies	dir. Philip Ford	USA
1947	The Beast with Five Fingers	dir. Robert Florey	Warner Bros, USA
1949	Voodoo Man	dir. William Beaudine	USA
1949	Mighty Joe Young	dir. Ernest B. Schoedsack	USA
1950	The Thing from Another World	dir. Christian Nyby; Howard Hawks	USA
1950	The Fall of the House of Usher	dir. Ivan Barnett	USA
1951	The Son of Dr Jekyll	dir. Stephen Friedman	USA
1952	Zombies of the Stratosphere	dir. Fred C. Brannon	Republic, USA
1952	The Black Castle	dir. Nathan Juran	USA
1953	The War of the Worlds	dir. Byron Haskin	George Pal Prods, USA
1953	House of Wax	dir. Andre de Toth	Warner Bros, USA
1953	Them	dir. Gordon Douglas	Warner Bros, USA
1953	The Beast from 20,000 Fathoms	dir. Eugene Lourie	USA
1953	The Magnetic Monster	dir. Curt Siodmak	USA
1953	Catwomen of the Moon	dir. Arthur Hilton	USA
1953	It Came from Outer Space	dir. Jack Arnold	Universal, USA
1953	The 5,000 Fingers of Dr T.	dir. Roy Rowland	Warner Bros, USA
1953	Creatures from the Black Lagoon	dir. Jack Arnold	Universal, USA
1954	The Phantom of the Rue Morgue	dir. Roy del Ruth	Warner, USA
1954	Robot Monster	dir. Phil Tucker	USA
1954	Revenge of the Creature		USA
1955	The Fiends	dir. Henri-Georges Clouzot	France
1955	It Came from Beneath the Sea	dir. Robert Gordon	USA
1955	Tarantula	dir. Jack Arnold	Universal, USA
1955	Day the World Ended	dir. Roger Corman	USA
1955	Godzilla	dir. Terry Morse	Inoshiro Honda, Japan
1955	The Creature Walks among Us		USA
1956	The Invasion of the Body Snatchers	dir. Don Siegel	USA
1956	The Pharaoh's Curse		Bel-Air, USA
1956	Zombies of Mara-Tau		USA
1956	The Gamma People	dir. John Gilling	UK
1956	The Quatermass Experiment	dir. Val Guest	UK
1956	The Cyclops	dir. Bert I. Gordon	
1956	Forbidden Planet	dir. Fred McLeod Wilcox	MGM, USA
1957	The Incredible Shrinking Man	dir. Jack Arnold	Universal/International, USA
1957	Voodoo Island		Bel-Air, USA
1957	The Curse of Frankenstein	dir. Terence Fisher	Hammer, UK
1957	The Blood of Dracula	dir. Herbert L. Strock	USA
1957	Daughter of Dr Jekyll	dir. Edgar Ulmer	USA
1957	The Black Scorpion	dir. Edward Ludwig	USA
1958	Frankenstein 70	starring Boris Karloff	USA
1958	Night of the Demon	dir. Jacques Tourneur	Sabre Films, USA
1958	The Fly	dir. Kurt Neumann	20th Century Fox, USA
1958	The Mummy	dir. Terence Fisher	Hammer, UK
1958	The Horror of Dracula	dir. Terence Fisher	Hammer, UK
1958	The Return of Dracula	dir. Paul Landres	USA

Year	Tile	Directors/Principals	Distribution
1958	Blood of the Vampire	dir. Henry Cass	UK
1958	Macabre	dir. William Castle	USA
1958	The House on Haunted Hill	dir. William Castle	USA
1958	Return of the Fly	dir. Edward Bernds	Associated Productions, USA
1959	Peeping Tom	dir. Michael Powell	MP Prods, UK
1959	Wasp Woman	prod. and dir. Roger Corman	USA
1959	Eyes without a Face	dir. Georges Fanju	Jules Borkon Prods, France
1959	The Stranglers of Bombay	dir. Terence Fisher	Hammer, UK
1959	Frankenstein's Daughter	dir. Richard E. Cunha	USA
1959	The Tingler	dir. William Castle	USA
1959	First Man into Space	dir. Robert Day	Producers Associates, USA
1960	Psycho	dir. Alfred Hitchcock	Paramount, USA
1960	Gorgo	dir. Eugene Lourie	UK
1960	Blood and Roses	dir. Roger Vadim	France
1960	The Fall of the House of Usher	dir. Roger Corman	USA
1960	Dr Blood's Coffin	dir. Sydney J. Furie	Cavaton, UK
1960	Thirteen Ghosts	dir. William Castle	USA
1960	The Two Faces of Dr Jekyll	dir. Terence Fisher	Hammer, UK
1960	The Brides of Dracula	dir. Terence Fisher	Hammer, UK
1960	The Village of the Damned	dir. Wolf Rilla	UK
1960	The Hands of Orlac	dir. Godfrey Grayson	UK
1960	Black Sunday	dir. Mario Bava	Italy
1961	Curse of the Werewolf	dir. Terence Fisher	Hammer, UK
1961	The Innocents	dir. Jack Clayton	20th Century Fox/ Achilles, UK
1961	The Damned	dir. Joseph Losey	Hammer/Swallow, UK
1961	The Pit and the Pendulum	prod. and dir. Roger Corman	USA
1961	The Premature Burial	prod. and dir. Roger Corman	USA
1961	Taste of Fear	dir. Seth Holt	USA
1961	House of Mystery	dir. Vernon Sewell	USA
1962	Tales of Terror	dir. and prod. Roger Corman	USA
1962	Terror of Dr Hitchcock	dir. Robert Hampton	Panda
1962	Whatever Happened to Baby Jane?	dir. Robert Aldritch	USA
1962	The Day of the Triffids	dir. Steve Sekely	UK
1962	The Diary of a Madman	dir. Al Westen	USA
1962	Kiss of the Vampire	dir. Don Sharp	UK
1962	The Birds	dir. Alfred Hitchcock	Universal-International, USA
1962	Harakiri	dir. Hasaki Kobayashi	Japan
1962	The Manchurian Candidate	dir. John Frankenheimer	USA
1962	Phantom of the Opera	dir. Terence Fisher	Hammer, UK
1963	The Haunted Palace	dir. Roger Corman	Alta Vista, USA
1963	The Man with X-Ray Eyes	dir. Roger Corman	Alta Vista, USA
1963	The Raven	dir. Roger Corman	Alta Vista/American-International, USA
1963	The Haunted and the Hunted	dir. Francis Coppola; prod. Roger Corman	USA
1963	The Haunting	dir. Robert Wise	USA
1963	The Terror	dir. Roger Corman	USA
1963	The Castle of Terror	dir. Antonio Margheriti	Italy
1963	The Spectre	dir. Robert Hampton	Italy
1963	War of the Zombies		Italy
1964	Kwaidan		Japan
1964	The Masque of the Red Death	dir. Roger Corman	Alta Vista/Anglo-Amalgamated, USA
1964	The Tomb of Ligeia	dir. Roger Corman	Alta Vista, USA
1964	Dr Terror's House of Horrors	dir. Freddie Francis	Amicus, UK
1964	Witchcraft	dir. Don Sharp	Lippert Films, UK
1964	The Earth Dies Screaming	dir. Terence Fisher	Lippert Films, UK
1964	Seance on a Wet Afternoon	dir. Bryan Forbes	UK
1964	Hush, Hush, Sweet Charlotte	dir. Robert Aldrich	USA
1964	Blood and Black Lace	dir. Mario Bava	Italy
1964	Castle of the Living Dead		Italy
1964	The Evil of Frankenstein	dir. Terence Fisher	Hammer, UK
1964	The Gorgon	dir. Terence Fisher	Hammer, UK
1964	The Curse of the Mummy's Tomb	dir. Michael Carreras	Hammer, UK
1964	Hysteria	dir. Freddie Francis	Hammer, UK
1964	Curse of the Fly	dir. Don Sharp	20th Century Fox/ Lippert Films, UK
1965	Repulsion	dir. Roman Polanski	Gene Gutowski Prods, France
1965	Jessie James Meets Frankenstein's Daughter		USA
1965	Fanatic	dir. Sylvio Narizzano	Hammer/Seven Arts, UK
1965	The Nanny	dir. Seth Holt	Hammer, UK

Year	Title	Directors/Principals	Distribution
1965	Dracula, Prince of Darkness	Terence Fisher	Hammer, UK
1965	Rasputin, the Mad Monk	dir. Don Sharp	Hammer, UK
1965	Onibaba (The Hole)	dir. Kaneto Shindo	Japan
1965	The Revenge of the Blood Beast	dir. Mike Reeves	Charles Griffiths Prods, UK
1965	The Face of Fu Manchu	dir. Don Sharp	Hammer, UK
1965	Devils of Darkness	dir. Lance Comfort	UK
1965	Monster of Terror	dir. Daniel Haller	USA
1965	Planet of The Vampires	dir. Mario Bava	Italian–International, Italy
1966	The Reptile	dir. John Gilling	Hammer, UK
1966	The Frozen Dead		Goldstar, USA
1966	It		Goldstar, USA
1966	The Plague of the Zombies	dir. John Gilling	Hammer, UK
1966	The Deadly Bees		UK
1966	The Skull	dir. Freddie Francis	Amicus, UK
1966	The Psychopath	dir. Freddie Francis	Amicus, UK
1966	The Projected Man	dir. Ian Curteis	UK
1966	Island of Terror	dir. Terence Fisher	Hammer, UK
1966	Carry on Screaming	dir. Peter Rogers	Anglo-Amalgamated, UK
1966	Theatre of Death	dir. Sam Gallu	
1967	The Mummy's Shroud	dir. John Gilling	Hammer, UK
1967	The Blood Beast Terror	dir. Vernon Sewell	USA
1967	Dance of the Vampires	dir. Roman Polanski	Cadre/Filmways, UK
1967	Frankenstein Created Woman	dir. Terence Fisher	Hammer, UK
1968	Night of the Living Dead	dir. George A. Romero	USA
1968	Rosemary's Baby	dir. Roman Polanski	USA
1968	The Torture Garden	dir. Freddie Francis	Amicus, UK
1969	Frankenstein Must Be Destroyed		Hammer, UK
1970	Scars of Dracula	dir. Roy Ward Baker	Hammer, UK
1970	Trog		Herman Cohen Prods, USA

Year	Title	Directors/Principals	Distribution
1970	Willard		Bing Crosby Prods, USA
1970	Blood on Satan's Claw		Tigon, UK
1970	Vampire Lovers	dir. Roy Ward Baker	Hammer, UK
1970	Count Dracula	dir. Jess Franco	Spain
1970	Horrors of Frankenstein		Hammer, UK
1970	House that Dripped Blood		Amicus, UK
1970	I, Monster		UK
1970	Incredible 2-Headed Transplant		USA
1970	Blood of Frankenstein	dir. Al Adamson	USA
1970	Count Yorga, Vampire	dir. Robert Kelljan	USA
1971	Blood from the Mummy's Tomb	dir. Seth Holt, Michael Carreras	Hammer, UK
1971	Murders in the Rue Morgue		Warner Bros, USA
1971	Tales from the Crypt	dir. Freddie Francis	Amicus, UK
1971	Thing with 2 Heads	dir. Lee Frost	USA
1971	Twins of Evil	dir. John Hough	Hammer, UK
1971	Countess Dracula		Hammer, UK
1971	The Omega Man		Seltzer, USA
1971	Return of Count Yorga	dir. Robert Kelljan	USA
1972	Frogs	dir. George McCowan	USA
1972	Tombs of the Blind Dead		Plata Films/Interfine, Italy
1972	Voodoo Heartbeat	dir. Charles Nizet	USA
1972	Doomwatch		Hammer, UK
1972	Vampire Circus	dir. Robert Young	Hammer, UK
1972	Abominable Dr Phibes	dir. Robert Fuest	USA
1972	Captain Kronos, Vampire Hunter	dir. Brian Clemens	Hammer, UK
1972	Blacula	dir. William Crain	USA
1972	Ben		Bing Crosby Prods, USA
1972	Creeping Flesh		Tigon/World Film Services, UK
1972	Vault of Horror	dir. Roy Ward Baker	Amicus, UK
1973	Voodoo Girl		American–International, USA
1973	Dr Jekyll and Mr Hyde	starring Kirk Douglas	NBCTV, USA
1973	Dr Phibes Rises Again	dir. Robert Fuest	USA
1973	Blood for Dracula	dir. Paul Morissey	Andy Warhol Prods, USA
1973	Frankenstein and the Monster from Hell		Hammer, UK
1973	From Beyond the Grave	dir. Kevin Connor	Amicus, UK
1973	Satanic Rites of Dracula		Hammer, UK
1973	Sssnake		Zanuck–Brown Prods, USA
1973	House of Dracula's Daughter	dir. Gordon Hessler	USA
1974	Living Dead of the Manchester Morgue		Star Films (Madrid)/Flaminia Produzioni (Rome) Spain/Italy
1974	Frankenstein, the True Story		Universal, UK
1974	Flesh for Frankenstein	dir. Paul Morissey	Andy Warhol Prods, USA
1974	The Exorcist	dir. William Friedkin	Warner Bros, USA
1975	The Ghoul	dir. Freddie Francis	Tyburn, UK
1975	Legend of the Werewolf	dir. Freddie Francis	Tyburn, UK
1976	Exorcist 2	dir. John Boorman	Warner Bros, USA
1976	The Omen	dir. Richard Donner	20th Century Fox, USA
1977	Carrie	dir. Brian de Palma	USA
1978	Invasion of the Body Snatchers	dir. Philip Kaufman	USA
1978	Alien	dir. Ridley Scott	20th Century Fox, USA
1978	The Manitou	dir. William Girdler	Enterprise Pictures, USA
1978	Texas Chainsaw Massacre	dir. Tobe Hooper	USA
1978	The Amityville Horror		USA
1979	Zombies Dawn of the Dead	dir. George A. Romero	Target–International, USA
1979	Zombie Flesh Eaters	dir. Lucio Fulci,	Italy
1979	The Shining	dir. Stanley Kubrick	USA
1979	Prophecy	dir. John Frankenheimer	Paramount, USA
1980	The Awakening	dir. Mike Newell	USA
1980	The Changeling	dir. Peter Medak	USA
1980	The Fog	dir. John Carpenter	USA
1980	Salem's Lot	dir. Tobe Hooper	Warner Bros TV, USA

Index

Page numbers in *italics* refer to illustrations

Acknowledgments

The publishers wish to thank the following individuals and organizations for their kind permission to reproduce the pictures in this book:

Alte Pinakuthek, Munich 81; Roy Ashton 40, 99 below left, 135; Photo by permission of ATV 156 above., 157; BBC Copyright 99 above right, 164; BBC Hulton Picture Library 65, 67, 86, 155 above and below left; Sarah Brown Artists Agency (David Carson) 159, 161; Camera Press Ltd. 155 below right; Bruce Coleman Ltd. (G. Zeisler) 90 below; Courtesy Collett, Dickenson, Pearce and Partners Ltd. Advertising 51 below; The Cooper-Bridgeman Library (Phaidon) 10, 18 below; Gift of Mr. and Mrs. Bert L. Smokler and Mr. and Mrs. Lawrence A. Fleischmann Courtesy the Detroit Institute of Arts 2–3; C.M. Dixon/Photoresources 154 right, 156 below; EMI Films 23; E.T. Archive 13 below, 130 above, 131 above; Mary Evans Picture Library 14, 35 above, 55, 84, 85, 106 above!, 108, 110, 115, (Harry Price Collection, University of London) 132; Alan Frank (Amicus) 6, 19, 22, 39, 48 below, 50, 54 below, 56, 106 below, 112, 113, 144–145, 146, 147, 152 above, 188; Denis Gifford endpapers 26, 30, 181, 184, 189; The Ronald Grant Archive 89; P. Keene 111; The Mansell Collection Ltd. 29, 66, 68, 69, 73, 105, 107, 109; W. McQuitty Outlook Films 151 below, 154 left; Chris Moore 177; National Film Archive/Stills Library 1, 12, 17, 20, 21 above, 24, 24–25 below centre, 25 above and below, 28, 32, 33, 34, 34–35, 35 below, 36, 37 above and below left, 41, 43, 44, 46, 48 above, 49, 51 above, 53 above, 54 above, 57, 58, 59, 60, 62–63, 72, 74, 75, 76, 77, 78–79, 82, 83, 91, 94 above left, centre and below, 95, 98, 99 above, 100, 101, 102, 104, 117, 119, 121, 122, 123, 124, 125, 126–127, 128, 129, 130–131, 133, 138, 139, 140, 141, 142, 143, 149, 152 centre and below, 153, 160, 162, 163, 165, 166, 167, 168–169, 171, 172–173, 175, 176; The National Gallery, London 11; Oslo Kommunes Kunstsamlinger 9, 92–93; Michel Parry 42, 45, 47, 61, 63; Francis Phillipps 18 above, 96; Popperfoto 21 below, 136 above, 137 above and below; Museo del Prado 15; Tom Rogers 37 below right, 52–53, 174; Thomas Schluck (NEL) 27, (Whelan) 31; The Tate Gallery, London 13 above; Thames Television 97 below, 99 centre and below right; Topham 70, 87, 90 above, 97 above, 103, 116, 136 centre and below; The Victoria and Albert Museum 71.

Our thanks also to Vivianne Croot, Carole Edwards, Marian Price and Ron Watson.